The Ravens of Odin

THE PRESS IN THE NORDIC NATIONS

THE PRESS I

The Ravens of Odin

THE NORDIC NATIONS

Robert G. Picard

IOWA STATE UNIVERSITY PRESS/AMES

Robert G. Picard is Associate Professor, Mass Communication Division, Emerson College, Boston, Mass.

© 1988 Iowa State University Press, Ames, Iowa 50010

Composed by Iowa State University Press from author-provided disks
Printed in the United States of America

First edition, 1988

Library of Congress Cataloging-in-Publication Data
Picard, Robert G.
    The ravens of Odin : the press in the Nordic nations / Robert G. Picard. — 1st ed.
        p.   cm.
    Bibliography: p.
    Includes index.
    ISBN 0-8138-1518-5
    1. Press—Scandinavia—History. 2. Scandinavian newspapers—History. 3. Journalism—Political aspects—Scandinavia.
I. Title.
PN5280.5.P53   1988   87–22750
078—dc19   CIP

To the memory of
Lars Erik Bertelsson Carpelan, 1913–1987
For his contributions to Finnish and Swedish journalism

CONTENTS

Preface, ix
Acknowledgments, xi
Introduction, xiii

PART ONE **Creation and Growth of the Press**
   1   History of the Nordic Press, 3
   2   The Nature of the Press, 26
   3   Freedom and Accountability of the Press, 43
   4   Press Economics, 56

PART TWO **Present-Day National and Regional Newspapers**
   5   Newspapers of Denmark, 83
   6   Newspapers of Finland, 96
   7   Newspapers of Iceland, 108
   8   Newspapers of Norway, 116
   9   Newspapers of Sweden, 124

Notes, 135
Bibliography, 141
Index, 149

PREFACE

This book is divided into two parts. Part One considers the history and content of the Nordic press and the social, economic, and political milieux in which it operates.

It provides a contemporary view of the important papers of Denmark, Finland, Iceland, Norway, and Sweden and the situations in which each paper carries out its functions. Recent developments and problems in the press of each of the five nations are reviewed and the efforts being made to deal with these issues are examined.

The text traces the development of the press in the modern history of the region and the effects of the press on the continued evolution of the nations. Because of the importance of the press in establishing liberal democracy and political pluralism, emphasis is placed on the political ties and activities of newspapers during the last two centuries.

The cultural, social, and political roles fulfilled by the press today are explored, as is the manner in which the press carries out those roles. The style and content of material in the press is also considered.

The emphasis on accountability to society through press councils, ombudsmen, and various approaches to news coverage, as well as the protections provided to press freedom in each nation and various legal accountability issues, are reviewed.

Finally, the economic bases of the press are considered, reviewing such topics as advertising, circulation, competition, and subsidies.

Part Two describes, by country, the most prestigious and largest newpapers as well as smaller provincial and political papers that are noteworthy as important elements of the press today.

Some papers mentioned in the text of Part One will not be found in Part Two. This occurs because these papers may no longer exist, may have declined significantly in size or import, or were important illustrations of specific issues or problems under discussion but do not have the influence or national recognition of other papers included in Part Two.

ACKNOWLEDGMENTS

This book could not have been completed without the assistance of scores of organizations and individuals who aided me on several trips to the Nordic countries. Credit must go to the Louisiana State University Council on Research, which funded part of the travel, and to the Louisiana State University College of Arts and Sciences and the Manship School of Journalism for providing release time that allowed the research to be completed and the book to be written in a timely manner. Significant contributions were made by the Nordic Council and the foreign ministries of each of the nations, which provided information, introductions, and other assistance.

In Denmark, hospitality and assistance were rendered by the Danish Newspaper Publishers Association, the Dagspressens Finansieringsfond, the Union of Danish Journalists, the Danish College of Journalism, the Danish Journalism Museum and Archive, the Nordic Documentation Center for Mass Communication Research, and the prime minister's staff.

In Finland, the Finnish Newspaper Publishers Association, the Union of Journalists, the Ministry of Traffic, and the Ministry of Foreign Affairs' Press Center were especially helpful.

Research in Iceland was assisted by staff members of the Icelandic Journalists' Union, State Radio, and the Administrative Office of the Parliament. The Norwegian research was aided by the Ministry of Finance and the Foreign Ministry.

In Sweden, research was completed with the help of the Swedish Institute, the Stockholm College of Journalism, the Press Subsidy Board, and the Press Council.

Acknowledgment must also be given for the hospitality and assistance extended by scores of newspaper publishers, editors, journalists, media scholars, government officials, and others whose personal efforts made it possible to complete the project more fully.

I wish to specifically thank Karl Thomsen, chief librarian, State

Library, Århus, Denmark; Eva Fønss-Jørgensen, documentalist, NORDICOM-Denmark; Thorsten Cars, press ombudsman, Stockholm; Kaarle Nordenstreng, professor, University of Tampere, Finland; Frank Hellstén, press attaché, Ministry of Foreign Affairs, Helsinki; Helgi Pétursson, reporter, Icelandic Radio; Birgitta Tennander, the Swedish Institute, Stockholm; Lars Furhoff, director, Stockholm College of Journalism; Karl Erik Gustafsson, professor, University of Göteborg, Sweden; Gustav Barfod, journalism librarian, Danish School of Journalism, Århus; Hans Larsen, Danish Union of Journalists, Copenhagen; H. P. Clausen, chairman of the Danish Media Commission, Prime Minister's Office, Copenhagen; Lars Wilhelm Carpelan, chief of information, Stockholm Information Service; Lars Erik and Ruth Carpelan; and Aaro Erkinheimo and his family.

INTRODUCTION

TWO RAVENS SIT ON HIS SHOULDERS and tell into his ears all the tidings, which they see or hear; these are Hugin and Munin. At the dawn of the day he sends them out to fly all over the world, and they come back at day-meal time; hence he knows many tidings.

Gylfaginning, ch. 38

The ravens that flew from the great hall Valhöll (Valhalla) each day on behalf of Odin, the battle god and ruler, provided information that allowed him to lead the Aesir tribe to the area that is now Scandinavia, to defeat his enemies in battle, and to be the wise and protective ruler of his realms.

Today, the descendants of this mythical ancestor rely on some of the world's most prestigious and active newspapers to understand their individual nations, the region, and the world, and to provide them news and information that permits them to rule these nations on their own. In its 300-year history, the press in the Nordic nations has provided singular examples of the role of the press in democratization, political development, and popular governance, and it has served as a model of social accountability by its continual emphasis on serving the social and cultural needs of the Nordic nations and protecting the rights of individual citizens.

The significant role of the press in these nations' political and social lives has remained constant. As democratic governance emerged and political pluralism flourished, the press became the voice of various groups of citizens and the influence of the press on the political process remains strong today. The importance of the press as an avenue for political discussion was recognized early, and the world's first guarantees of press freedom were established in this region, as were the earliest provisions guaranteeing access to public documents and providing protections to journalists' sources of information.

The press has maintained a strong tradition of serious coverage of events and ideas, with a significant local emphasis throughout the region. Nordic journalists have been cognizant of the effects of such coverage on society and have taken extraordinary steps to ensure that coverage is fair; respects the privacy, feelings, and reputations of individuals; and serves the greater needs of society. In doing so, Nordic citizens established the right-of-reply, pioneered the concept of press councils, and conceived the idea of the press ombudsman. Self-criticism and self-regulation began in an organized way in the Nordic countries early in this century, and those efforts have served as the prototype for self-regulation and self-criticism in other parts of the democratic world.

Twenty years ago, to prevent newspaper mortality and to preserve diverse outlets for opinion and the diverse voices they represent, Nordic nations began significant attempts to provide aid to marginal newspapers so they might survive and continue carrying the great number of divergent voices found in Nordic politics and social life. These efforts have gained considerable attention. The success that has been achieved in halting mortality and bolstering these avenues for opinion without government interference in content has led to changes in government press policies throughout the Western world.

The Nordic region (Fig. I.1) includes five sovereign nations – Denmark, Finland, Iceland, Norway, and Sweden – and three dependencies – Greenland and the Faröe Islands, which are associated with Denmark, and the Åland Islands, which are associated with Finland. Of the five sovereign nations, only three – Finland, Norway, and Sweden – extend above the Arctic Circle and less than a third of the landmass of each is located above the circle.

The three northernmost countries look very much like Minnesota and upper New England, with the majority of the land covered with forests, lakes, and land not well suited for agricultural use. The northern areas of the Scandinavian Peninsula (Norway and Sweden) are mountainous, rising to heights of 7000 feet.

Denmark, the southernmost of the five nations, juts from the European continent and is primarily flat with some rolling hills. The land is particularly well suited for agriculture and the nation is heavily dependent upon agricultural products for its economic base.

Iceland is the most unusual of the nations in geological and botanical terms. Located in mid–North Atlantic Ocean, the island is the result of thousands of years of volcanic activity; much of the nation is covered with not yet arable volcanic flows. Little vegetation of the

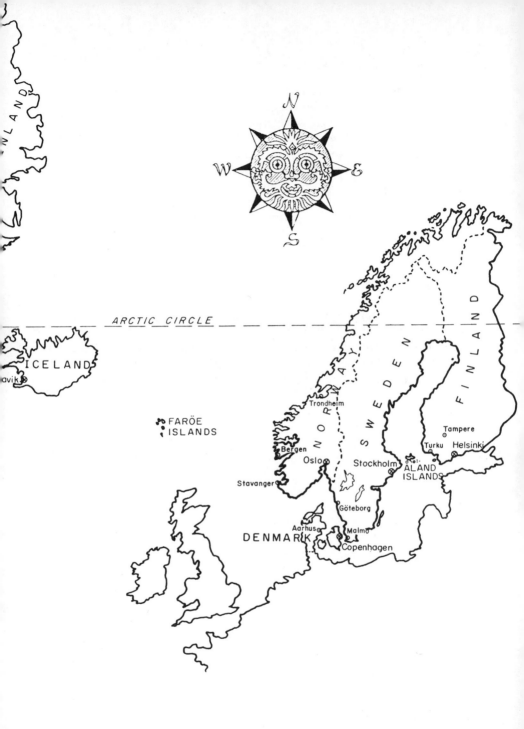

I.1. The five sovereign nations and three dependencies that constitute the Nordic region.

types most Americans know exists on the landmass, although efforts to plant forests and other vegetation are being made and the natural processes of botanical development are underway.

Climates in the region are milder than many people might anticipate, at least where most of the population reside. The Gulf Stream provides protective warm water and air to Iceland and then divides and enters into the North Sea and Baltic Sea.

The total population of the region is about 23 million, and the nations' populations range in size from about 250,000 in Iceland to 4–5 million each in Denmark, Finland, and Norway to a little more than 8 million in Sweden. In terms of national distribution, the populations are sparse, but in Finland, Norway, and Sweden, most are concentrated at the southern ends of the nations, near the Baltic and North seas.

A homogeneity exists between the nations that is stronger than that found in any other area of the world due to the common history, development, and similar linguistic and cultural backgrounds. Throughout modern history the region was held by Denmark and Sweden, and their activities influenced the developments in the conquered and discovered territories that became Finland, Iceland, and Norway.

Internal homogeneity of the population exists in each nation although the similarities have eroded slightly in recent decades as immigrant workers, particularly from the Mediterranean nations, have been assimilated into the population. Nevertheless, the homogeneity has led to a strong social consensus in terms of political-economic developments and social progress.

The population of the nations is highly educated and literate and enjoys some of the highest standards of living in the world. In terms of per capita Gross National Product, the five nations rank in the top 10 of the 24 members of the Organization for Economic Cooperation and Development (OECD). All the nations rank higher than the United States, except Finland, which is close behind.

Despite the lack of significant natural resources, with the exception of timber, minerals, and North Sea oil fields, the nations have achieved substantial economic growth and development through a wide range of agricultural products, high technology products, engineering and consulting services, and manufactured goods.

The citizens of these highly developed nations have an ideological propensity toward government involvement in society and have developed some of the West's most extensive systems of social welfare and state economic planning. Benefits such as public health insurance, unemployment benefits, and pensions are embraced throughout the region and are generally among the highest in the Western world.

The commitment to state involvement in such activities is not limited to the socialist parties in these nations, and is even embraced by the conservative bourgeois parties. This is not to say the parties are in complete agreement; they regularly differ on the extent to which benefits should be broadened and on the methods for raising public funds to pay for such government activities. Political debates are heated and participation is widespread both in local and national party activities.

In terms of political forms, the governments of all five nations are representative democracies, but constitutional monarchies exist in Denmark, Norway, and Sweden. The ruling monarchs are the heads of state, but prime ministers serve as the heads of government. In Iceland and Finland, the head of state is an elected president, but a prime minister serves as head of government as well. Denmark, Finland, and Sweden operate unicameral parliaments called the Folketing, Edhuskunta, and Riksdag respectively. Iceland has a bicameral parliament, the Althing, and Norway's bicameral parliament is called the Storting. The number of significant political parties in the countries ranges from 5 in Iceland and Sweden to 10 in Denmark. The predominant political orientation of the nations since World War II has been left of center.

All five nations have established state Lutheran churches, and more than 95 percent of the population of the region belong to the churches.

PART ONE

Creation and Growth of the Press

CHAPTER ONE

History of the Nordic Press

The history of the press in the Nordic nations has paralleled the history of democratic revolutions in the West but clearly has been shaped by the thousand-year struggle for supremacy between Denmark and Sweden, the development of populist agrarian and socialist parties, and the promotion of cultural nationalism elements that this chapter explores.

The emergence of antimonarchical sentiments and liberal democratic views helped promote the development of newspapers, as did the subsequent emergence of parliamentary government and multiple political parties, which established papers to promote their ideologies and policy proposals. In this century political, social, and economic changes significantly affected the structure of the press that was created during the era of democratization and altered the behavior of newspapers as well.

Although similarities exist between the historical developments in the Nordic nations and those of other Western democracies, the unique political and cultural context of the region produced political and press forms and functions not found in European or North American democracies.

Emergence of Print Communication

With the introduction of Christianity and the consolidation of the region into two kingdoms in the ninth and tenth centuries A.D., the struggle by the kings of Denmark and Sweden to control the Scandinavian Peninsula (now divided into Norway and Sweden) began. Until the early nineteenth century hostilities occurred almost constantly as the two powers battled to control Norway on the western edge of the peninsula and the southern portion of the peninsula that is now part of Sweden. The kings of Sweden also focused their attention on the east, where they endeavored to control the territory that is now Finland and part of the Soviet Union.

The territorial designs of the two nations were shaped by the early history of the region in which Vikings explored and raided much of Europe. The boundaries of their travels and pilgrimages are not yet certain, but it is clear that they reached as far west as the coast of North America and south to the Mediterranean.

By the thirteenth century the Scandinavians, no longer plundering Europe with raiding parties, began engaging in far-reaching commercial activities. Visby, on the island of Gotland in the Baltic Sea, became a major trading center of the Hanseatic League and served as an outlet for the goods of Swedish craftsmen.[1]

Settlement of Iceland, which later became another outlet for Nordic goods, was begun in the ninth century by the Norwegian Ingólfur Arnarson. Although some of the settlers came from Denmark and Sweden, most were from the leading families of Norway, or were related to them. As a result the residents of the island enjoyed a high standard of cultural and intellectual activities almost from its initial settlement.[2]

Printing reached the Nordic nations late in the fifteenth century, with the establishment of a press in Sweden in 1483. In 1526 the first press reached Iceland, the farthest major settlement of Scandinavian nations. Although apparently brought to Iceland by John Matthiasson, a Swedish priest, it was not used until it was established in Holar and operated by Jón Árason, the Catholic bishop, who used it for religious, literary, and polemical purposes. In 1572 the press came under the control of Gudbrandur Thorlaksson, the Protestant bishop, who continued religious control of what was printed.[3]

Following the development of printing presses, circulation of crude news publications reporting important political and economic events began among the clergy, aristocracy, and nobility of Europe. Because many of the early presses were held by religious organizations, much of the information was controlled by authorities of the Catholic and Protestant churches.

Corantos, primitive news sheets, began appearing regularly in London and other major European cities in the early seventeenth century. Similar publications began to appear at about the same time in the Nordic nations. The oldest known news sheet appeared in Strängnäs, Sweden, in 1624. *Hermes Gothicus* was edited by Olof Olfzson Enaeo as a propaganda vehicle for King Gustavus Adolphus II during the Thirty Years War, the conflict that pitted Protestants against Catholics in Northern Europe and led to Swedish conquests in Poland, Germany, and Russia.[4]

Den Svenska Argus, patterned after Britain's *The Tatler* and *The Spectator,* was published weekly between 1632 and 1634 by Olof von Dalin and carried the work of many of the nation's socially progressive writers and poets. Stromberg has observed that Dalin, "in delightful and lucid language and with consumate wit, often in allegorical form, attacked stale orthodoxy and its ally, intolerance, and preached a new doctrine of practical utility."[5]

Although the Swedish conquerors began publishing German-language newpapers in their occupied territories, the Nordic nations still did not have their own newspaper industry. Early news sheets had begun about the time such sheets appeared in other European nations; however, the educated, literate population was apparently content to rely on continental newspapers – particularly French newspapers, which had developed to the highest level of newspapers in the West by the 1630s – and did not attempt to develop and support indigenous newspapers in as timely a manner as their southern counterparts.

The establishment of public postal systems helped spur the Nordic newspaper industry, as it did throughout the world. Denmark's royal postal system was established in 1624, and in 1634 two German emigrants to Denmark, who gained a royal concession to publish news in Denmark, gave the region its first regular news from a regional source.[6] Eleven years later, the first Swedish paper, *Ordinari Post Tijdender,* appeared. This was a court newspaper, which carried news of the continuing Thirty Years War and survived to become the Western world's oldest known continuously published newspaper.[7]

In a pattern of ownership and control that was followed throughout much of the West and its colonies, *Ordinari Post Tijdender* was published by the postmaster of Stockholm, under the authority of the king. The postmaster used his position to gain information from subsidiary post offices around the realm and to deliver his product to readers.[8]

In Denmark the first real newspaper was edited by Anders Bording, who received a royal pension from King Frederick III for his work. Bording was such an able editor that he made *Den Danske Mercurius* the model for future Danish journalism and became known as the father of the Danish press.[9]

Newspapers began appearing in major provincial cities in Denmark and Sweden in the eighteenth century, and coverage of cultural and political issues began to increase.

The first paper in Finland, which had been a part of Sweden since the sixteenth century, appeared in Åbo (Turku). Published in Swedish by a group of professors, *Ett Tidninge Utgifne Af Ett Salskap i Åbo* became a tool for creating a national Finnish movement, and it concentrated more on disseminating nationalistic ideology and culture than news.[10] *Suomenkieliset Tieto-Sanomat*, the first Finnish-language newspaper, appeared in 1776 and was published by clergyman Antti Litzelius, who attempted to reach the small literate Finnish-speaking population. Litzelius discovered, however, that the educated Finnish-speaking population preferred Swedish-language papers and his paper soon folded.[11]

The oldest existing paper in Denmark (*Berlingske Tidende*) was started in Copenhagen in 1749 by E. H. Berling, under the name *Københavnske Danske Post-Tidender.*[12] Throughout the next three decades other individuals were provided charters to be the sole purveyor of news within a "stift," a defined geographical area of the nation. *Aalborg Stiftstidende,* founded in Ålborg in 1767 as such a paper, today remains one of the nation's important provincial papers. The growth of the press in Denmark and elsewhere began to make absolute control by monarchies more difficult, and in 1755, King Frederick V reluctantly relaxed censorship of economic news in Denmark.[13] In 1766 during the Age of Freedom in Sweden, the first constitutional guarantees of press freedom anywhere in the world were enacted. Although the period of freedom there was briefly interrupted by a return to strong monarchical rule, the principles promulgated in the eighteenth-century document were to influence later press protections in Sweden and other nations in the region.[14]

The early efforts to relax controls on the press in Denmark were extended somewhat in 1770 by a decree of Christian VII that won the praise of Voltaire.[15] Shortly thereafter, the country abolished censorship in its dependent territories, including occupied German states.

The first political paper in Finland, *Åbo Morgonblad,* emerged in the early 1770s in Åbo, where the first paper in that country had been founded. This paper differed from its predecessors by concentrating on political issues, although it continued the nationalistic cultural campaigns of previous papers. *Åbo Morgonblad* was published in Swedish, reflecting the continuing reality that the educated class that could afford the paper still preferred to read the language of the conquering nation and the homeland of most of the aristocracy and noblity.[16] In Sweden, meanwhile, economic, social, and political conditions had improved to the point where important regional papers could be established in Göteborg, Carlscrona, Norrköping, and Lund, and a daily newspaper, *Dagligt Allehanda,* appeared in Stockholm in 1767.[17]

The newspaper industry developed more slowly in Norway than in the other parts of the region because of the slow growth of population centers and necessary economic development and heavy censorship by Danish authorities. Early news sheets appeared infrequently during most of the eighteenth century; however, it was not until 1793 that the first newspaper, *Norske Intelligenz-Seddeler,* appeared in Bergen, violating a royal prerogative that granted permission only to Danish citizens to publish papers.[18]

A year after the first Norwegian paper appeared, the first regular news publication appeared in Iceland. *Klausturposturinn* was operated by Magnús Stephensen, who controlled the only printing press and used the paper to promote his social and political views and strengthen his position as chief justice.[19]

The rapid spread of presses throughout the region decreased the possibility for absolute control over newspapers and permitted the publication of information and ideas not previously authorized by monarchs or their representatives. At the same time, increasing discussions of the idea of popular government—especially after the American and French Revolutions—threatened the Nordic monarchies and they reacted with repressive measures. On February 7, 1790, King Gustav III of Sweden forbade the newspapers in that country to cover news events in France.[20] Later in 1799, a Danish decree mandated that all newspapers and pamphlets must be submitted to police for review before being sold.[21] After a brief attempt at popular rule in Sweden, the return to monarchical rule brought renewed controls on the press and delayed the continuing movement toward democratic government.

Beginnings of Modern Journalism

The early nineteenth century brought with it the last of the major military struggles for control of the region. In 1809 Sweden, which had struggled with Russia over parts of Finland since the sixteenth century, ceded Finland to Russia. Before the territory was turned over to the tsar, a correspondent for the *Swedish Intelligencer* went into the field of battle with the army of King Gustav IV Adolf, becoming one of the first recorded war correspondents.[22]

The long-standing struggle between Denmark and Sweden over Norway ended in 1814 when Denmark ceded the territory to Sweden after a Swedish invasion. The move followed increasing Norwegian opposition to the Danish monarchy, opposition that was reported and encouraged by newspapers in Norway.

Although Norway came under Swedish domination in 1814, it was allowed considerable autonomy in union with Sweden. The assembly set up to govern Norway recognized the importance of individual liberties, including freedom of the press, and afforded them some protection.

> Parallel with democracy went the assertion of personal liberty. It is a significant fact that the most universal demand which followed the news that the Danish absolute monarch had renounced his hold on Norway was the cry for freedom of the press. The Eidsvoll assembly hastened to proclaim freedom of the press and freedom of religion as principles of the new constitution – the latter, to be sure, extending only to Christian denominations.[23]

Because of the nation's underdevelopment, scattered population, and some administrative interference, however, newspaper growth continued to be limited and it was not until 1819 that the first daily newspaper, *Morgenbladet,* was established.[24]

By the 1830s foreign influences and technology, rising literacy, and increasing pressures for representative government throughout Nordic nations began to significantly alter the nature of the press. Norwegian journalism, which had lagged because of political and social conditions, began to mature rapidly. Political journalism increased with the development of municipal governments and nationwide reviews of politics began to appear.

In Denmark, which was beginning to redefine its internal and external relations after ceding Norway to Sweden and engaging in conflicts with Great Britain and Germany, a lively pamphlet press began discussions of individual rights and national governance. In 1834 the liberal newspapers *Kjøbenhavnsposten, Dansk Ugeskrift,* and *Fædrelandet* appeared and began to push for increased personal liberties and representative government. For the next generation, *Fædrelandet,* edited by Carl Ploug, dominated public opinion and the battle for popular participation in government.[25] In 1837 the Society for the Beneficial Use of the Freedom of the Press was formed and gained a membership of 5000 in its struggle to help papers such as *Fædrelandet.* The promotion of liberal ideals was not without risk, however. In an 8-year period, *Fædrelandet* was fined Kr 13,000. In the last half of 1843, one-tenth of all its issues were confiscated.[26]

The rapidly developing press of Norway was also supportive of liberal ideals. In 1843 the Danish king attempted to reduce its impact in Denmark by forbidding his subjects to subscribe to *Morgenbladet*.[27] Although the order undoubtedly reduced its circulation in Denmark, the paper grew and prospered and became one of Norway's leading journals.

The newspapers in Sweden also began promoting antimonarchy sentiments, and among the first to promote liberal ideals was the Stockholm paper *Aftonbladet*, published by Lars Hierta. The publication became a commercial success, partly due to its political leanings, but also because it was the first Swedish paper to combine news, commentary, and entertainment and to capitalize on the buying power of the growing middle class.[28]

Not surprisingly, the newspaper offended King Karl XIV Johan and was suppressed 14 times. Each time, Hierta defied the ban by changing the title to avoid the order. The paper appeared under the titles *Aftonbladet the Second, Aftonbladet the Third,* and so on, until attempts to suppress it were abandoned.[29] The loyalty of Hierta's readers was so strong that opponents dubbed him "King Lars" and his paper became known as the "Bible" of the Swedish people.[30]

During the mid–nineteenth century the liberal antimonarchy press in Sweden began expanding its readership outside Stockholm, and influential papers were founded in Uppsalla and Göteborg. Because circulation of a timely national newspaper was difficult due to poor transportation and communication capabilities, liberal provincial papers became important media of mass communication in the countryside. A liberal press that catered to the peasantry also emerged in Norway. *Folkebladet* began to strongly espouse Norwegian nationalism and *Statsborgeren,* edited by Peder Soelvold, contributed to the growing liberalization and nationalism.[31]

After the territory of Norway was ceded to Sweden in 1814, especially between 1830 and 1850, the press in Norway developed rapidly, fueled by the industrial expansion, increasing educational opportunities, economic development, and the development of municipal government and the local political press. Expansion of newspapers continued as high-speed presses replaced the older wooden letterpress technology, and in 1837 the artisans law removed the presses from the control of guilds.[32] By 1850 each city of any significance had at least one paper operating in it.[33]

Denmark had eight dailies at midcentury and liberalism had taken root sufficiently in Sweden so that Carl Daniel Forsell was able to pioneer radical journalism with the *Karlstadstidningen,* which supported communist ideology.[34]

The first regularly published Finnish-language paper to carry political as well as cultural material was founded in Helsinki in 1847. *Suometar* was founded by Finnish nationalists, following the example of the politician J. V. Snellman,[35] who started *Saima* as the first newspaper to seriously address subjects of interest to the politically active members of the population before it was suspended. Snellman was joined by other politicians and educators who played important roles not only in journalism but in setting the national political and cultural climate.[36]

J. L. Runeberg, who is considered the national poet of Finland, founded *Morgonblad,* and Z. Topelius, Finland's Hans Christian Andersen, started *Helsingfors Tidningar.* The papers played a major role in increasing nationalistic ideas and promoting Finnish culture.[37]

Reaction to the papers by the tsarist government was unfavorable; in 1850 rigorous censorship hampered the Finnish-language press. The Russians attempted to control the press, as they did the press in other parts of the realm, so that "radical" ideas that might threaten the empire could not reach the Finnish-speaking population. The controls became so rigid that *Suometar* had to give up both the foreign news and political commentary. To replace the official news that had previously been carried by *Suometar* and other private papers, the government started the inexpensive paper *Suomen Julkisia Sanomia.*[38]

While Finland was enduring the control of Russian rulers, Denmark was beginning to incorporate liberal ideals into its government. In 1849 a free constitution was constructed that enunciated the rights of the press and restricted censorship. Two years later a law intended to help protect public interests without resorting to censorship assigned responsibility for the content of unsigned articles to a single person, usually the editor or the publisher. The essence of the law was patterned after a Belgian law affixing responsibility, and it still exists today.[39]

Economic conditions were improving in Denmark, and in 1851 Carsteen Andersen Bille, an attorney, founded *Dagbladet* to cater to the growing petty bourgeoisie. Emphasizing foreign news and economic affairs, especially of interest to merchants, *Dagbladet* became an alternative to *Fædrelandet,* which catered to intellectuals.[40]

In Iceland in 1848 regular newspaper publishing began with the appearance of the weekly paper *Pjöðolfur,* which emphasized public affairs as well as general cultural and local news.[41] Freedom of the press was established by law in 1855, extending to the colony protections enjoyed by Danes.[42]

Rise and Growth of the Party Press

With the fundamentals of individual liberties protected and the establishment of the foundations of liberal democracies in Norway, Denmark, and Sweden, political parties began to grow and prosper throughout the region. To help propagate their ideologies and ensure that their voices could be heard in the political process, the political parties began establishing papers. Their actions set a pattern for the newspaper industries of the Nordic nations that is still influential today.

The first news agencies were established in the 1860s to serve the information needs of the rapidly growing newpaper ranks. In 1866 Eric Nicolai Ritzau founded the Ritzaus Bureau, which carried foreign news and financial information to subscribers in Denmark and southern Sweden. Within five years the agency was *the* news agency for Denmark.[43] A year after he began the Danish agency, Ritzau started Norsk Telegrambyrå in Norway with a partner, Alfred Fich, who acted as editor; they served the special needs of the Norwegian papers.[44]

The continuing struggle to promote democratic rule in Denmark helped increase the number of papers. Most papers that were established before midcentury and those operated by the church were nonpolitical and tended to support or at least not challenge the status quo – together with the old "stift" papers they came to form the nucleus of a press of the right.[45] However, the new politically affiliated press was clearly liberal and supported efforts for social change made by farmers, peasants, and intellectuals. Between 1866 and 1876, for instance, 19 Danish papers were started by the Farmers' party. These papers usually were backed by a local agricultural organization and operated for the purpose of supporting the political and economic views of farmers.[46] The Liberal party also helped spark growth in the industry by supporting newspapers in medium and large cities that championed liberal ideals.[47]

Thorsen has noted that the new dailies differed from the older ones by having a political standpoint. The provinces got journalist-editors who considered themselves the champions of an idea and aimed their efforts at the creation of a public opinion in favor of democracy and the Liberal party. The primary concern of the new dailies was politics, with the leading article and the parliamentary report often taking up more than half the columns.[48]

In Norway where parliamentarianism and political parties were not yet established, political discussion nevertheless arose. During the

1860s and 1870s arguments between conservatives and liberals were carried on in the existing papers and in pamphlets that promoted political discussions. It was not until the 1880s, however, that rapid growth of papers affiliated with political organizations began in Norway.

In Sweden the 1860s brought the establishment of *Dagens Nyheter*, which quickly gained a large circulation as an alternative to the liberal *Aftonbladet*. Like *Dagbladet* in Denmark, *Dagens Nyheter* catered to the growing middle class.[49]

In the 1860s Tsar Alexander II allowed the Finnish parliament to be reestablished after a 50-year absence. Until this time, Finnish nationalism had been expressed mainly on the cultural level, but with the formation of the parliament and the emergence of stronger political organizations, the promotion of nationalism in newspapers became more political.[50]

Previously, all Finnish papers except the tsar's official paper had been considered organs of nationalism, but with the arrival of parliamentarianism, the papers divided into two groups with different perspectives. The Swedish-language press supported the views of the aristocracy, who had a strong Swedish orientation, while the Finnish-language press concentrated on promoting the nationalistic views of the remainder of the population.[51] *Suometar* remained the paper of Finnish-speaking nationalists, and Swedish-speaking subscribers read the Swedish party's *Hufvudstadsbladet*. A third political group, the Liberal party, started *Helsingfors Dagblad* in 1862 to serve its needs. Seven years later *Uusi Suometar* became the organ of the Finnish party.[52]

Throughout the 1870s and 1880s the trend of politicization continued, with party-oriented papers emerging throughout the Nordic nations. Economic development and the establishment of regional trading centers sparked an increase of papers in rural areas. Like their counterparts in the cities, these new papers took on a decidedly political character.

In 1870 there were about 80 papers in Norway, split between the competing presses of the liberal Venstre party and the conservative Høyre party. The Liberal party dominated the capital and the eastern part of the country and the Conservative party dominated the western and southern parts of the country.[53]

In the last half of the century the development of socialist parties in the Nordic nations forever changed the nature of the press. The labor press began in Denmark in the 1870s and is second only to Germany's as the oldest in the world. In 1871 Louis Pio established *Socialisten* (later called *Social-Demokraten* and today *Aktuelt*, the oldest continuously published labor paper in the world) in Copenhagen and operated it until 1874 when it was taken over by labor unions.[54] About the same time, *Kolding Folkeblad* was founded by Chresten Berg as the mother newspaper of a chain of papers in Jutland. Published in Kolding, all these papers were alike except for changes on the advertising pages, an early example of advertising marketing strategies pursued by the largest newspapers today.[55] The operation was so successful that Berg started *Morgenbladet* as the first real liberal paper in Copenhagen. The paper, edited by Viggo Hørup, instituted reporting in contemporary language, which appealed to a wider audience.

In 1873 Christian Ferslew, who would become Denmark's only real press lord, started *Aftenposten* as a popular, nonpolitical daily for the masses, filled with entertainment and how-to stories. Two years later Ferslew brought the first rotary press to Denmark to help increase production speed so the demand for the paper could be met.[56] An innovator with production machinery, he later introduced typesetting machines and improved the use of his presses by printing morning and afternoon editions of a national newspaper, *Nationaltidende.*[57]

The rise of workers' movements in all the countries in the 1880s added more papers to the scene. August Palm founded *Socialdemokraten* in Sweden but was so undercapitalized that the first issues had to be printed in several small runs and he went into the streets himself to sell the first copies so the remainder could be purchased from the printer. From that small beginning, the newspaper developed into one of the nation's most influential publications and became the leading Swedish proponent of the socialist movement. As the movement grew, party officials saw the advantage of party organs and started nearly two dozen to serve readers in the major regions of the country.

The developing bourgeois parties gained support from many of the previously established papers, but party ties were based only on political agreement with the papers rather than on direct funding and ownership usually employed by the Social Democrats.

Socialist ideology also spread to Finland and the first labor paper there, *Työmies,* was established in 1895, even though the tsar maintained significant control in the country.[58]

In Denmark the labor movement continued to gain support throughout the country and *Demokraten,* published in Århus, became the chief mouthpiece for the movement in rural areas. The developing ideology of the leftist parties brought about the fragmentation of the Left and the Liberals. In 1884 Viggo Hørup, considered by many to be the greatest journalist of his time, left *Morgenbladet* to become editor of *Politiken* when it was founded by the radical wing of the existing Left.[59] Five years later Ove Rode increased competition in the industry by founding *København*. This boulevard paper was affiliated with the Liberal party and had an important influence on party policies and the literary community before it adopted the techniques of yellow journalism.

Emil Wiinblad became one of Denmark's leading journalists after he was named editor of the *Social-Demokraten* in 1881. Wiinblad became the best-known personality among Danish labor paper editors and helped change the solely ideological *Social-Demokraten* into a daily newspaper that covered both foreign and domestic news so workers would not need to subscribe to any other paper to receive important news and political rhetoric.[60] When Wiinblad took over the paper it had only 2500 subscribers but in 3 years he increased circulation to 18,000.

Socialist papers also began to gain strength in Norway, including two left-wing papers published in Christiana, *Dagbladet* and *Verdens Gang.* The extent of politicization in the Norwegian press can be seen in that there were 130 political papers operating in the country in 1885.[61]

As the turn of the century approached, 18 newspapers were operating in Iceland, and a printers' union – the first industrial union on the island – was formed.[62] It invited publishers to form their own federation for negotiations on wages and working conditions.[63]

Newspapers continued to be politicized and rising demands for more political rights and workers' rights did not escape the notice of monarchs.

The workers' papers in Finland differed from those in the other Nordic countries because they were purchased or given to the Finnish Labor party relatively early. Much of the labor press was established by selling shares to laborers and supporters in exchange for one vote per shareholder, no matter how many shares were owned. The Labor party ultimately purchased *Suomen Sosialidemokraatti* (the successor of *Työmies*) after a heated debate over who would control the paper, and the party operated it as a major vehicle for party viewpoints. Pentti Salmelin has observed that

> the Finnish Labour Press achieved its emergence within the space of a decade. The first Labour paper, the *Työmies,* was founded in Helsinki in 1895, but for the first years it appeared as the organization publication of the workers' associations for promotion of social reform, and came out only once a week. The change of this Helsinki paper to a six-daily publication and the establishment of local Labour papers in the other big industrial centres, Turku and Tampere, meant the actual establishment of the first Labour press group.[64]

The Finnish Labor party papers developed successfully as labor association publications and began changing into general circulation newspapers, with an increasing demand for improved content, which was met by the news agency Suomen Tietotoimisto, Finska Notisbyrå. Though the agency, begun under the editorship of Woldeman Westzynthius in 1887, had the approval of the Russian government, it encountered official intrusion into editorial decisions throughout the Russian rule of Finland as the government endeavored to quench the increasing thirst for news.

The campaign to "Russify" Finland was begun by the governor general in the 1890s, and to promote his goals, stringent controls were placed on the press, especially those newspapers that appealed to nationalistic political and cultural feelings. Some papers were abolished and new papers could not be established without a permit. During the height of the campaign in 1898 and 1899, nearly 500 censorship actions were taken by officials, including regular confiscations of newspapers and deportations of journalists. At least 47 papers were ordered to suspend publication as a punitive measure and 24 papers were completely shut down. Eero Erkko, who opposed the Russification of Finland, began *Päivälehti,* which promoted Finnish nationalism until it, too, was suspended by the tsar's censors in 1904.[65] The process kept the press in line and halted the growth that had been experienced in the Finnish newspaper industry.

At the turn of the twentieth century 177 papers were being published in Sweden, including *Stockholms-Tidningen,* which first appeared in 1900.[66] This paper was addressed to the lower middle class and sold at a single copy rate 80 percent below its competitors. The reduced price was made possible because the publisher, Anders Jeurling, increased the cost of advertising and began the first real attempt to build a dual source of income from advertisers and readers.[67] *Stockholms-Tidningen* became the first of Sweden's true mass papers and gained 100,000 circulation shortly after its founding.

The Danish press also began to show rapid improvement and expansion through focusing on the problems of its readers and by moving toward a popular press format. Henrik Cavling, editor of *Politiken,* introduced practices he had learned while observing the commercial press during travels in the United States. He introduced human interest stories, gave foreign news a "bright" touch, and introduced the concept of putting breaking news on page one and pushing advertisements and cultural articles to the inside pages. He also imported a Marinoni press with built-in folding and pasting machines so he could produce a 16-page paper, a first for Denmark. In 1904, he introduced

Ekstrabladet as an afternoon supplement to *Politiken.* Cavling's activities helped shift the Danish press from a cultural and polemical press to one that concentrated on popular information and political activity.

The first two decades of the twentieth century are considered the classical period of the four-paper system in Denmark. Under that system, each of the larger towns had four papers that represented different political viewpoints. Roughly, they represented the middle classes of the towns, the farmers, the workers, and the small land holders, yet they were not strictly speaking class presses. The ruling principle of each group was not a narrow class interest, but a general political outlook, capable both of attacking outsiders and of repelling those factions of the population to which the newspaper in question usually catered.[68]

Editorships were important political positions and only a few of the early newspaper editors were originally professional journalists. The importance of ties between papers and the parties they represented was not lost on political activists. In Denmark, members of parliament representing the Radical-Liberal party formed The Free Press, an organization that helped small papers throughout the country that presented the party's viewpoints. Most papers associated with the party used the name *Venstreblad,* preceded by the name of the province in which they appeared.

Liberal party papers accounted for a large number of the papers in the country, and by 1903, 83 papers were members of the Association of Liberal Newspapers. The labor press reached a circulation of 100,000 by 1906, with its circulation divided among 32 papers. About half of the Labor party's circulation was in Copenhagen and the other half was in the provinces. The labor press actively supported the party and the Copenhagen-based *Social-Demokraten* began publishing a regular daily page of party information to serve the needs of party officials.

The labor press of Denmark differed from that in the other Nordic nations in that it was linked economically as well as politically almost from its beginning. As early as 1888 the party had placed its newspapers under the direction of a special newspaper committee, which worked to use the resources of the existing papers to start new ones throughout the country and to ensure they had adequate financial support. For example, *Social-Demokraten* subsidized *Demokraten* when it was founded in Århus. This arrangement, unique to Denmark, was possible partly by the close contact between the labor unions, the original owners of the labor press, and the political party and partly by the solidarity of the workers.[69]

In Finland, growth of the Labor party made it possible for the party to begin providing loans and other financial assistance to papers after the turn of the century. In 1909 the party proposed the creation of a special tax within the party that would increase membership fees to support labor papers. The plan was patterned after that of Sweden, where Social Democrats had earlier levied a party tax on behalf of their papers.[70] The plan met with strong opposition in Finland, however, and it was abandoned.

Efforts to increase the number of papers supporting the Finnish Labor party were thereafter stymied by the lack of money to purchase new papers. The lack of resources forced the party to continue to rely on *Työmies* as a national paper until after independence was achieved, despite the difficulties of circulating the paper throughout the country and the fact that it never really became a successful paper. Like other papers in Finland, the labor press still faced censorship and, because of its political stances, was subjected to special regulations as the attempt at Russification continued.[71] After the constitutional reform of 1906, control of the press was eased slightly and the Farmers' party founded *Ilkka* in Vaasa to promote its views.

Political parties began blooming in Iceland in the early twentieth century, and the conservative Home Rule party and the liberal Independence party emerged as the dominant parties at that time. The first daily newspaper, *Visir*, appeared in 1910 and was associated with the Independence party.

War, Peace, and Structural Change

The years surrounding the First World War brought change to the press in the Nordic nations. The three sovereign nations – Denmark, Norway, and Sweden – proclaimed neutrality, but public opinion in the nations was divided. For example, the Swedish agency Svenska Telegrambyrå fell under the control of German sympathizers and the British helped organize a rival agency to "balance" the coverage with an anti-German, pro-Allies view.[72]

During the war professionalism reached Sweden's newspaper industry and organizations for advertisers, journalists, and publishers emerged. A fair practices commission, Pressens Opinionsnämnd, was also established and evolved into the modern press council.

In 1917 the Social Democratic party press of Sweden suffered a blow when a leftist faction split with the party and managed to gain the support of party papers in the northern part of the country. As the split widened the new leftist party managed to start several other papers to support its views. However, the majority of the Social Democratic papers in southern and central Sweden remained loyal to the party.

The Russian Revolution and the continuing turmoil in Europe were used by the Finns to assert their independence in 1917. Because of the historical importance of the press in promoting nationalism and political parties, efforts were made to protect press freedoms under independence. An act of 1919 guaranteed that "Finnish citizens shall enjoy freedom of speech and the right of printing and publishing written or pictorial presentations without any previous authorization." The act also defined the rights and responsibilities of editors and the conditions under which suppression or confiscation of issues would be permissible.[73]

In 1920 the number of papers in Sweden peaked at 240, with the average paper being small and having a circulation of less than 1000.[74] In large cities each significant party had a newspaper or aided one that supported its ideology. In many communities, even in the provinces, as many as six papers were produced locally. The bourgeois papers, generally the largest and independently owned, normally dominated the markct, and since their owners sought to create profit, the papers were not primarily outlets for party ideology as was the case in the labor press.

Many reasons are given for the peak in the number of Swedish newspapers, but clearly, good economic conditions, strong political activity, and the relatively inexpensive cost of starting papers contributed. The increased number of papers required a considerable amount of information for publication, and difficulties with the previous news agency, combined with a desire for participation in its management, led Swedish publishers to form a cooperative agency, Tidningarnas Telegrambyrå, in 1921.

The decade contributed a change in the competitive nature of newspaper publishing. The competitive forces afflicting newspapers in other parts of the developed world began to appear in the Swedish papers as they, too, began to compete with each other more and more as interchangeable products.[75] During the 1930s those forces, as well as the economic turmoil that afflicted the capitalist world, began making it economically difficult for smaller papers, and by 1940 the number of papers had declined to 207.[76]

The Social Democratic party, although the largest party and the party controlling government at that time, lost the most papers because they tended to be small, economically unsound regional papers. In 1936 to combat the threat of the loss of vehicles of expression, the Social Democrats founded Arbetarpressens Forlagsaktiebolag, a press support foundation. Shortly thereafter, some of the smaller right-wing parties set up a similar organization, Unitas, to combat similar problems among their papers. In 1932 *Aftonbladet* was transformed into the nation's first modern evening paper, giving extensive space to entertainment, columns, and sensational news coverage.

The number of Norwegian papers peaked at 247 in 1930 and the number of locations in which papers were published peaked at 111. Though the 1930s were a golden age for the political press in Finland, with ties between parties and papers remaining strong, the Communist party did not enjoy the benefits of Finnish independence and press freedom. Despite the Communist party and press being prohibited altogether during the years 1930–1944, communist papers began growing and maturing in other nations.[77] For example, the communist paper *Arbejderbladet* began publication as a daily newspaper in Denmark in 1934. During the Finno-Russian War (1939–1940), fought over military rights in borderlands shared by those two nations, the paper was subjected to the considerable animosity of many Danes because of its Soviet sympathies. Nevertheless, the paper survived.

Anticommunism had been felt earlier in Finland, where it resulted in the curtailing of civil liberties and the banning of the Communist party. In the late 1920s the Communist party of Finland pursued an aggressive labor policy through the Confederation of Trade Unions and adopted a political stance similar to that of the Communist party of the Soviet Union. These actions split the socialist and communist alliance in the trade union group and in many other joint political activities. The policies of the Communist party also sparked the emergence of anticommunist organizations, called the Lapua movement after violence against communists in Lapua. They received wide attention by resorting to regular violence against the party and its sympathizers. The most radical of these organizations was the Safeguard Finland Association (Suomen Suojeluslitto), which was primarily composed of rural veterans of the 1923 civil war.

The Edhuskunta, the Finnish parliament, was asked to consider legislation restraining the Communist party press in the spring of 1930, but the proposal met with severe opposition by members of the Communist, Socialist, and Swedish People's parties. While the measure was still under consideration, anticommunists stilled the press by destroying the communist paper in the town of Vaasa. Members of the local Suojeluskunta (civil guard) and the police force were involved in the planning and execution of this act. The perpetrators, who had ostentatiously given themselves up to the police, went to trial, which marked the beginning of a new phase of violence. The communist lawyer for the printing press was seized by a mob, beaten up, and driven out of the province with a warning never to set foot in it again. The Lapua movement declared that it would not tolerate the reappearance of the communist paper in question.[78]

The paper did not reappear as the government, without legal authority, banned all communist newspapers in mid-June, including the national paper *Tiedonantaja*. Later it began moves to outlaw communism and arrested all the Communist party members of parliament for treason. By November 1930 anticommunist laws were passed and the party was forced underground for almost 15 years. When it was permitted to reorganize, it started the paper *Työkansan Sanomat* in Helsinki, which has been published since 1946.

The concept of press responsibility embodied in the Swedish Fair Practices Commission was adopted in Denmark in 1938. A law setting up a Board of Denials and Corrections was enacted and the board was charged with handling disputes between citizens and newspapers over factual errors. The law also stipulated the responsibilities of editors and made them legally responsible for the entire content of their papers, except for signed articles, for which the author was held responsible.[79]

The Second World War created serious problems for the Nordic press due to the occupation of Denmark and Norway by Germany and the defeat of Finland by the Soviet Union. The Swedish government espoused neutrality in the conflict, partly due to the ties of the royal family to German royalty and partly out of desires to avoid defeat and occupation. The government quieted newspapers that exhibited vehement critical opinions of the Nazis. These actions sparked a great deal of discussion about the implications to freedom of the press, and the limitations of existing Swedish press protections became clear.

In its efforts to help support the nation's claims of neutrality, the government confiscated the offensive issues of the paper *Göteborgs Handels-och Sjöfarts-Tidningen,* which usually included editorials and cartoons opposing Hitler. They also confiscated newpapers containing violent pro-Nazi pieces. The confiscation was possible because the government resurrected a defunct statute, but as William Shirer noted, whether all this appeased Hitler or not is questionable.[80]

The war also lessened the influence of foreign governments on the Swedish press, but as indicated earlier, the papers were not opposed to taking sides in the conflict.

The occupation of Norway brought with it the closure of many Norwegian newspapers and the incarceration and execution of journalists. Those who managed to stay on the job began publishing poetry containing seemingly innocent words that alluded to patriotic themes and symbols understood by Norwegians.

As a result of the persecution of the press and journalists, underground papers, relying on news gathered from hidden shortwave radio receivers, developed. About 300 such papers, ranging from a few hundred copies per issue printed on mimeograph machines to newspapers with a circulation of 20,000 printed on a secret press, kept the people informed of the developments in the war and helped increase morale. There was a large radio audience in Norway for the British Broadcasting Corporation (BBC), and when the Germans and their collaborators in the Quisling government seized the radio receivers, these underground papers assumed an even greater role.[81]

With the invasion of German forces, radio stations and newspapers in Denmark came under the control of the Danish Foreign Ministry beginning April 9, 1940. They were placed under direct German control in August 1943.[82] All foreign news and editorials that related to international developments had to be cleared by censors. Any criticism of Germany and German activities was forbidden, of course, and military news was sharply controlled. In spite of the censorship and seizures during the occupation, the activities of the Danish journalists were a model of courage.

During the months that followed the invasion, newspaper sales declined because the public distrusted the content and discussions of political issues had disappeared. Despite pressure from German officials, however, no Danish paper sided with Germany or supported national socialism during the occupation. The dailies carried articles from the occupation authorities, but they clearly labeled the sources of the material and refused to print attacks on the Danish government.[83]

Within a year of the invasion, the Communist party of Denmark was banned and the action brought a flurry of protests. The party paper, *Land og Fog,* began publishing secretly and ultimately attained a circulation of over 125,000 as a fortnightly publication.[84]

De Frie Danske, an underground paper founded by journalists who had lost their jobs at legal papers and working journalists who wished to help print truthful accounts of war events, eventually attained a circulation of 20,000. *Frit Danmark* was established as a monthly paper in April 1942 and by the end of the year also had a circulation of 20,000, which later rose to 145,000. During 1942 there was a phenomenal growth in the number of illegal newspapers and by the end of the year, nearly 50 papers with a combined circulation of 300,000 were appearing in the country.

Publishing underground papers was not without risk, but the

perils did not stop the illegal press. In autumn 1942, *De Frie Danske* was raided and its staff jailed; the editor of *Frit Danmark* was arrested also, but the remaining staff managed to continue publishing the newspaper. By the end of 1943, 166 newspapers with a combined circulation of 2.6 million copies existed. Continual searches by authorities hampered the activities of the illegal printers, and in the spring of 1944 the Germans found 18 illegal printing presses and made mass arrests of the journalists and printers involved.[85]

To serve the needs of the mushrooming underground industry, an Illegal Press Coordinating Committee and an Illegal Press Joint Association Newsroom were formed to help distribute supplies and information. In 1944, Information—a news service that had once been legal—served 254 illegal newspapers with total circulation of 11 million. It operated under the direction of the Freedom Council's Press Committee and was organized so that it was not only able to provide daily information to Danish papers but was able to smuggle information to Sweden, where the Danish Press Service used it on nightly radio broadcasts and distributed it worldwide.[86]

The circulation and influence of the underground press during the occupation exceeded that of the legal press. Journalists employed creative devices to help readers understand what they could not say outright.

> Suggestive headlines appeared in print and layout editors placed German reports in ironical juxtaposition, thus inviting readers to draw their own conclusions. The provincial press, in particular, out of immediate touch with censors in Copenhagen, often ignored regulations and played up the few Allied victories and played down the continuing string of German victories. Even Copenhagen newspapers carried on a running though hidden struggle with the censors and their German mentors. The flashy afternoon newspaper *Ekstrabladet* once printed an entire article with double spacing between the lines, thus making it easier for readers to read between them.[87]

The end of the war brought major changes to the newspapers of the Nordic nations. Some of the Danish underground papers attempted to capitalize on their success and continued to publish. Competition began to reduce the number of papers available throughout the region, however, and the face of the newspaper industry began to be altered radically. In Sweden the introduction of afternoon tabloids altered the newspaper environment. For example, *Expressen* was established by *Dagens Nyheter* and *Aftontidningen* (later replaced by *Aftonbladet*) was established by the Confederation of Trade Unions.

Between the end of the Second World War and 1970, the number of Danish papers declined from 207 to 116.[88] In Norway, between 1946 and 1966, provincial cities producing more than one local paper decreased from 33 to 9.[89] Until 1946 the Finnish press was dominated by political newspapers, but by 1970 the number of politically independent papers had grown 60 percent due partly because more than 40 Finnish newspapers folded, were incorporated into other papers, or were transformed into other types of periodicals. Most of the papers that closed were party papers that ranked second, third, or fourth in their market area.

By the 1950s the failure of newspapers throughout the region had begun to create a serious imbalance between newspaper affiliation and party strength. In Finland the biggest loss of papers was on the political right.[90] In Sweden the Social Democrats were hit hard and were especially damaged by the loss of *Stockholms-Tidningen* in 1967.[91]

Because of the changes in the number of newspapers representing particular party views and their electoral strength, new ways in which public funds could be used to stem the tide of newspaper deaths and the concentration of ownership were considered. In the 1960s various subvention plans were proposed and a variety of subsidy, loan, and cooperative programs were begun.[92]

In 1965 the Swedish government instituted subsidies to political parties to support information activities, including subsidizing papers sympathetic to the various political parties. Five years later it instituted a loan fund for modernization of newspaper equipment and facilities, and shortly thereafter the government began providing direct subsidies to the papers to offset production costs.[93]

The Danish government helped establish the Dagspressens Finansieringsinstitut in 1970 to provide loans for modernization and expansion; similar loans are now available in Iceland and Norway. Increases in government funding also made it possible for newspapers to make better use of preferential postal and telecommunication rates and to begin cooperative publishing and distribution efforts.

Recessionary economics in the region during the late 1970s and early 1980s has created a growing concern about the high levels of state funding for the press, but it is clear that the aid has generally halted newspaper mortality throughout the region and made it possible to maintain a wide variety of voices that could not survive in a solely commercial market. Recent discussions of state aid for the press have concentrated on ways to cap or slow the growth of such aid programs and on means of using the existing funds to promote the establishment of new papers, particularly weeklies, to replace some of those lost during the postwar period. Means are also being sought to encourage more cooperation between papers in their capital-intensive operations, such as printing and distribution.[94]

The early history of the Nordic press parallels that of liberal democratic nations because it was government related – operating by charter or fiat of the authorities. The press began a transformation into a pluralistic institution, free from undue government control, as the liberal ideal of democracy spread in the Nordic region. Newspapers became vocal proponents of personal liberties and played significant roles in bringing about democratic political institutions.

The growth of multiple political parties, however, had a much greater influence on the Nordic press than that in much of the West. The development of political organizations, particularly Socialist and Populist parties, during the nineteenth century brought with it the establishment of hundreds of newspapers that promoted party ideas and interpreted the news. These papers became important factors in national and local political activities. As the Nordic region evolved from two into five nations, the newspapers helped by becoming strong proponents of nationalism and indigenous culture, particularly in Norway and Finland, and continued to promote political activity.

The Nordic press has not escaped the commercialism that developed in the Anglo-American press in the past century, but its content and marketing were less affected. The closing of newspapers and the concentration of ownership in the Nordic region were caused by the competitive economic system, however, and the remaining papers have struggled to maintain political diversity and not to evolve into the purportedly "objective" press of North America. Also, the Nordic press has managed to escape many of the dangers of rejecting much serious news and cutting out circulation in "undesirable" areas, found in the marketing approaches to news evinced in the Anglo-American newspaper industries and developing in other Western nations' press industries. As a result the Nordic press has continued to provide serious information, commentary, and cultural discussions that have become increasingly difficult to find elsewhere, especially in the common English-language press.

The political nature of the press is expected to continue, although the number of papers aligned with each political party will continue to fluctuate. In the aggregate, the number of papers closely tied to political parties will probably decline as the parties replace many small, expensive papers with fewer but larger papers designed to serve wider audiences and as some privately owned papers reduce political rhetoric for commercial purposes.

Current press developments, however, indicate that there is a desire for the press to continue its role in political and social processes and to extend access to and participation in the press to the widest possible audience. Pluralism in communicators and media units seems to be the goal of current press planning and support.

CHAPTER TWO

The Nature of the Press

Roles

The basic roles of the Nordic press are much the same as those of the press in the other developed nations of the world. They include the three functions identified by Harold Lasswell: surveillance of the environment, correlation of the different parts of society in responding to the environment, and transmission of social heritage, with a fourth function, entertainment, suggested by Charles Wright.[1]

While such informational and entertainment activities have been a part of the Nordic press since the beginning of publishing history in the region, three other activities have gained significance since the nineteenth century and are now among the most important functions, even in the smaller regional papers: (1) education, including the creation and transmission of cultural information; (2) discussion and political mobilization; and (3) the creation of profit.

The order of importance attached to these roles and objectives varies from nation to nation, however. In Denmark, for instance, where the main role of the press historically has been to create and educate opinion, business considerations have remained secondary. Although there is concern to maintain stable financial bases for Danish newspapers, the industry is not viewed as a profitable one, so investments there are not made for profitability alone.

In Norway, cultural, political, historical, and social education has remained the prime purpose of newspapers. John Merrill has observed that the "one theme—unity of serious intent—runs throughout the entire Norwegian press system."[2] It also has been noted that

> the Norwegian press of today gives a clear picture of the structure of society, its functioning and functions, as well as of every imaginable aspect of national life and culture. It covers all the subject matter in which the public could be interested, and it provides for all facets of public opinion.[3]

The educational and political roles of the press in the Nordic nations are much more visible than in the United States. The educational

26

role involves the discussion and consideration of those elements of society and culture that affect human life. In addition to expositions and coverage on traditional cultural matters (art, music, theater, cinema, literature, and criticism), Nordic newspapers include philosophy, architecture, economics, social policy, heritage, and other aspects of such humanistic inquiry (Fig. 2.1).

The cultural role is not just a matter of content, but also one of mass manufacture and mediation of ideas and images to define and transform society. This is evident in the particular importance given educational material, particularly information for isolated individuals, including rural and agrarian readers. The information and discussion helps to explain and develop the collective mental environment that has led to the unique Nordic view of society and the role of the individual in that society.

In Norway where education is still considered a primary goal of the newspaper industry, cultural and historical articles are incorporated into the papers in numbers well beyond those ever seen in the most literate papers of North America or continental Europe. Kronikks (chronicles), found almost daily in newspapers of every size, are essays on a variety of cultural, social, or political topics that tackle the issues with a thoroughness and thoughtfulness rarely observed elsewhere. And the material is written so that even those without higher education may benefit from the content.

In Denmark the high level of education of the populace allows the use of thoughtful pieces as well, but citizens are not so isolated as their Norwegian counterparts and other publications and cultural-educational institutions reduce the need for as much educational material.

Swedish papers also include cultural pages, although they are not as plentiful as in the past. David Jenkins notes the extensive use of debates by which newspapers either argue with one another (by featuring editorial opinions from other papers that contradict or agree with a particular stand) or the different contributors attack one another within the same paper—and occasionally both occur.[4] Participants in such discussions and essays are often educators, political figures, or individuals with recognized expertise in the topic of discussion. These kulturella pages survive today due in part to the lack of widely distributed literary and artistic journals in the country. Because educators are among the regular contributors to cultural pages, discussions often focus on the results of scholarly research, including dissertations and monographs, which help keep the public apprised of current ideas and explanations in educational circles.

The importance of protecting and promoting indigenous culture is

SE ABC 800
HOS ABC-SPECIALISTEN
T·D·X

Högkonjunkturen nära för den svenska industrin

INDUSTRI–
KONJUNKTUREN

Anita Kratz

Konjunkturbarometern närmar sig högtryck. I över ett år har den svenska industrins konjunktur pekat uppåt och närmar sig nu samma läge som under den senaste toppen 1979/80.

1964 66 68 70 72 74 76 78 80 82 84

Dyr dollar - guld faller

Karin Henriksson

Dennis kräver ny åtstramning

Bo Östlund

Rederisamarbete för nordisk export

Oförändrat riktpris mål inför Opecmöte

Karin Henriksson

Enighet prestige

Fem fraktioner

Bo Östlund

2.1. Business and economic sections began proliferating in the 1970s and serious papers, such as *Svenska Dagbladet*, devote extensive space to such coverage. This page from that Swedish paper reports the effects of prosperity on the nation's industries and the objectives of OPEC decisions. (Reprinted with permission)

well recognized on both the local and national level by the Finns, who adopted the cultural material approach from the Swedes during Swedish rule of their nation (Fig. 2.2). A particular form of cultural promotion is the newspaper *Sabmelas,* which is published to help maintain Lapp culture. The paper is distributed free of charge to all Lapps, pays particular attention to Lapp activities and cultural expressions, and provides other educational and informational material in their own language.[5]

The importance of promoting regional and national cultures in all the Nordic nations is magnified by their relatively small sizes and the impact communication of cultural forms and values from other societies can have on local cultures. To promote and maintain the cultures, the majority of newspapers pay particular attention to cultural activities on both the local and national levels. Griffiths notes that the press in Iceland, "although primarily a vehicle for news and polemics, has its role to play in the nation's cultural life. In particular, it carries frequent examples of new work by local poets and critical dialogues in the form of readers' letters on subjects of literary and artistic importance."[6]

A recent study of the roles of the press at the Stockholm Institute of Economics found that Swedish journalists view the roles of the newspaper as (1) being a watchdog on government, (2) providing a forum for public discussion, (3) acting as an educator, (4) providing political information and seeking mobilization, and (5) providing entertainment, in that order of importance.[7]

A study at the Swedish Journalism School in Stockholm identified the objectives of newspapers as (1) informing readers about current events, (2) providing advertising, (3) fostering opinion, and (4) offering diversion and entertainment. The study added, however, that the major objectives of Swedish newspapers is to provide a profit to their owners.[8]

The political role of the Scandinavian press moved to the forefront with the promotion of democratic ideals against monarchical rule and with the development of political parties during the nineteenth century. The press became intimately connected to a political public of the classical democratic type, and it also became a local phenomenon, an indigenous institution.[9]

It is in this political role that the media assume their greatest power – as actors in the decision-making processes of a society (Table 2.1). A 1982 study of the role of media in the decision-making processes of Norway found that the media provide the organizing link that makes possible mutual exchange between citizens and representa-

Käsityöläisviulut eivät kiinnosta ostajia

Viulunrakennusnäyttelyssä voi kokeilla, miten valioviulu soi.

US — Kaustinen (Harri Kuusisaari) — Nyt ei ainakaan kukaan voi väittää, että kansanmusiikkijuhlat olisivat kuivia, lausahti Kaustisen kansanmusiikkijuhlien puheenjohtaja Vilho S. Määttälä, kun puoli päivää jatkunut sade piiskasi juhlakenttää.

Kantria intiaanimusiikin vivahtein

Pelimannimatrikkeli ilmestynyt

Päivän puheenaihe: Ei ole puheenaihetta

● Tätä on julkisuus: tutkija Juha Partanen (vas.) on rajautunut kuvasta pois, samoin professori Jaakko Lehtonen (oik.). Jäljelle jäävät Erno Paasilinna, Liisa Kulhia, Leena Kirstinä (mm. sijaintinsa ansiosta) sekä Jörn Donner.

Kulttuurihenkilöt keskustelevat ja Kulhian kampaus

"Vastustamme reumatismia ja reilua peliä"

Missä olet, oppositio?

MARKETTA MATTILA

Mestaritöitä

HEIKKI AALTOILA

2.2.   Serious discussions of cultural materials are prevalent, even in small papers. This kulttuuri page from the mid-sized Finnish paper *Uusi Suomi* is similar to Swedish kulturella pages and kronikks found in Norwegian papers. The main discussion on this illustrative page is buyers' views of violins. (Reprinted with permission)

Table 2.1. The Ten Most Influential Nordic Papers

Paper	Country
Aftenposten	Norway
Berlingske Tidende	Denmark
Dagens Nyheter	Sweden
Göteborgs-Posten	Sweden
Helsingin Sanomat	Finland
Information	Denmark
Morgunbladid	Iceland
Politiken	Denmark
Svenska Dagbladet	Sweden
Jyllands-Posten	Denmark

tives. But, the report noted, the Norwegian media were not merely channels of communication, but also formulators of policy through suggestion, conveyance of reaction to proposals, and creation of a public climate regarding issues and proposals.[10]

An earlier study noted four ways in which the Norwegian press was an integral part of and played an active role in the political system: (1) they constituted the most important medium for debate and molding of opinion; (2) they were in a better position than other media to act as "the fourth estate," able to expose errors and defects to public scrutiny and to draw to the attention of the public the problems that remain to be solved; (3) the daily press was in a better position than other media to take up matters of current interest, and to do so more thoroughly than possible in the electronic media; and (4) no other medium could replace the daily press in the life of the local community.[11]

In Sweden, the press maintains an important political role partly due to the allegiances of most papers to various ideologies and parties and to the amounts of information and commentary the papers carry.

> Unlike the United States, there are few news magazines or polemical journals in Sweden, and their main functions are assumed instead by the daily newspapers. It is in their pages that the political and social issues of the day are debated, and a constant watch is kept on Swedish officialdom. There are few countries where the Press is so important to the total political process as it is in Sweden.[12]

Because historical development of the Nordic press has strong ties to political movements and parties, most newspapers today maintain party affiliations or support basic socialist or bourgeois views. Although the degree of commitment varies from paper to paper, the majority publicly attest to their affiliations on the masthead or opinion pages. Even those papers that espouse neutrality and independence carry an exceptionally high proportion of political news and comment because almost every topic is political. In addition to the overt political machinations surrounding government, the close symbiotic relationship of government with economic, social, and cultural policies and other activities that affect almost every citizen results in the politicization of almost every issue a newspaper might cover.

Denmark historically has manifested a four-newspaper system in which each town had four newspapers representing the Conservative, Social Democratic, Liberal, and Radical-Liberal parties between the late 1800s and the First World War. While most papers had small circulations, they were spread throughout the provinces and many papers published special neighborhood editions for towns too small to warrant their own papers.

The number of newspapers in Denmark was able to grow until the time between the two world wars because of the limited number of pages, the importance of political arguments, and the relatively inexpensive costs of production. However, since the 1920s the provincial press underwent concentration and attrition, which was pronounced from 1935 to 1943 and increased more rapidly after about 1950.[13]

The number of local, independently owned papers in the Danish provinces dropped from 133 in 1920 to 45 in 1971. With the death of multiple competitors in provincial areas, readers there began to make more use of the popular Copenhagen dailies, which exhibited a wide variety of political orientations. Despite the increase in the use of the capital dailies, their number fell from 19 in 1905 to about a half a dozen today.

In spite of the nationwide mortality, all major political viewpoints are still represented in the Danish newspapers today. In some cases the views are provided by a local paper committed to a particular ideology or party, and in other cases the viewpoint is served by a paper nationally circulated out of Copenhagen.

A study of the structural changes in the Danish press industry has found that these changes have not significantly reduced political activity per se. "It can be clearly observed that it still reacts as a party press during campaigns – favouring its own party to a high degree."[14]

A paradox of the political links of the press is the disparity between the size of political parties and the number of papers supporting each party. The political affiliations and size of circulation of newspapers do not necessarily translate into votes at the polls. This disparity between voters' party preference and newspaper circulation is clearly seen when comparing the results of elections and the figures of newspaper-party affiliation.

Although Sweden has a greater proportion of the largest papers in the Nordic countries, the political influence of larger papers in Sweden is not as strong as would be anticipated because they are wide-coverage papers, attracting readers who do not share similar political opinions because of better content (Table 2.2). Many of the smaller narrow-coverage papers, according to the paradigm, are circulated only to political converts and have a much stronger impact on readers.[15]

Table 2.2. Ten Largest Nordic Papers

Paper	Country	Circulation
Expressen	Sweden	531,000
Helsingin Sanomat	Finland	450,000
Aftonbladet	Sweden	390,000
Dagens Nyheter	Sweden	386,000
Göteborgs-Posten	Sweden	285,000
Ekstrabladet	Denmark	250,000
VG	Norway	240,000
Aftenposten	Norway	230,000
Svenska Dagbladet	Sweden	210,000
B.T.	Denmark	200,000

Annamari Mäkinen has argued that the provincial press in Finland has rapidly lost its political "color" and that the Finnish press in general has given up its political affiliations much more quickly than most of the other Nordic presses. However, the Center party has been the most successful at maintaining affiliation in rural areas, she notes. Part of the trend toward rural independent papers can be attributed to mergers of party papers into single independent papers and the assertion of independence of coalition party papers to help them become the largest papers in a market.[16]

In terms of political leanings, about 40 percent of the Danish press is associated with the bourgeois parties (center and right parties) and only about 10 percent with the parties on the left. About half of the nation's daily papers consider themselves independent, but normally support the policies of the bourgeois parties.

In Finland about 60 percent of the papers claim independent status, 28 percent support the right and centrist parties, and 12 percent support the left parties. In terms of national political representation, 42 percent are left party representatives and 58 percent are divided between 6 center and right nonsocialist parties.

While the Finnish press has played an active part in the partisan political discussions of the nation since parliamentarianism was introduced, its approach toward the policies and activities of the executive branch of government, particularly those involving foreign policies, has been quite subdued. Part of this unwillingness to undertake critical discussion of the policies involves the delicate Finnish-Soviet relationship and the policies of President Urho Kekkonen.

With the passing of the Kekkonen presidency in 1982, the International Press Institute (IPI) noted a change toward a more adversarial attitude on the part of the press. Perhaps the majority of the formerly cautious media relaxed in the less disciplined and more debating political atmosphere of the post-Kekkonen era.[17]

Icelandic papers are rather evenly divided in terms of political support: 40 percent of the press support the socialist parties, 40 percent support the center and right parties, and only 20 percent separate themselves entirely from party support.

In Norway a large number of papers call themselves independents, but regularly support various parties. In terms of political orientation, the leftist parties have less support in the press (about 40 percent of the papers) than the center and rightist parties, although the socialist press (labor) represents the single largest bloc of newspapers in the nation. In the parliament, however, socialists have 49 percent of the seats.

The pattern of newspaper–party affiliation in Sweden shows the great disparity between left and right: 73 percent of the papers represent the view of right and center parties and only 16 percent represent socialist parties. A little more than 10 percent of the papers assert independence from party affiliation. Socialists account for 53 percent of the representation in the parliament while right and center parties account for 47 percent.

The primary role of the press in the political process is to promote specific views, usually those of the party with which a particular paper is associated or with whom its editors usually agree. It also serves as a catalyst for political mobilization. But even in presses directly owned or funded by parties, one sometimes finds that the agenda set by the party differs from that of the political agenda of the press. For example, in Norway recently officials of a variety of parties supported the development and establishment of local radio stations but their newspaper editors took differing stances out of fear that the establishment of advertising-funded radio would harm the economic status of the press. On the whole, however, party newspapers tend to promote a political agenda and political programs that match those of the parties with which they are associated.

Those who study communication and its influence on individuals' behavior in the Nordic nations have a difficult time determining whether the party agenda and activities most affect individuals, whether the agenda and activities of a politically oriented press create the largest effect, or if a combination of each affects citizens.

Style and Content

Nordic newspapers, for the most part, present sober and thoughtful presentations of news and information and generally shun sensational presentation and content. That distinction is somewhat true even among the evening tabloids, which employ the techniques of less serious papers but generally do not attempt to match the sensationalism of the tabloid press of Great Britain or the United States. Although the daily press tends to be less formal than newspapers in the United States or Europe in language or presentation, the readers are still provided with serious material, which is reported in depth.

Styles of presentation differ between the quality press (usually the morning newspapers in the major cities) and the popular press (the evening tabloids); however, both types of papers carry considerable social and political debates. Board has noted that while Swedish tabloids tend to be less informative about domestic and foreign affairs than the morning papers, "both types of papers devote considerable space to the presentation, often quite pungent, of political opinion."[18] Merrill has noted that Danish papers have an overall tone of "neatness and dignity, yet of friendliness and warmth. Stories are usually written in language that in the United States would be called 'light' or 'folksy.' "[19] Danish tabloids, however, are the most sensational of the Nordic newspapers. Recent headlines such as "Boy Behind Bloodbath at his Grandmother's" (*Ekstrabladet*) and "Near Drowning in Asphalt Bog" (*B. T.*) give an idea of the type of front-page headlines favored by these street-sale papers, although one usually finds less colorful material on the inside pages.

Norwegian newspapers were rather slow in adopting the techniques of modern writing styles and presentations, for prior to the First World War the press "was tied to tradition in regard to form and content but in the last forty or fifty years it has developed amazingly, being much more in contact with contemporary evolution outside of Norway."[20]

In recent years the adoption of the summary lead and retirement of strict narrative chronological presentation have brought Norwegian reporting much more in step with journalistic presentation throughout the region. Part of this transformation has resulted from the increasing availability and use of material from news and feature services and the development of journalism education programs, which serve as guides for good journalistic practice.

In addition to distinctions made between the serious daily press and the popular press in the region, distinctions also must be made between the national capital-city oriented papers and the provincial press. Provincial papers tend to have much closer ties to their readers than national papers and separate themselves from the big city dailies by placing greatest emphasis on local issues. In Denmark the chief difference between the Copenhagen city papers and provincial presses is in the direct relations of the provincial dailies with their readers, because the editors and reporters tend to have strong familial and social ties to the area they serve—they are deeply involved in the local issues.[21]

A UNESCO study noted that Danish provincial presses exercise considerable influence on political affairs. Generally these papers consist of 6–8 pages and give good coverage to national and international news.[22] They usually avoid sensationalism in dealing with such issues and provide briefer coverage than the larger national papers. Local content is also important and regional newspapers make extensive efforts to draw information from the small towns within their market areas.

Similar distinctions divide the Norwegian provincial and national press, but the amount of international and national news tends to be more limited in the small provincial papers. These papers try not to compete with but supplement the large city or national papers with strong local coverage and discussion of important local issues and political debate that the large regional and national papers cannot provide.

In Sweden mortality has reduced the number of provincial papers in most towns to only one local daily, which competes with the national and regional papers. Although most provincial papers have a local monopoly as a daily provider of local information, a few towns have competing dailies and many have competition from papers that publish at least several times a week, thus improving coverage of local issues. Competition within their area of circulation gives newspapers a greater motivation for investing in costly local content. At the same time, newspapers with good economies have greater possibilities for using local contents as a means of competition.[23]

Nondaily newspapers in Denmark tend to handle the entertainment functions of the press and do not enjoy the influence of the dailies. Many of these papers devote considerable space to cultural material and local news from towns too small to warrant a local daily or much coverage in the provincial and regional dailies.

The Swedish nondaily press with its strong local coverage also has restricted circulation. However, unlike Danish weeklies they enjoy a larger amount of influence. Many are published by political parties and organizations and were at one time daily papers that were forced to reduce their frequency when economics made it difficult for more than one daily paper to survive in a single market. Many of these nondaily papers provide well-written coverage and discussion of local events and political issues, as well as news on local families and social activities that are appreciated by readers.

Nondaily newspapers are widely circulated in Finland, as well, and they, too, concentrate much of their coverage on community groups, churches, businesses, political organizations, and other items ignored by the larger provincial papers. These weeklies have an average circulation of about 5000 subscribers, but despite their relatively small size, are well integrated into community life; more than 90 percent of households subscribe in the 310 communities served by Finnish local weeklies.

Nordic journalists generally have adopted professional standards that separate fact from opinion, which results in fairly well balanced reporting. This occurs despite the fact that many journalists are politically active in their communities and it is not unusual for public representatives to be journalists. The large amount of space devoted to commentary, debates, and editorial exchanges provides significant opportunities for journalists to offer their political views, and thus most are content to offer their opinion separately from their ordinary news coverage.

Editorial opinion throughout the Nordic region is generally devoted to local expression though a few commercial syndicated editorial services exist. This is not to say that papers do not carry opinion material not produced in-house. Papers often carry commentary produced by members of the political parties with which they are affiliated and, especially in Sweden, carry selected editorials appearing in newspapers in other parts of the country, thus giving rural columnists access to wider national audiences.

Despite such exchange policies, much of the commentary appearing in the papers is locally or regionally produced by individuals from a wide variety of occupations, although educators, politicians, and journalists are the most regular contributors.

It is difficult to find an acceptable definition of objectivity, but it is probably fair to say that the journalistic standards of the Nordic press are comparable to those of the American press. However, when the intellectual reputation of the Nordic journalists and editors is compared with that of their American counterparts, the Nordic journalists and editors are more highly regarded as intellectuals.

In Sweden a perquisite of the extensive commentary by journalists is the prestige attached to them, especially to the editors of respected papers, who are frequently scholars in their own right and who are usually atop the hierarchy of national status. Because of the tendency of the Swedish press to quote editorials of other papers, editors of provincial papers frequently develop national reputations by association.

In regard to the subjects of gossip and titilating information about personalities, the Danish papers tend to print more than papers in the other Nordic nations; operating at the opposite end of that spectrum are the Finnish papers. Also, in Finland coverage of criminal acts tends to be handled in a more factual, unsensational fashion and is limited to more serious offenses than in all the Nordic press. Thorsten Cars, the Swedish Press Ombudsman, notes that coverage of crime is much different than it was 50 years ago: "Criminal reporting has changed for the better, there is less sensationalism, less bloody detail, less invasion of privacy of the victim or the criminal" (author interview, Stockholm, June 1984).

Throughout the region the privacy of individuals is prized and the press tends to respect personal privacy to a much greater extent than anywhere else in the West, although the Danish press is more apt to violate this general rule (Fig. 2.3). In Sweden, for instance, the press stopped printing the names of victims and suspects in the 1930s and today will print the names of convicted criminals only if they are public officials or have been convicted of especially heinous crimes. While Sweden tends to protect the privacy of suspects and convicted criminals more than other nations, Swedes argue that the practice is justified because it helps rehabilitation and the return of the individual to society.

Nevertheless, there is support for relaxing those rules in some cases. Thorsten Cars reports that recent signs indicate that the press wants to loosen restrictions on the publication of names of criminals, particularly in serious cases involving drugs or public officials (author interview, Stockholm, June 1984).

Nordic papers devote considerable amounts of space to foreign news, due in great part to their nations' dependence upon exports and foreign trade and the strategic importance of the region in East-West relations. The emphasis on foreign information has increased since the

Politiet tog ingen chancer mod tysk pistolpige

Her stopper den vesttyske pistolpiges Danmarksturné. Hendes to følgesvende har ladt hende i stikken og er stukket af.

I de tre tyskeres bil finder URO-patruljen hurtigt en pistol med fem skarpe skud. Den fjernes forsigtigt.

Efter fundet af den skarpladte pistol tager URO-en ingen chancer. Den 23-årige pige bliver lagt i håndjern.

4: **Hverken håndjern eller betjentenes spørgsmål kunne få pistolpigens tunge på gled med en forklaring om, hvorfor hun og hendes to kammerater kørte rundt med en skarpladt revolver.**
Foto: Hans Karpheden

Af Palle Polar

En ung »uskyldigt« udseende vesttysk 23-årig pige pistolpige fik i går uden for fristaden Christiania ufrivilligt afbrudt sit besøg i Danmark.

Under stor dramatik blev den unge pige anholdt. Politiets URO-patrulje tog ingen chancer og lagde hende i håndjern. Politiet havde fået kik på de unge menneskers bil.

To stak af

De var dog ikke interesserede i at tale med »URO«-patruljens folk og prøvede at stikke af.

Politiet optog forfølgelsen, og de tre unge nåede ikke mange meter uden for fristaden, før deres bil var bragt til standsning De to mænd nåede at flygte, mens kvinden blev anholdt. Ved en ransagning i bilen fandt politiet i handskerummet en revolver med fem skarpe skud. Den 23-årige pige er fast kunde i det vesttyske politis kartotek. Hendes to følgesvende eftersøges for øjeblikket.

Kæmpe-razzia

Ud over den vesttyske pistolpige har URO-patruljen anholdt 22 udlændinge, repræsenterende det meste af kloden. Den storstilede razzia blev indledt på grund af den kommende weekends Roskilde Festival. Politiet har været i Christiania det meste af torsdagen.

Alle de anholdte var i besiddelse af narkotika lige fra hash til de helt hårde stoffer. Vagthavende i URO-patruljen oplyser, at de af dem, der ikke er efterlyst allerede, er udvist af Danmark.

Foruden pistolpigen har URO-patruljen anholdt en vesttysk narkokonge. Han prøvede at flygte i sin bil, men blev indhentet og måtte overgive sig. Han var i besiddelse af hårde stoffer og 70.000 kr. i kontanter.

Udvises

Vagthavende oplyser til B.T. at han også er en gammel kending af det vesttyske politi, og flere gange har været efterlyst gennem interpol. Han har flere fængselsdomme for narkohandel den seneste for fire et halvt års fængsel.

De anholdte, der ikke er efterlyst, er allerede udvist af landet.

2.3. Crime coverage tends to be sober and respectful of the privacy of victims and suspects. Most papers do not carry identifiable photographs or names of suspects, but Danish papers are more likely to violate the general rule—as in this story by *B.T.*—which includes a photograph of an arrest.

Second World War and many larger papers now have bureaus outside the region to help supplement coverage from national wire services and external services such as Reuters, Agence France Presse, Associated Press, United Press International, Deutsches Presse Agentur, and TASS.

Criticism of Nordic newspapers in decades past often focused on the lack of content or depth in coverage of foreign developments, but that criticism is no longer applicable, except in the small, local press. Local readers are not denied that information, however, because most readers supplement the local paper with one of the large national papers that place emphasis on such issues. Television has also had an impact on the coverage of world news by rapidly increasing the visual images of the world and by expanding the psychological horizons of the Nordic citizens.

Icelandic newspapers place greater emphasis on international news than papers in other Nordic nations. This, of course, is due to the nation's small size and its greater dependence on economic and political conditions outside Iceland. Much of the nation's economy and development is dictated by events outside its boundaries. Finnish papers also devote considerable space to foreign news because of the nation's distance from many of the events in the world and its dependence on foreign trade for a large amount of its economic activity. The importance of foreign developments to all aspects of the economy makes such developments interesting to even the small farmers in isolated regions of the country. This situation contrasts markedly with the situation in Finland a half century ago, when the nation was not only physically, but culturally, isolated. At that time little foreign reporting, on-the-spot reporting, or investigative reporting was found in the bulk of the press.

Economic and business news has attracted an increasingly large audience since the 1970s and the amount of editorial space devoted to such news has also risen, especially in Denmark and Sweden where large segments of their industrial economies are affected by such information.

Political coverage has improved in recent years, particularly in Norway and Finland where such reporting tended to be less aggressive. Finnish papers traditionally had been less critical of national leaders and public policies than the press of other nations, but that tradition is changing and leaders of political parties, parliament, and even the president of the nation are uneasily adjusting to the new style of critical reporting.

Effects of the new adversarial relationship are leading to some criticism of the press by authorities. President Mauno Koivisto recently expressed his displeasure with the speculative coverage of national military policies, saying that the interjection of the press into such discussions damages the government. Speaking at the closing ceremonies of the Finnish parliament, Koivisto criticized the handling by the press of a revelation, by a professor of international relations, that the 1947 Treaty of Paris (ending hostilities with the Soviet Union) did not prohibit Finland from possessing nuclear weapons or prohibit deployment of nuclear weapons on Finnish soil by other nations if the Finnish government agreed.

Press coverage of the debate over the revelation was rigorous because of the espoused neutrality and antinuclear weapons policies of Finland. It was also amplified because when reading between the lines, the "other nations" referred to clearly meant the Soviet Union. Newspapers barraged the public with information and discussion on the subject and the headlines charged that Finland could be used by the Soviets to pressure Norway with nuclear arms. Such items, accompanied by illustrations of mushroom clouds, etc., clearly disturbed Finnish authorities. Koivisto felt the coverage damaged Finnish relations with both Norway and the Soviet Union and blasted the press, saying, "Not only have we heard speculations about what is possible within the confines of our international treaties and what is not, but indeed conjectures have been published as to what our neighbours will do in times of crises."

Adjustments to the adversarial stance of the press are coming slowly, but incidents such as this have not led to any government actions against the press—except for expressions of displeasure.

Norwegian officials are also adjusting to changes in the style of political reporting. The adoption of investigative journalism and an increasingly questioning attitude by reporters, who are no longer content to automatically print what government officials provide them, has led to the publication of independent confirmations of government pronouncements and alternative explanations for national developments.

An early feature of the Nordic press that was adopted later by much of the press in the United States is the heavy sectionalization of newspaper content. A relatively new section of the Nordic papers is for cartoons, which are now found in papers throughout the region—satirical political cartoons are widely employed, especially in Denmark. In recent years newspapers have begun printing entertainment comics as well as many U.S.-produced comics, which are translated into the Nordic languages (Fig. 2.4). Popular comic strips include Peanuts, Donald Duck, Blondie, Hagar the Horrible, Sad Sack, Garfield, and B.C.

2.4. A comic page from the Danish paper *Aktuelt* illustrates the extensive use of comic strips popular in the United States. (Reprinted with permission)

CHAPTER THREE

Freedom and Accountability of the Press

Freedom

The traditional aspects of press freedom, safeguards against undue government interference with expression, have a long history in the Nordic region.

Sweden was the first nation in the world to guarantee freedom of the press, placing strong protections for the press in its King-in-Council Ordinance Concerning Freedom of Writing and Publishing in 1766. First in the world of its kind, this law deserves to be looked upon not only as a most interesting consequence of political and ideological developments in eighteenth-century Sweden but also as the forerunner of the broader Swedish press laws of 1810, 1812, and 1941. It is also the forerunner of the many, often more limited, freedom-of-the-press provisions in the constitutions of almost all countries of the world today.[1]

The law, passed by the Swedish parliament (Riksdag) during the Age of Freedom, contained 15 major provisions outlining what was covered by the freedom to publish and the exceptions to that freedom. Especially interesting is the introductory material that clearly establishes the philosophical ideas behind the concept and the benefits that accrue to society when its citizens can freely debate subjects of social significance.

Today, press freedom in Sweden is guaranteed by what is undoubtedly the world's most extensive constitutional protection for the press. The Freedom of the Press Act, the fourth document of the constitution, includes 14 chapters with 123 articles guarded by rigid guarantees that make changes in or withdrawal of any freedoms extremely difficult. The act was embodied in the constitution in 1949, replacing an 1812 provision.

The constitutional guarantees are somewhat unusual because they guarantee not only freedom of the press in the conventional sense but also guarantee the citizen the widest possible access to official documents, except those of a secret nature.[2] This access provision echoes a similar provision placed in the 1766 law, which stipulated that certain records of government agencies would be open and available to the public and the press.

Denmark's constitution of 1849 recognized the importance of discussion and information in the press and paragraph 91 of that document stipulated that everyone has the right to publish their opinions in print, but they may be called to account for them before the law: censorship and other preventative measures can never again be introduced.[3]

In the new constitution, promulgated in 1953, Article 77 abolished all censorship: "Any person shall be at liberty to publish his ideas in print, in writing, and in speech, subject to his being held responsible in a court of law."[4] The provision, a clear repetition of the principle embodied in the constitution 100 years before, reasserted the principles of press freedom that had been abrogated during the Nazi occupation of the nation.

Finland, which gained its independence from Russia as a result of the 1917 revolution, promulgated its constitution in 1919 and provided the press the right to publish without prior restraint. The Finnish Freedom of the Press Act, passed that same year, qualified the constitutional provisions by defining the few restrictions to press freedom, the rights of editors, and official conduct in disputes over press information.

Iceland, independent of Denmark since 1944, continued the Danish tradition of press freedom and incorporated similar provisions into its new constitution: "Every person has the right to express his thoughts in print, but is responsible for such utterances before the courts. Censorship and other restrictions on freedom of the press may never be enacted."[5]

Freedom of the press in Norway historically came under provisions of press law of Denmark, but after cession of the area to Sweden in 1814, national leaders established a constitution that provided the basic structure of press freedom as it is today. That document was intended to protect the people against Swedish efforts to keep Norway a dependent territory and to provide the means by which the Norwegian press could continue to promote nationalism and carry on political discussions about the country's future without interference from Swedish rulers.

The Norwegian constitution reads:

> There shall be liberty of the press. No person must be punished for any writing, whatever its contents may be, which he has caused to be printed or published, unless he wilfully and manifes-

tly has either himself shown or incited others to disobedience to the laws, contempt of religion or morality or the constitutional powers, or resistance to their orders, or has advanced false and defamatory accusations against any other person. Everyone shall be free to speak his mind frankly on the administration of the State or on any other subject whatsoever.[6]

Norway does not have an additional press law that clarifies or expands these provisions, as is the case in Denmark and Finland.

Because their constitutions and press laws provide some of the strongest protections of press freedom that exist in the West, the Nordic nations are regularly classed among the highest in the world in terms of press freedom.

A study on freedom of the press in the world placed all the Nordic nations in free-press categories, with all but Finland in the highest category. Finland was placed in the second highest category, which bore the caveat, ". . . free press system, but for shorter period or with less evidence of stability." The status of Finland can be explained as being due to its short history as an independent nation at the time of the research (it had been a sovereign nation for less than 50 years) and to the fact that it had undergone a civil war, two wars with the Soviet Union, and the turmoil of the Second World War during its short existence. Despite the freedom-of-the-press conflicts that arose due to those exigencies, a basic and deep commitment to freedom of the press was recognized and upheld in the nation.[7]

Another study of press freedoms in the world, using the Press Independence and Critical Ability Index, ranked all the Nordic nations in the highest category of press freedom with the exception of Iceland, which was not analyzed in the study.[8]

Subsequent analyses have continued to rank the Nordic nations in the highest categories of press freedom, with Sweden and Norway being ranked above the United States. However, even these nations have some controls on information, although they are generally recognized as legitimate government interference in information dissemination.

No nation can have absolutely no controls and thus achieve absolute press freedom, because, as Ralph Lowenstein asserts, "the country in which it existed would have these unusual characteristics: no economically weak press units, no publishing chains or broadcasting networks, no government advertising and virtually no contempt or libel laws."[9]

Social observers in the Nordic region do not view freedom of the press as merely the absence of such restraints but also the presence of conditions that provide the effective ability of citizens to take part in the communication process, i.e., freedom of expression in the mass media is based on two interrelated criteria: that citizens shall be enabled, without unreasonable financial sacrifice, to spread information and express their views; and that citizens shall be able to choose between messages with different political biases. Therefore, the structure of the mass media shall make provisions for a many-sided approach to all situations.[10]

This view recognizes the importance of positive press freedom, which includes the existence of conditions in which diverse ideas may flow freely, as well as negative press freedom, which is represented by the prohibitions on action against press freedom. Proponents of positive press freedom recognize the duty of the state to promote such conditions and ensure their continued existence.

This second aspect of press freedom has gained support rapidly in the region as part of the ideology of democratic socialists. Their philosophy has been put into practice in public policies toward the media during the past 20 years.[11] Many of these policies are part of government economic policies toward the newspaper industry, which will be discussed in Chapter 4.

Other evidences of the importance attached to providing the effective ability for the press to carry out its functions are found in the significant access to government information legislation and protection of journalists' sources.

Some form of guaranteed access to government information exists in all the countries. Sweden's tradition of access has existed for 200 years and recent legislation limits the ability of government to classify information. Most of the right to inspect documents is embodied in the unique Freedom of the Press Act, which grants the constitutional right to members of the mass media and to the general public to read mail addressed to the prime minister or any minister or other member of government; all documents, with certain exceptions due to security or integrity aspects; and all background materials for commissions and bills being processed. Having read any of these materials, the media also has the right to inform the public of their contents. Therefore, journalists from the staffs of the Swedish news agency Tidningarnas Telegrambyrå, from the various newspapers, as well as from the Swedish Broadcasting Corporation's radio and television departments are stationed in various government offices.[12]

This access to material has resulted in the embarrassment of a number of governments when sensitive information about their activities was discovered in letters to ministry officials or in other documents.

Finland passed an access provision in the early 1950s, the Act On Publicity of Official Documents, which affirms the right of citizens to review government documents but permits the exclusion of foreigners from reviewing some documents. The statute also stipulates that documents excluded from the access law will be classified for only 25 years, after which they are to be made public.

Norway passed a Freedom of Information Act in 1970 that opens the files of government administrative offices to any member of the public. This act has helped spur the increasing investigative approach of the Norwegian press by providing access to information that was not as readily available before.

The importance of human as well as documentary sources of information is well recognized in the region, and journalists enjoy some of the strongest protections of sources found anywhere in the world. Protection of sources in Swedish law has been provided in some form since 1766, with that protection being increased as various new press acts and constitutional provisions were enacted.

Today, Swedish journalists are prohibited from disclosing the identity of a source without the consent of that source and public officials are forbidden to ask for the identity of sources. The only exclusions from this law involve disclosure that a judge may require during the course of a trial involving high treason, espionage, or other extremely severe crimes. In practice, however, Swedish journalists enjoy nearly total protection of their sources, including government officials, during their day-to-day reporting efforts.

Finnish law also requires professional secrecy of journalists, except in some court cases where unusual exigencies make disclosure a necessity. Journalists are specifically permitted to withhold sources' identities from legislative and administrative bodies and authorities.

Norwegian journalists have had specific legislative authority to shield their sources from exposure since 1951. However, the act which provided this privilege includes a provision that a journalist may be ordered to identify a source in some trials or face imprisonment, but such situations are extremely rare.

Danish journalists do not have a legal requirement that they conceal sources of information, as do Swedish journalists, but protection of those sources is an accepted journalistic practice and sources are rarely identified under duress. Although they have the power to force disclosure, Danish courts have rarely used their authority to do so, recognizing the social benefits of shielding sources.

Accountability

Press accountability to society for the privileges and rights granted is manifest in two ways in the Nordic press: (1) self-criticism and self-regulation and (2) laws designed to ensure accountability.

Self-criticism and self-regulation are much more widely accepted in the Nordic region, both among the populace and the press itself, than they are among citizens and the press in other Western nations. As a result, significant contributions to the practice of voluntary self-criticism and self-regulation have been made in the region and much of this pioneering work has been used as the impetus or model for the few efforts to promote self-accountability in other nations.

The two main contributions to voluntary accountability have been the press council and the ombudsman. Accountability is also enforced by law and government regulation. Nordic governments' activities in this area have been restrained, as they have in all nations that deeply believe in the concept of press independence. The most important government-enforced accountability measures involve the fixing of journalistic responsibility for material published, national security issues, obscenity, and defamation.

Press Councils. The concept of self-criticism and self-regulation by the press can be traced to the development of the Fair Practices Commission (Pressens Opinionsnämnd) in Sweden in 1916. This self-regulatory group was the first press council to be established in the world and was founded in the wake of extensive criticism of press performance, especially by members of the Riksdag. Members of the press set up the organization to help improve their practices as well as to deal with press malpractice and poor conduct to avoid government intervention. In 1923 the commission adopted a code of ethics for the press that stipulated what would be considered good conduct for journalists.

The council, which was reconstituted in 1969, considers complaints against members of the press and can initiate investigations against practices it considers unworthy. The council has legally binding contracts with almost all the press in Sweden that require offending newspapers to print the council's decisions and criticisms and to carry out the council's directions. Since 1969 contracts include a provision that allows the council to levy a symbolic fine up to $400 (U.S.) a year for serious violations or refusals to carry out council directions.

Finland and Norway followed the lead of Sweden by setting up press councils in the 1920s. Like the Swedish council, the councils in both these nations include nonjournalist members. The Finnish council, established in 1927, was reestablished in 1968 as the Council for Mass Media (Julkisen Sanan Neuvosto) and can issue a judgment against units of all media in the country—and has done so in about one-quarter of its cases. Council decisions must be published or broadcast by the offending publisher or broadcaster. The council cannot issue fines, as in Sweden, but relies upon the moral suasion of its findings as punishment. The Finnish council will not consider cases that are also being considered by legal authorities.

The Norwegian press council, established in 1928, was reconstituted in 1972 to include members of the public and to permit newspapers to present their side of an issue more completely. If the council rules against a newspaper, that paper must publish the finding, which will then be distributed throughout the nation by the national news agency. Although the council, which may act on complaints or initiate investigations on its own, has no enforcement authority, its judgments are well regarded.

The press councils in Finland, Norway, and Sweden helped set the stage for other councils that were established in the first quarter of the century and served as models for most councils established thereafter. The self-regulatory impetus in the press was diminished in the 1930s when economic pressures and the rumblings of fascism diverted attention away from press performance issues. By the 1960s, however, concerns about press performance reemerged throughout the developed world and a second wave of press council development took place.

During this second developmental period, publishers in Denmark set up a press council in 1964 that acts only on complaints brought to the organization. It is the weakest of the councils in the region and operates with voluntary compliance of publishers. An earlier body handled some of the same duties but was disliked by many journalists because of its ties to the government. In the Danish press law of 1938, a Board of Denials and Corrections was set up to mediate disputes between the public and newspapers when papers refused to publish a citizen's reply to published prejudicial information. The board included two members nominated by each of the professional organizations in the industry and a high-court judge who presided over the activities of the board.

The narrowness of the scope of the board and some support for establishment of a press council similar to that of Sweden's led to the institution of the press council in the 1960s. However, acceptance of that council is not as broad among journalists and publishers in Denmark as acceptance has been for other councils in the region.

Iceland does not have a press council, but because of its small population and the general accessibility of the publishers and journalists to the public, is able to deal with public complaints in a less formal manner.

Ombudsman. When the Swedish Press Council was reorganized in 1969, the position of press ombudsman was created to help facilitate self-discipline by investigating complaints against the press and working with newspapers to gain corrections, explanations, and amplifications without necessarily bringing the dispute to the press council itself. The position was created amid harsh public criticism of press performance. It was alleged that the newspapers lacked respect for ethical rules and that the press council was ineffective. Critics pointed out the fact that a number of violations of good newspaper practice were not brought before the council, and the ombudsman was an answer to this criticism.[13]

The press ombudsman represents the general public in disputes and attempts to mediate complaints the public has against a newspaper. In addition the ombudsman acts as a prosecutor to investigate complaints or initiate actions against the press. If the ombudsman's mediation or initial requests for actions by a newspaper are not accepted by the paper, the issue is presented to the council for judgment.

This unique aspect of the Swedish press self-criticism mechanism helps reduce the work of the press council and makes it possible for the council to concentrate on more significant disputes. It also provides a mechanism by which average citizens may gain assistance in bringing complaints forward and having them handled by someone with influence within the press community.

Ombudsman Thorsten Cars says that the most frequent complaints today concern errors in reporting or result from someone being criticized without being given a fair chance to respond. Such problems are usually mediated without going to the press council, but Cars believes there is a pattern to these problems because some journalists have a "tendency not to check for a response because it might not lead to a story" (author interview, Stockholm, June 1984).

Cars also says that the provincial papers are more responsible and more eager to respond to complaints than the city papers, which tend to be larger and more confident of their practices.

The concept of the ombudsman as citizen advocate is a uniquely Swedish institution that had its genesis early in this century in an effort to help protect citizens' rights in encounters with administrative authority and to ensure due process of law. Today, the citizen advocates represent the public against government bureaucracy and against antitrust actions by businesses involving consumer issues, and in media disputes. The press ombudsman is employed by a special foundation, which separates the office from the media and the government, and the primary function is to help avoid litigation. The first two ombudsmen, Lennart Groll and Thorsten Cars, were both judges prior to their selection for the post and their selection lent strong credibility and prestige to the position.

The office of ombudsman has been a source of discomfort for some journalists because of its critical stances. In recent years it has been criticized by members of the press for being too "legal" in its language and approach to issues, for not understanding the special problems of reporters and the press, and for emphasizing small errors within articles rather than taking into account the articles as a whole. Nevertheless, the ombudsman's position in Swedish press self-regulation appears secure and general support for the concept exists among the press.

Since the press ombudsman post was created some 15 years ago, the concept has been accepted by individual papers in various parts of the West. Some papers have hired an ombudsman to represent the readers and to criticize the paper's performance on various issues. However, the use of a press ombudsman as an offshoot of the press council or for the industry as a whole has not been widely accepted.

Legal Accountability

The Nordic press enjoys a situation in which legal accountability is limited to the most serious violations of public and social interests and rights. Two major foundations of legal accountability are involved: (1) that there be no prior censorship of material and (2) that a single person in each paper be accountable for the content of the paper.

Throughout the region, papers may publish at will, except in extraordinary circumstances involving national security. This situation is similar to that found in the United States, where prior restraint is ideally limited to extraordinary cases that pose significant and dangerous threats to security. At the same time, however, laws in the Nordic nations make papers accountable for what they print and this accountability is specifically placed upon the management of the press.

Fixed Responsibility. The concept of fixed responsibility is widely accepted in Scandinavia and it is usually the editor who is legally responsible for the content of the publication. Under this arrangement it is impossible for journalists, editors, or publishers to disavow responsibility for what is published in the event of legal disputes, and it eliminates the necessity of making a legal determination of who made the decision or error that caused the problem.

Denmark adopted such a requirement in its 1849 constitution and reaffirmed the principle in its press law of 1938. Under the Danish law the editor of the paper is legally responsible for the contents of the paper, except for the articles signed by an author, in which case the author is responsible.

In Sweden a responsible publisher must be designated for each paper. In most cases the editor is so designated, because the editor has daily control of the paper. In cases where charges of defamation, violation of national security laws, or obscenity are brought against a paper, the penalties are imposed on the responsible publisher. Similar provisions are found in the other nations of the region due in great part to the historical and cultural developments that link them to the Danes and the Swedes and to the forms of government and administration practiced in their nations.

National Security. Issues involving information related to national security necessitate that the press and the government carefully ensure the protections of the free press while at the same time protect the security of the citizens. Efforts to meet the two goals take many forms throughout the democratic world, and the efforts of the Nordic nations are among the least intrusive.

In Denmark, papers have a wide latitude in which to discuss military and security issues. Prohibitions on security of information apply only to narrow topics, which the government may specify as requiring extraordinary secrecy, and to some military operations.

Similar restrictions exist in the other Nordic nations, but the amount of information that is considered related to national security is generally limited. Because military-industrial complexes are not as well developed or grounded in the political environments as they are in the United States, the influence of military agencies in Nordic governments is limited and clearly subservient to political apparatuses. Even though the military does not enjoy the power bases the U.S. military does, Nordic observers have noted a slight tendency to overclassify military material, but the tendency is not nearly as strong as that found in the United States or the United Kingdom.

In 1979 two journalists from the Norwegian paper *Ny Tid* (New Times), an author, and a former intelligence agency employee were tried for violating national security regulations. The case involved more than the mere publication of overclassified data, however: the offense was publishing information about illegal activities undertaken by the Norwegian Intelligence Service 20 years prior to their revelation by *Ny Tid*. The author was charged with making lists of intelligence staff members using information from public documents and sources. The government alleged that the act endangered state security when compiled into a completed work. All the defendents were convicted and sentenced.

The Swedish press earlier had gone through a similar difficulty after *Folket i Bild/Kultur Front* published allegations of Swedish intelligence activities that violated Swedish law and involved committing illegal acts in Finland. The writers were charged with violation of espionage laws and the case resulted in the conviction and jailing of writer Jan Guillou. Later, officials brought charges against the editor when the paper criticized the handling of the case by the Swedish High Court. The editor, Greta Hofsten, was accused of demeaning the authorities, under a 1936 law designed for use in periods of unrest that had only been invoked once before. Hofsten was acquitted, but the incident is an indication of the sensitivity of officials to cases involving national security and how they handled such incidents. Public outcry over government actions led to changes in Swedish law that stipulate that when information on security matters is collected or used for publication, any trial on the matter must be made under provisions of the Press Act rather than under espionage statutes.

A unique problem relating to national security is found in Finland, the only Western democratic nation to share a border with the Soviet Union. Because of historical developments, including more than three dozen wars with Russia in modern times—two of which were in the middle of this century—the Finns necessarily walk a fine line in their relations with the Soviet Union and view events that lead to troubled relations as major threats to national security.

Although the press does not face any significant legal restrictions on discussions of Finnish-Soviet relations or comments on world events involving the Soviet Union, the press in the past has tended to moderate the tone of its discussions and commentary. The situation between the two countries today is not as tense as in previous decades and editors are more open and opinionated in their dealings with Soviet-related affairs than in earlier years when self-censorship was more regularly practiced. For example, editors freely criticized Moscow's policies toward Afghanistan and the shooting down of Korean Airlines Flight 007 by the Soviet Air Force.

Libel. Because the Nordic societies have a high regard for individuals and their place in democratic society, there are strong protections against libelous communication. However, unlike the situation in the United States, libel actions are not often heard in the courts because most disputes that might lead to libel actions are covered by right-to-reply laws and are voluntarily handled by individual members of the press, or are mediated by the press councils.

In Sweden when cases cannot be handled outside the courts, libel cases are tried by juries. These jury trials are a departure from the normal Swedish judicial process and are found only in cases involving press law. The judge may overrule the jury's decision only to find the responsible editor not guilty. The judge may not overrule a not guilty verdict.

Under Swedish law only individuals can seek the legal remedy for defamation, and the accusation is tried with a view to the spirit and intent of the article(s) in question, rather than the mere wording under dispute. The editor-in-chief is held responsible for libel against private persons. According to ombudsman Thorsten Cars, theoretically, this kind of offense is punishable by imprisonment for about a month but decades have passed since an editor-in-chief last incurred such a penalty and fines and/or damages are the only penalty employed in practice. The amount of money involved in both instances is usually very small, corresponding to a couple of thousand dollars plus the plaintiff's legal costs, which can be somewhat higher.[14] Swedish courts handle only about 10 libel cases a year and only a fourth are usually decided for the plaintiff. When the plaintiff loses the suit, he or she can be ordered to pay the legal costs of the editor-in-chief; this provision dissuades many from filing suit.

Danish journalists have a broad area in which they may comment upon public and private figures, but strong defamation laws make it possible for associations as well as individuals to bring defamation actions. Most observers agree that Denmark has more libel disputes than any other Nordic nation. This may be because it has not had a long and strong tradition of a press council and its papers tend to be more sensational and less respectful of individual privacy than others in the region.

Finnish law, in addition to its ordinary defamation provisions, includes a statute that provides strict penalties for libeling foreign heads of state. This provision, which was enacted while Finland was a grand duchy of Russia and was intended to end derogatory comments about the tsar, has not been used since well before Finland gained its independence.

In at least two of the Nordic nations, libel is punishable as a criminal act. Both Denmark and Finland have provisions that permit jail sentences, usually short, for serious breaches of the defamation law such as the papers refusing to comply with the right-to-reply provisions of those nation's laws.

CHAPTER FOUR

Press Economics

The economic situation of the Nordic press has both similarities to and differences from the press in other Western nations. Because it operates in a capitalist system, it competes in two markets: advertising and readership. The performance of individual newspapers in each market affects their performance in the other.

In larger papers in the region, the advertising market provides the majority of income, but large papers account for only a small fraction of the total industry. Most papers are relatively small and advertising accounts for well less than half of their income. To make up for the smaller advertising income, these papers rely more heavily on circulation income, assistance from social or political organizations, and state subsidies.

Because the bulk of the Nordic newspaper industry is locally oriented in both content and advertising and the number of competing papers is generally higher than elsewhere in the West, newspapers operate at low profit levels if they operate at a profit at all. The low profit levels, which have been aggravated over the last four decades by rapidly rising production costs, have kept the industry from becoming a target for commercial concerns interested in using the press as a profit center. As a result, there are few newspaper chains or groups as they are known in the United States and other Western nations. Instead, much of the ownership is held by not-for-profit organizations including foundations, cultural and labor organizations, and political parties.

Circulation

Newspaper circulation in the Nordic nations is among the highest in the world, and Sweden has led the list of newspapers sold per capita for a number of years. Iceland and Finland are also high on the list and all the Nordic nations have higher circulation per capita than found in the United States. Distribution of newspapers is well established and the reading of more than one paper in a household is common. The use of provincial or metropolitan dailies is often supplemented by small, local nondailies and/or afternoon tabloids.

A study of newspaper distribution by social class in Sweden found that the reading of at least one daily paper is virtually universal in Sweden, even in the working class.[1] Other research has shown that Swedes spend an average of 30 minutes each day reading newspapers, a figure that has remained relatively stable over several decades.[2] Circulation throughout the region has been relatively stable as well, but editors and publishers – as in the United States – are concerned by indications that young people are using newspapers less than their parents. Like their counterparts in other Nordic nations, the publishers are beginning to consider means for combating or adjusting to that trend.

In Finland the average household receives 1.5 newspapers – in metropolitan Helsinki that number is 1.9, probably due to the number of papers available and the heavy competition among afternoon papers. Despite an already high readership and the introduction of television throughout the country, Finnish papers increased their circulation almost 3 percent between 1970 and 1980. Norway has 166 papers that have a circulation of nearly 2.5 million with each edition; this is an average of 1.6 papers per household.

Television is growing as a supplier of news throughout the region, and younger people are relying on it more than their elders as a source of news and information. However, the increased use of television among all age groups has not yet resulted in an appreciable loss of circulation. As with papers in other areas affected by the introduction of television, Nordic papers have added television sections to provide their readers with programming and news and information about television.

The most important form of newspaper sales is subscriptions, which are generally well established due to a variety of factors, including geographical distribution and climate, as well as cultural patterns. This is especially true of the serious morning publications. The subscription rate in Denmark is 90 percent for the morning papers and in Finland the rate is about 97 percent; only 3 to 4 percent are sold on the newsstand. Similar figures are encountered in the other nations as well. Those figures change, however, when one looks at the afternoon press, which like tabloid papers throughout the West, relies upon newsstand sales to afternoon commuters for the bulk of its circulation.

Most newspapers are relatively small and cater to a local audience. The average paper in Norway, for instance, has a circulation of about 5000. In Sweden the typical provincial newspaper has a circulation of about 32,000 and a similar paper in Finland typically has a circulation of just under 30,000.

Large national or regional papers circulate more widely, but the number of large papers is small in each nation. In Sweden the large papers account for half the total circulation in the country and the 60 major regional papers account for 30 percent of the circulation; only 6 papers have circulations above 200,000, only about 10 have circulations above 100,000, and less than 24 have circulations above 50,000.

In Finland only 1 paper exceeds 200,000 circulation, only 4 have more than 100,000 circulation, and only 16 have circulations above 50,000. Two Danish papers surpass the 200,000 mark, but only 4 exceed the 100,000 mark and just 9 have circulations in excess of 50,000.

Danish and Swedish papers rely on cooperative distribution and delivery companies that do away with the need for papers to maintain their own distribution organizations; this saves substantial amounts of money for the papers. Under these plans a delivery person working in a neighborhood or delivering papers to newsstands will deliver all the papers for that neighborhood or newsstand, thus eliminating duplicate efforts and the need for a greater number of distribution vehicles. These distribution cooperatives operate as not-for-profit organizations and are viewed as service organizations to reduce costs to a point the individual papers could not reach using their own personnel.

In Finland the leading newspapers in each geographical region use their distribution systems to carry other papers, in what amounts to a joint distribution system, and thus lower their own operating costs. Icelandic papers rely on private delivery systems for their circulation, a possibility that is accounted for in part by the small size of the nation.

In all the nations, postal systems are used regularly for distribution of small papers or those distributed to especially remote areas. Despite increases in postal rate advantages for publishers in the past decade, the costs of postal distribution have risen significantly. Publishers are concerned that the rising costs will force them to set up other delivery systems or drop especially costly circulation.

The introduction of newspaper delivery by air in the late 1970s helped the large Norwegian newspapers increase their market area; however, there was little effect on the largest segment of the press — the predominantly small, local papers that are found in small towns throughout the nation.

Price regulations in Iceland control the price that newspapers may charge for subscription, and the monthly rate for all papers is now set at 240 kronur ($8.50). The regulation is advantageous to *Morgunbladid* (the most influential Icelandic paper), according to competing publishers, because it makes the paper the best buy for consumers since it contains the largest amount of editorial content and advertising.

Advertising

Advertising provides the bulk of the revenue for most large Nordic newspapers, and its contribution represents as much as 50 to 75 percent of the revenue of the major newspapers. That amount is smaller for many of the tabloids and small local papers.

In all the Nordic nations, however, newspaper advertising accounts for the largest portion of the national total of advertising expenditures. The amounts spent by advertisers are comparable to or exceed those of advertisers in other European nations in terms of per capita spending.

Finnish papers receive about 73 percent of their income from advertising, which is nearly two-thirds of all advertising dollars spent in that country. In 1983 newspapers received more than 3.5 billion Finnish markka in advertising revenue ($580 million). Danish papers received 1.56 billion kroner ($156 million) in advertising income in 1983, with about one-third of the amount being accounted for by the Copenhagen daily papers alone.

No specific advertising figures are available for Norway because no organization compiles such figures, but government estimates indicate the figure passed 2 billion kroner ($335 million) annually in the mid-1970s, three times the estimate given for the mid-1960s. Economic stagnation in the late 1970s and 1980s undoubtedly slowed growth of the figures in this predominantly rural country where demand for advertising has been lower than in other Nordic nations.

While advertising expenditures have grown steadily over the past several decades, publishers are concerned about the effect of new media on advertising revenues. Throughout the region the development of free circulation advertising sheets has concerned publishers and many have started their own to keep competitors out of their markets or to extend their own ability to market advertising to consumers. And, until recently television and radio have been noncommercial in the region, but governments – faced with rising operation costs and the demand for more programming–are considering new channels, cable systems, and other alternatives that may be fully or partially funded by advertising.

Icelandic television, which carries commercial advertisements, has not affected the advertising revenue of the nation's major newspapers and publishers of those papers are not seriously concerned about television. Part of their confidence comes from the fact that broadcasting hours are relatively short and the number of advertisers and potential advertisers on national television is limited. However, the proposed commercial radio outlets and local cable systems have publishers of small-town papers worried because the small-town papers are concerned that local advertisers who do not have large advertising budgets may reduce newspaper ad expenditures and move some of their advertising to other commercially based media. Helgi Péterson of the state-operated broadcasting company notes that instead of drawing money from the newspaper advertising budgets, television has increased the advertising budgets of companies.

Devastating economic conditions struck Iceland in the 1970s and 1980s when the fishing industry declined; high government investments were made in the fishing industry, geothermal energy, and in social spending programs; and the worldwide recession simultaneously sapped the economy. The economic conditions harmed newspapers because inflation (as high as 60 percent), combined with monetary and fiscal policies to combat the economic problems, reduced buying power, slowed production and sales, and reduced advertising expenditures. By the mid-1980s efforts to control the economy and better financial conditions throughout the developed world improved the situation.

Danish publishers are deeply concerned about the effects the new electronic media will have on their financial situations because efforts are underway to establish new television and local radio channels, cable systems, and related services that are expected to drain as much as 200 million kroner ($20 million) annually from newspaper coffers. To combat that possibility, publishers have joined together to experiment with teletext services and are seeking to provide news and public affairs information to the new media. To stem their expected losses in ad revenue, the publishers are also seeking ad sales franchises in the new media if the government implements proposals that the new media be supported by advertising.

In recent years the rapid appearance of free circulation advertising papers has worried Danish publishers and many responded by establishing supplemental advertising papers to their normal daily publications. About 300 free ad sheets are regularly published by existing newspapers to supplement their income and prevent competitors from entering their advertising markets.

Newspaper space utilized for advertising in Finland increased by 40 percent during the 1970s, with the greatest increases occurring in the provincial papers. Overall, newspaper revenues have increased steadily since the mid-1970s and have stayed ahead of inflation for more than a decade.

The development of department stores and grocery store chains in the past two decades has been a major contributor to the growth of newspaper ad revenues, although this market base, too, is being pressured by free advertising papers. Many publishers have started their own advertising sheets, distributed in the stores without cost, to compete with the free advertising shoppers. The Finnish Newspaper Publishers Association has been working to ensure its members do not start such ad sheets in markets served by other newspaper publishers.

The competition from advertising sheets has not been compounded by television advertising. Although the Finnish government permits advertisements on television, television advertising now accounts for only about 10 percent of advertising expenditures and has not appreciably cut into newspaper ad expenditures. Finnish radio does not carry advertising.

The introduction of cable television systems and other new technology has concerned Finnish publishers, but the larger publishers – like their large counterparts in the rest of Europe and North America – have involved themselves in the operations of the systems so they will derive profits that might be drained away from their newspaper operations.

In Norway ambitious experimentation in new media has induced many Norwegian papers to become involved in electronic advances in an attempt to protect advertising revenues and keep competitors out of their markets. In recent years Norway has been dubbed "one big media laboratory" because of its trial cable operations (CATV), local radio, satellite broadcasting, and other activities in the new media.

Commercialization of local radio, which was opposed by most newspapers but now is supported by much of the press, and the introduction of CATV systems in rural cities operated by newspapers have helped change the nature of Norwegian communication and audience patterns, and they may affect newspaper readership and revenues in the future. The participation of the press in these projects, however, may lessen the impact on the total operation of the press.

Although Swedish publishers face no competition from radio and television, the spread of advertising papers has increased advertising competition throughout the nation. That competition is being studied by a government-sponsored commission on press problems. Efforts by manufacturers and marketing companies to promote television advertising are being combated by publishers, and there is strong resistance to such ads from other sectors as well, which will undoubtedly delay their appearance.

Efforts to improve marketing of advertising space throughout the region have established a wide variety of cooperative advertising sales organizations and networks. In Sweden, for instance, 47 different cooperatives exist that allow joint advertising in all the papers that are members of the co-ops. The co-op sizes range from 2 to nearly 70 newspapers, and the cooperatives are most often linked to multiple members of political party papers. Such cooperatives exist throughout the region. They help reduce the costs of marketing advertising space and arrange package deals that make many small newspapers attractive prospects to major advertisers.

Labor Issues

The newspaper industry in the Nordic region is almost completely unionized, with unions representing clerical and white-collar workers, as well as journalists and backshop personnel. With the exception of Denmark, relations between workers and employers have not been overly confrontive in recent decades.

Journalists' unions in the region have a long history of protecting workers' interests and represent more than 90 percent of journalists in the five nations. Historically, journalists have achieved better pay scales than throughout much of the West, with Danish journalists being recognized as the best paid in the world and Swedish journalists close behind.

The Finnish Union of Journalists, the oldest union in that country, has negotiated wage scales for the average journalist that are on par with those of assistant professors in the nation's universities. The pay scales are somewhat lower than those in Denmark and Sweden because the union has sought collective agreements covering all journalists and has directed its efforts at raising the minimum pay scale rather than the maximum. Eila Hyppönen, general secretary of the union, feels that although individual agreements would have ended in higher pay scales, the collective agreement achieved the overall improvement for journalists. The collective approach has managed to raise that scale between 25–30 percent in the past decade, and although the Finnish journalists' union has not indexed wages to inflation rates, real wages have nevertheless managed to stay ahead of inflation for at least a decade.

Icelandic journalists have not been as fortunate. Due to the instability of that nation's economy and government wage-restriction policies, wages have dropped significantly in recent years and the union is now seeking to regain income lost to inflation. Nevertheless, wage scales are high by U.S. standards, with the average salary near that of entry-level university professors.

Danish journalists also have suffered declines in real wages (6–8 percent) since 1980, according to union officials, and increases have not kept up with the inflation rate. Although the compensation level has dropped, the pay scales are still high. However, they are now roughly equivalent to those of other Nordic nations, although they are not as high by comparison as they were in the 1960s and 1970s when they were the world's highest.

Along with the drop in wages, Danish journalists have been faced with unemployment problems. In 1984 the unemployment rate among journalists was 8 percent, down from a staggering 10 percent at the height of the recessionary period of the early 1980s.

Generally, working conditions throughout the region are good. Many journalists are provided with private offices in contrast to traditional newsroom settings in which journalists in North America usually work.

The highly organized Swedish journalists' union, like its Nordic counterparts, has been actively working to help direct national press policy and deal with the issues of new newsroom technology. The introduction of such technology in Sweden and Norway was heavily debated on the basis of health, pay, and job security. These issues have been less controversial in Denmark and Finland.

Finnish journalists negotiated extra pay for working on video display terminals (VDTs) in the mid-1970s and Danish journalists reached a similar accord more recently. Danish journalists' concerns over the new technology revolved around fears that it might widen the gap between the high and low pay scales by creating two classes of journalists – high-tech employees (VDT users) and low-tech employees (typewriter users) – with different levels of pay. Danish journalists also have negotiated an agreement providing for protection of stories and compensation for use on the experimental teledata systems.

In recent years Finnish journalists have been concerned with undermanning, which results in extensive overtime work, sometimes uncompensated for salaried journalists. Although the union suffers less than 1 percent unemployment, its members feel significant efforts must be made to reduce forced overtime and provide better compensation. In 1980 a Christmas-season strike by the union shut down newspapers at the height of the holiday advertising time and resulted in some concessions on working hours and wage increases, but problems still remain in the area of overtime hours. Despite such disputes, labor-management relations in Finland are considered generally good.

Labor relations in the Danish newspaper industry have been traditionally confrontive, due to strong, well-organized, well-supported, politically active unions. In the 1970s and 1980s labor-management issues have focused on disputes over the introduction of labor-saving new production technology and its effect on union members. The typographers' union in particular has fought for strong wage increases and overmanning through job security measures. After continuing disputes in the 1970s, a bitter strike in 1981 closed the Danish papers before 40 percent of the typographers were dismissed and wage increases of 4 percent were granted to the remaining workers. The reduction of personnel brought Danish newspapers into line with manpower levels appropriate for the new printing technology.

Typographers and newspaper publishers are now debating issues surrounding the introduction of pagination systems, but the negotiations are less bitter than those over job security and overmanning when modern cold-type composition and offset presses were introduced.

In Sweden the utilization of some new technology has been slowed by printers who have also sought to preserve existing jobs. For the most part, however, the transition to cold-type technology was accomplished by the end of the 1970s without the serious confrontations experienced in Denmark, and Swedish labor relations are much friendlier.

Today, the Swedish printers' union is concerned about government efforts to promote cooperative publishing houses for small newspapers and other efforts aimed at reducing production costs at individual papers. Job security concerns have prompted most of their activities and the union has gained support from the journalists' union.

Generally, solidarity between journalists and printers is stronger in the Nordic nations than in other Western nations. When journalists struck Finnish papers in 1981, for instance, printers refused to publish the free circulation advertising sheets in order to bolster the economic pressure on the publishers.

Production

Newspaper publishing is a labor intensive industry, which requires considerable mechanical equipment and large quantities of material in the form of newsprint, ink, and related supplies to produce the final product. The costs of acquiring, maintaining, and operating the equipment are high, and as technology changed the industry from hot-type composition and letterpress printing to phototypesetting (cold-type) and offset printing in the 1960s and 1970s, smaller papers in the region were financially squeezed by acquisition costs for the new equipment and changeover costs.

The larger newspapers in the region were able to accommodate the innovations and, on the whole, the Nordic industry adopted the technology much more quickly than many of its European counterparts. While most of the smaller papers had to defer purchases well into the 1970s, some organized cooperative houses to acquire the newer equipment, thus publishing several papers at the same location. The Social Democratic press in Denmark began to concentrate its printing in two major houses in the 1960s, and other papers not associated with parties began contracting for printing at larger houses or entered co-ops themselves.

The largest papers in the country are improving their printing presses to increase the number of pages that may be produced and to allow four-color printing. Smaller papers, which did not have resources to convert to cold-type and offset printing when they became readily available in the past two decades, are now doing so or making plans to replace existing equipment in the next 5–10 years. Some assistance is available for these projects through government-backed loans, which were doubled in 1984. In previous years the loan amounts available were very low and were used mainly to help purchase electronic typesetting equipment. However, with the increase in available funds, it is expected that some loans will be made to help in the acquisition of new presses by small publishers.

Though in the recent past most papers lost money or only managed to break even, in the last 5 years the economic outlook for Danish publishers has improved significantly. The majority of the Danish press was foundation owned or operated on a not-for-profit basis, which made it more difficult to modernize and adjust to the changing media situation. The overmanning requirements of the typographical union when labor-saving equipment was installed also kept operating costs high. With the reduction in backshop personnel in 1981 and improved economic conditions in Europe as a whole, the newspaper situation has improved to the point that many papers are now producing modest profits. Indications are that most papers, even those that are privately owned, are reinvesting their resources in equipment that will help improve operations or in related information-delivery systems.

In Iceland the socialist parties and the large paper *Visir*, later *DV*, set up a joint publishing company to handle the majority of the nation's daily newspapers and reduce operating costs through bulk purchases, cooperative printing, and the acquisition of new equipment that would lower publication costs. In 1972, a common printing facility for all Icelandic dailies except *Morgunbladid* was established. It would not have been possible for many of the papers to undertake the modernization effort alone, but they were able to do so as a cooperative effort; they received help from the Norwegian labor press for the project.

Despite the advantages of the cooperative system, *DV* has withdrawn from the co-op and now contracts with *Morgunbladid* for its production requirements. The departure was sparked by scheduling disputes between *DV* and other papers over which paper should be printed first.

Swedish newspapers were some of the earliest to adopt new printing technologies, and the transition to offset printing and phototypesetting was completed well before the new technologies spread throughout the industry in the other Nordic nations. The second wave of newspaper technology, electronic composition from VDTs in the newsroom, has reached most of the major papers and is now spreading to provincial papers as well.

A few cooperative ventures appeared in Sweden, with the most unique being a joint newspaper company created at Visby in 1972. In it two newspapers with differing political orientation created a joint venture that combined personnel, offices, and equipment of the two papers into a firm that would publish two editions, one under the nameplate of each paper, with the only difference being a unique editorial page in each edition. That venture lasted until 1984, when the papers completely merged. The new paper is now one edition with separate opinion material from each of the cooperating political organizations.

In other parts of the country, cooperation, mainly in the area of shared printing equipment, is slowly being tried. The Social Democratic press is planning some centralized printing plants in an attempt to reduce production costs, and other newspaper groups are considering such efforts. Those efforts have been slowed, however, by the great resistance of many newspaper operators to give up their presses. They reason that if they don't have their own presses, they lose their identity.

Throughout the region, the large papers are replacing their presses due as much to growth beyond the present capabilities and the desire for four-color printing as to wear on the machines. Smaller papers are in the same situation, but the much-increased investment for replacement presses is expected to force many, especially in Denmark and Sweden, into cooperative efforts.

Finnish publishers have been relatively progressive in adopting new technologies for production, and many of the papers were among the first in the Nordic region to convert to cold-type technology. During the changeover, agreements were reached with printers and other production personnel to handle the concerns for job security. The Finnish papers were not subjected to the difficult conversion process that Danish papers have felt in recent years.

Because the Nordic nations are a prime source of newsprint due to extensive forestry industries, one might expect that the cost of paper would be lower. However, by comparison to the U.S. prices, newsprint prices are relatively high but are generally in line with those paid throughout middle Europe. It is the high cost of transportation and the lower use of newsprint by individual papers in the region that helps keep the costs high when compared to the United States.

Ownership

The types of newspaper ownership in the region vary to a greater degree than found in other nations of the world, and four major types are readily found in the Nordic nations: family ownership, public ownership, foundation and related not-for-profit ownership, and organization ownership.

In Sweden, for instance, some papers are owned by editors and their families, while others, such as *Svenska Dagbladet,* are owned by a not-for-profit firm in which ownership is held by 150 of the nation's largest companies. Other papers are owned by political parties or labor organizations; this is the case of *Aftonbladet,* which is owned by the Swedish trade unions.

Danish papers also exhibit a variety of ownership patterns as well. *Information* has been employee-owned since 1970, and *Berlingske Tidende* was recently sold by the Berlinge family to a not-for-profit company founded with the aid of a number of Danish companies, a development similar to that of *Svenska Dagbladet*'s ownership.

The trend to new forms of ownership is especially strong in Denmark where profits traditionally have been absent or low for small- and medium-sized newspapers, and well below the rate of return for other

investments for larger papers. In many cases where foundation ownership has been established, the papers are directed by boards made up
of educators, philanthropists, and representatives of the cultural industries. Political figures are usually not well represented on these boards.
This is not a rejection of the political role of the press, however. Political figures have active roles in the ownership and operation of papers
associated with and owned by political parties and affiliated organizations.

The move toward foundation ownership is not without criticism.
Managers of these enterprises and other observers note that the foundations have been and will be faced with greater demands for employee participation in the management of the enterprises. Others argue that creation of foundations does not always reduce the influence
of the previous owners. As noted by Torben Krogh, editor-in-chief of
Information, this is especially true where owners of large papers have
named friends and colleagues to the boards of directors of the foundation and thus have maintained a measure of managerial and editorial
control (author interview, Copenhagen, June 1984).

Political party ownership of papers is fairly common throughout
the region, but that ownership usually is not directly by the party
apparatuses. Instead, members and party officials own shares but have
limited ownership rights. However, some papers are directly owned by
a party, as is *Arbeiderbladet* in Norway.

In Denmark most of the Social Democratic press is owned not by
the party but by the trade unions associated with the political organization. In terms of total circulation, the Social Democratic press accounts
for about 5 percent of newspapers sold. In addition to ownership, the
unions also provide subsidies to the papers to improve their economic
situations. Trade union ownership of the socialist press exists in Sweden and Norway as well.

Private chain ownership is not as prevalent in the region as it is in
middle Europe and North America because the potential for profit is
limited by the small markets and limited availability of advertising
revenue in small towns that make up the bulk of the newspaper
markets. However, a few families do own newspaper chains, but the
size of the chains is limited. The largest family chain in Sweden is that
of the Bonnier family, who owns controlling stock in *Dagens Nyheter*
and *Expressen* and has other publishing holdings, including the nation's
largest book publisher. In terms of newspaper circulation the group
controls about 20 percent of the nation's circulation, mostly due to the
strength of its morning and evening papers in Stockholm. The second
largest chain in Sweden, the Hjorne group, controls about 8 percent of
the national circulation.

Swedish journalists have been active in attempts to limit the power of newspaper groups due to self-protective and ideological concerns. Lars Furhoff, head of the journalism school in Stockholm, attributes their success at limiting the power of owners to the fact that "journalists in Sweden are 95 percent organized [in labor unions] and very active regarding press policy and abuses of power by newspaper owners." Nevertheless, chain ownership is increasing, and Furhoff credits this to political organizations buying papers from commercial operators for use as political papers in party newspaper chains. He says that "profit does not equal the bank rate and there is a low return on investment [in the newspaper industry], so political chains can easily buy papers." When commercial chains purchase Swedish newspapers, however, it is usually to buy out and shut down a competitor or to invest in a new market and "run the competition out of the market" (author interview, June 1984).

The largest publishing company in Finland, Sanoma Oy, has been controlled by the Erkko family for nearly 100 years. The firm owns two of Finland's largest papers, the morning edition *Helsingin Sanomat* and the evening tabloid *Ilta Sanomat,* as well as a number of regional papers. It accounts for about 10 percent of the total newspaper circulation in Finland. The company also publishes the Finnish edition of *Reader's Digest* and women's, children's, and general interest magazines. Despite its size, Sanoma Oy does not own a large number of papers. The other newspaper chains that exist in Finland tend to be small, rural family operations, so chain ownership is not a significant problem in the country.

The Norwegian newspaper industry contains none of the commercial chains and press groups found in other parts of the West. A few small family groups operate papers in several small towns, but their influence is not significant. A similar situation is found in Denmark.

This is not to say that there are no newspaper groups in the nations, however. For economic and political reasons, most of the political press is organized into cooperative editorial gathering, advertising sales, and group purchasing associations. This is true not only of the papers owned directly by parties or affiliated organizations, but also of privately owned papers that associate themselves with a political party.

Newspaper Mortality

The number of newspapers throughout Europe generally reached its peak in the two decades preceding the Second World War, and separate from the damage of that war, underwent significant mortality in the years following. However, by Western standards the aggregate mortality suffered in the region was not heavy; the mortality was less than 25 percent of the total number of newspapers, but most of that loss was attributable to losses in the Danish and Swedish press. Pertti Hemánus has observed that in Denmark and Sweden the decline has been so drastic (Denmark has lost 51 percent and Sweden 39 percent) that, unlike in Finland and Norway, the overall composition of the press has changed fundamentally. But competition between newspapers has decreased in all the countries and more and more cities have become one-paper cities.[3] These observations do not take into account the situation in Iceland where, despite changes in the actual newspapers appearing and other structural shifts, the number of papers has not declined but has increased slightly since the war.

In Finland, with the exception of a few large cities, municipalities are the sites of only one locally produced newspaper. The overall number of Finnish papers has been reduced by about 18 percent since the war, but their number stabilized in the late 1970s. Finnish journalist Ari Jarvinen says that this change is partially due to state subsidies introduced during the 1970s, new technology utilized in the printing field, and good economic growth in the country during that time (videotape interview, World Journalism Resources Unit, 1980).

The industry in Denmark, which was known for its four-newspaper system even in relatively small provincial towns, suffered rapid and significant mortality in the late 1940s and early 1950s, after which it achieved a measure of stability. The loss of half of its papers (Table 4.1) rocked the nation as the provincial towns moved toward supporting one newspaper when production costs squeezed out papers, particularly those with less than 3000–5000 circulation. The surviving papers thus had improved circulation and advertising bases, which provided additional economic strength for their survival.

The Swedish newspaper industry also suffered dramatic losses, but underwent the change more slowly. A study found that the decline occurred at a relatively constant rate between 1945 and 1970. Since the loss of newspapers occurred at a slower pace than in Denmark and

Table 4.1.   Daily Newspaper Mortality since the Second World War

Country	Percentage
Denmark	51
Finland	18
Iceland	0
Norway	16
Sweden	39

most of the papers lost were small, structural changes in individual markets were absorbed more easily by the remaining papers. But the political and cultural effects of the loss were taken seriously and resulted in the creation of the most extensive state subsidy system for newspapers in the democratic world. As a result the mortality of Swedish papers has ended and competition has been maintained as a direct consequence of the subsidies. These subsidies have been increased in line with rises in costs and sufficient compensation has been extended to the competitively disadvantaged; thus, some unprofitable newspapers have survived.[4]

The causes of the rapid death of newspapers in the last four decades have been the subject of considerable research and discussion, but most scholars and newspaper industry representatives have agreed the cause has not been a reduction in readership, a drop in advertising, or merely the increasing production costs. Anthony Smith has argued that certain major shifts are occurring in the types of newspapers that have remained profitable. In the case of the Nordic nations the mortality has resulted from the increasing popularity of afternoon tabloids and the growing popularity of papers not associated with political parties.[5]

The majority of researchers credit changes in profitability to increasing urbanization and other social changes taking place since the Second World War. Socialists credit social bases, that is, the structural bases of capitalism, for mortality and monopolization of the press.

John Hohenberg attributes the problems of the Swedish press to competition from television and the development of large mass-circulation dailies.[6] While bearing out his views on the development of new dailies, however, Swedish researchers and others in the region have generally discounted the impact of television.

For nearly a decade the "circulation spiral" paradigm, offered by Lars Furhoff, has been accepted as an explanation of the causes of mortality. Its theoretical bases have application as an explanation for mortality throughout the West. The theory suggests that the newspaper that has achieved the highest density of distribution also enjoys the largest market potential—the largest number of readers within the territory in which advertisers are interested. This attracts an increased flow of advertising, and thus, larger resources to support the competitive stratagems and low copy prices by which new readers and further advertising will be gained.[7]

Furhoff points out that the leading papers also are able to determine the standards of editorial, production, and distribution quality expected by readers and potential readers. Therefore, competing papers are pressured to live up to those standards, and as those papers attempt to meet the demands, their economic difficulties increase. In other words, according to the circulation spiral theory, some papers will spiral out of existence if quality and circulation are not maintained, because the loss of these elements forces the papers into less advantageous, and ultimately mortal, economic conditions.

Economist Karl Erik Gustafsson, who recently suggested modifications to the theory, explains the spiral as the smaller of two competing newspapers being caught in a vicious circle; its circulation has less appeal for advertisers, and it loses readers if the newspaper does not contain certain attractive advertising. A decreasing circulation again aggravates the problems of selling advertising space. The spiral continues downward to the point where the paper can no longer sustain itself.[8]

Although Gustafsson supported the basic elements of the spiral theory, he proposed that the real indicator of a newspaper's success was not merely its circulation, but its percentage of coverage within a particular market area. He showed a positive correlation between household penetration and economic success, causing him to argue that "only a household coverage of 50 percent or more makes a newspaper indispensable to advertisers. Mere circulation strength is not the real indicator of a newspaper's competitive strength."[9] Gustafsson also noted that it is possible for more than one newspaper to have a household penetration of more than 50 percent in the same market area and projected reasonable prospects for survival for each.

State Intervention

An important aspect of the economic milieu of Nordic newspapers is government intervention. As a whole, state intervention in press economics is higher in the region than any other area in the democratic world.

All governments intervene in press economics to some degree through a variety of state activities, but among the Nordic nations, a study ranks the intervention in Sweden, Norway, and Finland (in that order) as being the highest, while intervention in Denmark and Iceland is the lowest.[10] This intervention occurs in three main categories (advantages, subsidies, regulations), which are subsequently divided into a dozen subdivisions (Table 4.2).

The advantages include preferential tax rates or exemptions from some taxes; preferential postage rates; preferential telecommunication rates; and preferential rates for newspapers distributed by rail, air, and sea transport. The subsidy programs include subsidies for training and research grants, production costs and grants to encourage economic improvements in the industry, loan and loan guarantees, government advertising expenditures, financial aid to agencies to defray the costs of telegraphic and radio systems, and financial aid to political newspapers and other informational activities of political parties. Intervention by regulation involves ownership and price regulation.

State intervention in press economics increased rapidly in the region during the past 20 years, fueled by concerns over rising newspaper mortality, commercialization, and the diminishing outlets for political and social viewpoints. During the last part of the 1960s, government committees were established in each country to study the problems of the press and propose public policies for dealing with the difficulties, especially the diminution of voices for political parties. The first Swedish commission finished its work in 1965 and resulted in the subsidization of political party informational activities, including funds for sympathetic newspapers. The Finnish committee presented its reports in 1967, which resulted in similar subsidies, while the Norwegian report resulted in direct support to smaller newspapers, in the form of a loan fund and new tax advantages.

In comparison with the policies of Sweden and Norway, Finland was more concerned with preserving party papers in each city than with preserving overall national availability of voices. Sweden and

Table 4.2. State Intervention in Press Economics in the Nordic Nations

Intervention	Denmark	Finland	Iceland	Norway	Sweden	Total
Advantages						
Tax rates	x	x	x	x	x	5
Postal rates	x	x		x	x	4
Telecommunication rates		x		x	x	3
Transportation rates		x		x	x	3
Subsidies						
Education and research grants	x	x		x	x	4
Other grants and production subsidies		x		x	x	3
Loans and guarantees	x		x	x	x	4
Government advertising	x	x	x	x	x	5
Aid to news agencies		x		x	x	3
Aid to political parties		x	x	x	x	4
Regulations						
Ownership regulation					x	1
Price regulation			x			1
Total	5	9	5	10	11	

Norway wanted to preserve papers to ensure that multiple voices were available throughout each country, but they did not attempt to preserve as many papers in each city.

The rationale for support was clearly based on political considerations. In Sweden, the decline of newspapers resulted in the Left, particularly the dominant Social Democrats, having fewer outlets for their political opinions. This was believed to be especially damaging to the party because the electoral strength in Sweden is skewed to the left, while existing newspapers are skewed to the right. This imbalance between orientation of newspapers and political representation was a major cause of the early efforts to institute press support measures. The rhetoric used to justify the action – that democracy requires multiple viewpoints – was picked up by other parties, which joined in the effort to gain support for the press and thus aid their own papers as well.

Denmark took a different approach to its problems, partially because the loss of newspapers had almost ended by the 1960s and partially because of a stronger commercial influence in the country. There was also significant opposition to direct government funding of the press due, in part, to its experiences in the Second World War. When the press commission issued its report in 1969, the proposals concentrated on fiscal advantages and the establishment of a government-backed loan fund.

Iceland, which did not suffer the mortality found in the other nations, did not experience the impetus for state intervention found in the other Nordic countries. When moves have been undertaken to increase government assistance, the strong Conservative party has created insurmountable stumbling blocks. As a result intervention has been limited to political party informational subsidies, bulk purchases of newspapers by the government, government ad purchases, and regulations affecting circulation and ad sales prices.

Government subsidy does not guarantee success. At least two new daily papers were established as a result of Swedish newspaper subsidies, but they ultimately failed. In 1981 the Social Democratic party restarted its serious morning paper, *Stockholms Tidningen,* which had perished in 1967. The paper reached a circulation of 40,000, but despite the significant subsidies it received from the government, it could not gain sufficient advertising or circulation to support itself and was shut down again in 1985. The party was forced to choose between funding it or the evening paper *Aftonbladet,* and *Aftonbladet* won the support.

Another paper, *Göteborgs Handels-Och Sjöfartstidningen,* also died in 1985 after just 18 weeks of publication. The privately owned paper was described as a total disaster by some observers. Although the paper used the name of the well-known Göteborg paper that had died earlier because of its inability to achieve a balanced economy, the new version managed to reach a circulation of only 18,000 with 3.5 pages of paid advertising daily before it was closed.

However, there are some weekly papers that have been launched successfully as the result of subsidies. Since 1976 a total of 15 new weekly papers have appeared as the result of establishment grants: 5 have local distribution, 7 have regional distribution, and the remaining 3 have national distribution. Since Sweden has only about 100 daily papers and 40 weeklies, the appearance of 15 new papers is significant. Once established, the papers became eligible for the significant production subsidies that are the mainstay of the Swedish subsidy system. The main political beneficiary of the new papers has been the Center party, with which the majority of the papers are affiliated.

The costs of intervention increased rapidly as the programs instituted in the 1970s increased costs of previously established state aid, the number of recipients increased, and new grant and subsidy policies were instituted. These removed the discretion of awarding or withholding funds from administrators and resulted in aid being provided even to papers that did not require assistance.

The increasing costs were combined with the rising costs for other social and industrial programs but were offset by steady economic growth, high savings rates, and increasing foreign trade during the late 1960s and early 1970s. The worldwide economic recession of the 1970s fueled large trade deficits, unemployment, deficit spending to finance increased demands on social welfare programs, double-digit inflation, and declining productivity throughout the region. All these events affected state assistance programs for the press as government austerity programs were instituted to hold down increases in funding for many of the programs.

In Finland, the amount of aid was deliberately restrained during the mid- and late-1970s, despite inflation and rapidly rising production and distribution costs. Since 1980 some attempts have been made to increase aid to make up for past losses, but subsidy and advantage levels have remained below those that would have been reached had aid increased with demand and inflation.

The Finnish telecommunication subsidy, which was 1 million Finnish markka (FIM) ($165,000) in 1971, grew to only 3 million FIM ($500,000) in 1980. Selective subsidies grew from 7.5 million FIM ($1.25 million) in 1971 to 32 million FIM ($5.3 million) in 1980, but much of that increase was due to program expansion rather than increasing aid for individual recipients. When more favorable economic conditions were achieved in the early 1980s, the funding for the postal rate reduction was raised from 250 million FIM ($42 million) in 1981 to 338 million FIM ($56 million) in 1984. The telecommunication subsidy then jumped from 3 million FIM ($500,000) in 1980 to 4.1 million FIM ($685,000) in 1982. Selective subsidies were increased from 32 million FIM ($5.3 million) in 1980 to 42.9 million FIM ($7.2 million) in 1983, as were expenditures for political party aid.

Finnish government officials are concerned about finding ways to redirect aid to the most marginal newspapers. According to Niilo Laakso, ministerial counselor for the Ministry of Traffic, which administers the bulk of press subsidies, the lack of coordination among various press aid programs will be the subject of a new government study group. The group is expected to make recommendations that will reduce the number of aid recipients and provide mechanisms for the administrators of various subsidy programs to coordinate efforts on behalf of the most needy enterprises. Means of keeping down costs of press support are being sought and efforts will be made to find ways that the industry can reduce its costs as well (author interview, Helsinki, July 1984).

Kaarle Nordenstreng, professor of journalism at the University of Tampere and a member of the government commission on newspaper subsidies, helped shape Finland's subsidy system in the early 1970s. He believes that the saturation point for funding is fairly close, and when that point is reached, there will be no more increases for some time (author interview, Tampere, July 1984).

Sweden's Riksdag limited most government spending in the late 1970s, and the press aid system did not escape the actions of the moderate government that had gained power in the mid-1970s. When the Social Democratic government regained power in 1982, restraints continued. Although much of the revenue that supports subsidies comes from a 4 percent advertising tax, the economic conditions afflicting the economy as a whole slowed ad activity and, thus, the government income from the tax. Production subsidies, which quadrupled from 1971 to 1976, increased only 65 percent between 1976 and 1980. Between 1980 and 1984 they rose 50 percent to a total of 369.1 million kronor (SKr) ($46.1 million), but were then frozen. Loan funds, which amounted to 24.2 million SKr ($3 million) in 1969, have never been increased, except for a transfer of the cost of administration from one account to another that pushed that amount to 25 million SKr ($3.1 million) in 1984. From 1976 to 1984, grants for the establishment of new papers rose from 2.6 million SKr ($325,000) to only 3.8 million SKr ($475,000), despite rapidly increasing use and applications for the funds.

Lars Furhoff, a member of several media funding commissions established by the Swedish government in the past three decades, believes that newspapers will have to begin to adjust their budgets to absorb more costs in the future. Newspaper subsidies are big and the country, which is in debt, has capped social welfare programs. Press subsidies will soon be capped as well (author interview, Stockholm, June 1984). To prepare for that event newspaper managers in Sweden must look for ways to reduce costs or cooperate with other papers so the lack of increases in aid does not catch them unexpectedly.

Gunnar Öberg, editor of *Gotlands Tidning,* one of the major recipients of aid from a number of subsidy programs, says the Swedish subsidy board is beginning to get coercive with competing or strategically located newspapers in its efforts to promote cooperation in such areas as production, printing, and purchases. The board is starting to use the threat of withholding aid as an inducement to promote the cooperative efforts which many newspapers have rejected up until this time (author interview, Visby, June 1984). Öberg also expects that a new government commission on subsidies will recommend that the Riksdag restructure the production subsidy system to reduce the number of recipients which would increase the funding that could be made to more needy papers despite a capping of the funding level for the program.

Norway's subsidy costs grew from 15 million kroner (NKr) ($1.9 million) in 1969 to 70 million NKr ($8.8 million) in 1975, but the growth of those funds has now been limited below inflation rates by government in an attempt to keep expenses down.

According to Sigurd Klakeg, senior executive officer of the Ministry of Finance, efforts to change the methods and formulas for funding papers in Norway are also planned; action should begin on those changes shortly. The conservative government that was elected in 1981 wishes to change the formula for production subsidies to limit program expenditures. It also wishes to introduce a type of selective subsidy system in which aid can be directed more efficiently toward those papers with marginal economies, thus reducing the need to continually increase the amount of expenditures for press aid (author interview, Reykjavik, June 1984).

In Denmark where loan funds are guaranteed by the government, a 4-million-kroner (DKr) ($400,000) limit placed on the funds in 1975 remained in place until 1984 when the amount was doubled and an additional 6 million DKr ($600,000) was authorized for loans to plan the establishment of new papers and for selective loan funds for religious papers.

The press commission, which ended its work in 1984, chose not to abandon Denmark's traditional avoidance of extensive press subsidies. However, Karen Siune, who served on the commission, says it moved farther toward press aid than the government wished by urging distribution subsidies for papers circulated throughout the country and by suggesting aid for alternative publications. Direct aid for newspapers was not sought by the commission, Siune says, because there were so few papers left in need of help that direct subsidies were not seriously considered (author interview, Fugslø, August 1985).

Denmark's aid efforts, which have never relied on subsidies but rather on loans and advantages, will also be restricted by economic conditions for some time. The possibility of extensive new subsidies is exceedingly low, according to Asger Lund-Sørensen, counselor to the prime minister, because the Danish government has no interest in funding dying industries (author interview, Copenhagen, June 1984). Instead of relying on subsidies, the government has and will continue to rely on loans to promote press modernization and efforts aimed at making papers more economically sound.

In Iceland, which experienced the worst economic conditions in the region, levels of state support have remained constant and the effect of that aid has diminished as costs have raced ahead of inflation.

Arguments for increasing aid have been muted. Arni Gunnarsson, editor of the Social Democratic paper *Althýdubladid,* which suffered significant economic reverses when the party lost control of the government, says that even his party is not promoting significant increases or new party aid; the party is afraid of pressing the issue too hard. He believes that if a party cannot help itself in a situation like this, it has not only financial difficulties but political difficulties as well (author interview, Reykjavik, June 1984).

Although there have been disagreements among the various political parties in the different nations as to whether or not the amounts of aid should be increased, there is a strong consensus across the parties that existing aid programs should be continued. But according to recipients of the aid and program officials, changes in eligibility for aid and the capping of some aid programs should be expected in the near future. Removing from aid programs the newspapers that do not need the aid for survival, increasing cooperative efforts between papers to reduce the amount of aid needed, and promoting better sales and management practices are now being considered. The reactions of the governments during the recessionary period and their current efforts would seem to indicate a commitment and willingness on the part of those governments to continue funding press programs, albeit while taking closer looks at the effectiveness of and need for assistance.

As long as the Nordic nations continue to perceive newspapers as playing an important role in national political, cultural, and social debates, it would seem reasonable to conclude that the governments that intervened in press economics in order to preserve multiple outlets for opinion will continue to do so. However, the experience of the past decade indicates they will not do so at levels of funding that are absolute, but that funding will be dependent upon the existing economic situation and their ability to fund other social services that provide an immediate direct assistance to individual members of their societies.

PART TWO

Present-Day National and Regional Newspapers

CHAPTER FIVE

Newspapers of Denmark

National Newspapers

Aktuelt. This tabloid is the most serious of Denmark's popular tabloids and does not rely on the sensationalism of *Ekstrabladet* and *B.T.* The paper concentrates primarily on Danish news and features, with heavy coverage of sports, arts, and political debate.

Usually about 44 pages in length, the paper has a circulation of about 60,000 weekdays and 125,000 on Sunday. The paper is associated with the Social Democratic party. Called *Social-Demokraten* until it was renamed *Aktuelt* in 1959, the paper has the distinction of being the oldest continuously published labor paper in the world (Fig. 5.1).

Berlingske Tidende. This paper is not only Denmark's most prestigious paper but one of Europe's most important newspapers as well. Its content reflects the serious tone and coverage expected of a paper with such a reputation. Like its major competitor, *Politiken, Berlingske Tidende* carries a significant amount of national and international news, financial information, political debate, and discussions of art, culture, and social issues (Fig. 5.2).

Normally about 44 pages in length, the paper has a circulation of 120,000 daily and 200,000 on Sundays.

The paper is independent of political parties but generally supports Conservative party viewpoints. It is the oldest existing paper in Denmark, having begun publishing in 1749.

Børsen. An economic paper, much like the *Wall Street Journal, Børsen* places particular emphasis on Danish and international economic and business news and carries short articles on general national and international news that may affect its readers (Fig. 5.3).

The paper, which is published in tabloid format, is cleanly designed and usually about 44 pages in length. Advertisers of business

Dobbeltmorder snart fanget

Bagside

aktuelt

**Stor rift
om holding-
selskaber:
En fed
skattefidus**

Side 7

Fredag 29. juni 1984 - Nr. 178
Uge nr. 26 - 113. årg. - Kr. 3,75

Multinational ekspansion i Danmark:

2148 JOB ER SOLGT PÅ ET ÅR

Sid

Sommer i Aktuelt

Sommer er det, selv om det tilsyneladende ikke er gået op for vejrguderne. Den årlige turist-invasion er startet forlængst, og Aktuelt har spurgt nogle af dem, hvorfor det lige blev Danmark i år.

Samtidig har københavnerne også fået nye fritidsmuligheder midt i storbyen med åbningen af det tidligere militære skydeterren for offentligheden — et eldorado for botanikere, ornitologer og andet godtfolk. Og så vil Aktuelts meteorolog Hubert Hill i øvrigt ikke udelukke, at vejret bedrer sig i weekenden.

Side 4, 19 og 21. Foto: Per Daugaard og Jørgen Schiøtt.

**Anker:
De unges
studie-
gæld en
katastrofe**

Side 14 og 15

5.1. *Aktuelt* is the current version of the historic paper *Social-Demokraten*. This front page te the capture of a double murderer and the effects of multinational companies on the job mark Denmark. (Reprinted with permission)

84

5.2. *Berlingske Tidende* is now the oldest existing newspaper in Denmark. In this recent issue the front page celebrates the arrival of summer and the victory of a national cyclist in an international race. (Reprinted with permission)

85

Børsen

Dagens tendens

Dag til dag rente..12,750 —1,125 Eurodoll. (6 mdr.) 12,62
Oblig.rente gns..... 14,55 +0,08 Dollar/Krone ...1.025,75
Aktieindeks .... 182,02 —0,53 D-mark/Krone 367,00
Eff. kronekurs .... 87,59 —0,20 D-mark/Dollar ... 2,7970

Fredag den 29. juni 1984 ☐ Nr. 124 ☐ Uge nr. 26 ☐ 89. årgang ☐ 5,50 kr. ☐ Tlf.: (01) 15 72 50 ☐ Telex: 22 90

Børsen i dag:

■ Der bør også være mulighed for at yde realkreditlån på Grønland, mener Byggeriets Realkreditfond - side 2

■ Industriminister Ib Stetter har besluttet, at organisationerne næste år må vinke farvel til støtte til i alt 58 konsulenter - side 2

■ A. P. Møller går nu ind i linietrafik med containerskibe mellem det fjerne Østen og Vestafrika - side 5

■ DSB's underskud er faldet med 20 mio. kr. i forhold til 1982 - side 12

■ Danmark har en høj kreditværdighed, siger lederen af den japanske bank i København, Mitsui Trust & Banking - side 22

■ Verdens største private bank, Citicorp, disponerer over enorme lobby-kræfter, der på flere områder tvinger lovgivningen i knæ - side 16

■ Det første hold elever på den nye fireårige presefotograf-uddannelse starter til efteråret - side 19

■ A/S Roulunds Fabriker er inde i en særdeles gunstig udvikling med en fornem fremgang i salg og overskud - side 7

■ A. P. Møller har skrevet kontrakt med det japanske rederi, Hitachi om forlængelse af fem containerskibe - side 5

■ Danmarks fire første cand. linc. merc'er i italiensk har netop afsluttet deres eksamen fra Handelshøjskolen - side 18

■ Det er lykkedes Carlsberg i Malaysia at opfylde den malaysiske regerings krav om 30 pct. indenlandsk ejer- og lederskab - side 30

■ Rejsebureauernes billeteksperter koster SAS et tab i Danmark på omkring 80 mio om året - side 31

■ Den tyske metalarbejderstrejkes ophør fjerner en alvorlig belastning fra erhvervslivet, og forliget svækker ikke dets konkurrenceevne. - side 8

■ Tre diskontohop presede fonds op på fondsbørsen i går - side 38

■ Dollaren faldt i går troda gunstige amerikanske handelstal - side 38

Fondsb....	38	TV.........	42
Ledere	10	Udland ...	8
Opinion ...	11	Valuta......	38
Råvarer ...	37	Vejret	42
Søfart.....	37	Øjet.........	42

Udlandet bag størstedelen af sidste års firma-opkøb

Swedish Match overtog HTH-Køkkener, Norsk Hydro fik fuld kontrol over KFK og Kuwait Petroleum overtog Gulf Oil

Udenlandske koncerner tegnede sig for 24 af de i alt 104 virksomhedsopkøb, som fandt sted i Danmark sidste år. Disse 24 virksomheder tegnede sig til gengæld for 64 pct. af omsætningen og 65 pct. af kapitalen i samtlige opkøbte selskaber. Tungest vejer overtagelse af Gulf Oil og et norsk firmas overtagelse af Dumex - Bagsiden

Direktør H. C. Bang, Handelsbanken — har endnu ikke hørt noget fra banktilsynet.

Anva henter direktør i Daells Varehus

Varehuskæden A/S, der drives af har håndplukket si direktør, Mogens ka, 51 år, hos konku ten Daells Varehu anset ham som enen tør for kædens fire retninger fra 1. augu

Mogens Trepka af Jørgen Skovlund, de nylig opsagde sin sti som administrerend rektør for at gå til F gaard Radio. Ifølge b for FDB og Anva, Anva bestyrelse ansættelsen af Mog Trepka ønsket at s sig realiseringen a ekspansion for Anva.

Mogens Trepka e til Børsen, at han stemt ikke smækker dørene i Daells Varu og hvis han som me ne virksomhedsle ikke skal gro fast i v somheden, er det no skal skifte.

— For mig er de drømmeopgave, jeg Et. ønskejob, siger gens Trepka. Om sin år i Daells Varehus s han, at han var mee at opbygge Daells B hus både i Glostrup Krystalgade i Køb havn, og at han været med til hele re verlingen og den forn sesproces, der forvan de det gamle varehus et moderne varehus.

Den fornyelse har m beundret udfra tænkt, at sådan no måske også kunne fo gå andre steder. Og m det jo netop stillet mi til rådighed for An Også måske for en yd ligere fornyelse af for ningen på Vesterbrog i København, siger M gens Trepka.
K.J

Tilsyn: Nej til speciel bank- for- sikring

Handelsbankens forsikringsordning etableret sammen med Hafnia accepteres ikke - Side 2

Lønramme- sag på fire pct. trækker ud

Arbejdsgiverkredse mener at Metal ikke vil løbe risiko for nederlag i arbejdsretten før kongres - Side 4

Max Søhring: Arbejdsgiverne siger så meget, men vi tager den tid der er brug for.

Børsen- AIM: Rege- ringens flertal er intakt

De konservative noterer markant fremgang på bekostning af Venstre og CD - Side 6

I den katolske kirke er kommandovejen fra præst til pave kort og direkte. Foto: Nordisk Pressefoto

Top- karakter til katolsk kirke for fin ledelse

Skriftemål og tredelt hierarki væsentlige elementer - Side 13

I dag: Job

5.3. Stories about the effects of foreign operations on Danish firms, such as the one featured this front page of *Børsen,* are typical of this serious business paper. (Reprinted with permission

products and services make heavy use of the publication; advertising often makes up at least half of the content. *Børsen* has a daily circulation of 35,000.

B.T. A 44-page afternoon tabloid, *B.T.* features heavy sports coverage and a mixture of short news and feature items haphazardly combined in a modular makeup. It is the least serious of Denmark's major newspapers (Fig 5.4). However, *B.T.* is published by the same company that publishes the more serious morning paper *Berlingske Tidende.*

This independent paper that supports the Conservative party has a daily circulation of about 200,000 and, like its main competitor, *Ekstrabladet,* carries a nude woman's photograph in each issue, much like the tabloids of Great Britain.

Ekstrabladet. This national tabloid specializes in feature stories, human interest stories, and sports and entertainment information (Fig. 5.5). A journalistically aggressive paper, it often carries out community improvement campaigns and crusades against perceived wrongs. The paper is Denmark's largest daily with a circulation of about 250,000.

Ekstrabladet is usually 44 pages in length and often uses four-color printing to highlight articles and photographs. As in *B.T.,* each issue ordinarily carries a photograph of a nude young woman, a feature not found in the newspapers in other Nordic nations.

Although not as politically oriented as other papers, *Ekstrabladet* does not ignore politics and often supports Liberal party views. The paper is published by the same firm that publishes *Politiken.*

Information. A thoughtful daily newspaper, *Information* traces its history to the struggle against Nazi occupation of Denmark when it served as the news service for underground papers. After the occupation ended, it inherited a large amount of money from a resistance organization to help it become a newspaper.

Today the paper is an independent liberal publication that concentrates on long articles and discussions of social and political issues (Fig. 5.6). It provides important daily national and international news but is more interested in providing context and explanations of events. The paper has been described as a cross between the *New York Times* and the *Village Voice.*

44 sider   Fredag 29. juni 1984   Uge 26   3,75 kr.

Skatteyderne betaler Foighels rejsefråds

ISRAEL-TUR BRUGT TIL FAMILIE-BESØG

B.T kan idag af-sløre, hvordan skatteminister Isi Foighel sammen med et helt lille hof af embedsmænd hæmningsløst har turet rundt til eksotiske steder på kloden. Formålet har de fleste gange væ-ret fuldstændigt betydningsløse. En rejse til Israel faldt meget belejligt sammen med, at Foighels datter, der er bosat i Israel, havde fået barn.

SIDE 4

Sølvhøj: Jeg kan blive fem år til hos Margrethe

SIDE 10

Gunnar Nu jubler: Jeg topper hitlisten

SIDE 15

5.4. This front page of *B.T.* features a story about the celebrity status of the pope and a story about a tax official who took a government-funded trip on which he visited his family in Israel.

88

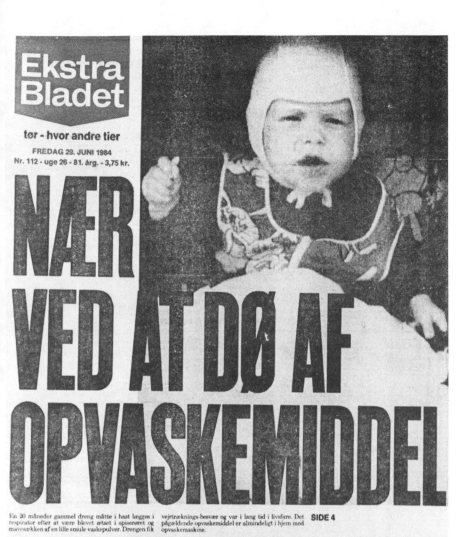

Ekstra Bladet

tør - hvor andre tier

FREDAG 29. JUNI 1984
Nr. 112 - uge 26 - 81. årg. - 3,75 kr.

NÆR VED AT DØ AF OPVASKEMIDDEL

En 20 måneder gammel dreng måtte i hast lægges i respirator efter at være blevet ætset i spiserøret og mavesækken af en lille smule vaskepulver. Drengen fik vejrtrækknings-besvær og var i lang tid i livsfare. Det pågældende opvaskemiddel er almindeligt i hjem med opvaskemaskine.

SIDE 4

QVIST SPONTANT HYLDET I TIVOLI

SIDE 25 I SOMMER EKSTRA

Det tog ti minutter før Tivoli Revyen kom i gang i aftes. Årsag: I ærkeslagen sad Ole Qvist og fik hele salen til at gynge med på 'og det var Danmark'.

5.5. This present-day version of *Ekstrabladet,* the Danish national tabloid, heralds the near death of an infant in a dishwasher. (Reprinted with permission)

89

Information

Fredag 29. juni 1984
UAFHÆNGIG AF PARTIPOLITIK · UAFHÆNGIG AF ØKONOMISKE INTERESSER
40. årgang nr. 149. Pris 4,75 kr. ₀₀₀

Lægers forsøg

LÆGER kritiserer ikke hinandens arbejde. Ikke åbenlyst. I hvert fald. Det er der århundreders tradition og gode argumenter for.

Lægen skal i alle måder være en *gentleman*, indskærpede allerede den engelske læge Thomas Percival, da han for snart 200 år siden nedfældede de forslag til en medicinsk etik, som har været kollegial vejviser for senere læge-generationer.

I 1700-tallets England lå allehånde udøvere af den såkaldte lægekunst i evindelig strid. Kirurgerne, der oprindeligt var barberer og først måtte i barberådet skifte sig ud fra friserfaget, tottedes med medicinerne og apotekerne om omverdenens gunst og respekt. Men det var en åben lægekonflikt under en tyfus-epidemi på sygehuset i Manchester, som i 1791 fik Percival til at supplere de lægeregler, som bl.a. græskeren Hippokrates fra turistøen Kos to tusind år tidligere havde nedfældet, med -et sæt af regler for professionel opførsel i relation til hospitalslæger og andre medicinske videnskabsinstitutioner.

Senere af Percival udvidet til almengyldige moralske forskrifter for alle læger.

En hellig dyd er, at læger ikke rejser offentlig kritik af hinandens arbejde. Kun når der en læge groft udnytter patienternes tillid eller sætter ikke blot liv, men et *rigtigt* liv på spil, må andre læger blande sig. Og så skal deres motiver virkelig være -rene og ærefulde-, betonede Percival.

Man må derfor gå ud fra, at Danmarks førende talsmand for lægeetiske regler, professor dr. med. Povl Riis, har -rene og ærefulde- motiver, når han nu i fuld offentlighed tager afstand fra sine kollegers LSD-forsøg i de gale tressere på Frederiksberg Hospital.

DE FORSØG var ikke forsøg, mener Povl Riis. De fulgte ikke de lægefaglige spilleregler for *videnskabelige* forsøg. Derfor kræver de ikke de *videnskabs-etiske* regler, som Povl Riis har været med til at udforme. bl.a. i den såkaldte Helsinki-deklaration nr. 2 fra 1976, lyder professorens ræsonnement.

Der kan være rene og ærefulde grunde til, at Povl Riis ønsker at værne om lægevidenskabens forsøgschance i en fremtid med utrolige bio-tekniske muligheder og derfor distancerer sig fra kollegers spild ren med menneskeskæbner. Men det kan også være en besnærende måde at glide uden om sagens kerne på.

Uanset om man vil kalde afdøde overlæge Einar Geert-Jørgensens og kollegers LSD-forsøg for videnskab eller ej, er de udtryk for en klar overtrædelse af fundamentale menneskerettigheder.

Til enhver forsøgsmos essentielle nyttiveardi, deres videnskabelighed eller mangel på samme kan begrunde, at læger kaster uforbeholde patienter fra 11-års alderen ud i madet med et psykedelisk helvede, blot fordi en overlæge -...gerne ville se, hvad der sker, når man kun giver stoffet og i øvrigt lader patienten i fred uden for som indgreb eller andre behandlingen ...-

Danske læger burde være de første til at fordømme den slags uhyrligheder.

HVOR ER DET, vi tidligere har hørt læger forklare sig med, at de gerne ville se, hvad der sker? Var det ikke i kz-lejren Buchenwald? I Blok 46, der under SS blev omdannet til «Afdelingen for tyfus- og virusforskning», hvor læger blev påført tyfus, gul feber, kopper, kolera, difteri og fik sine dineres dødsforløb nøje registreret.

Eller i Auschwitz og andre lejre, hvor tyske forskere rekvirerede -med egne ord - «associale» sigøjner-bastarder-, jøder, bolsjevikker, prostituerede og andre «undermennesker» til forsøg. For en ren, hvad der sker-, når mennesker udsættes for iskoldt vand, for gasser, gifte, smitsomme sygdomme, brandbomber og andet, som den nazistiske krigsmaskine skulde undersøge.

Den nære end lo år lange mediciner-sag, som fulgte under Nürnberg-processerne efter Anden Verdenskrig, blev ikke kun en amerikansk helt op ger med den nazistiske grusomheder under en krig.

På forhånd frakendte amerikanerne de begåede grusomheder enhver videnskabelig værdi, men de anklagede læger havde i deres forsvar netop hentet frem lange videnskabelig søn s-seletse. Nogle af dem var ifølge en amerikansk. militære-læge -revolutionerende- og ville -spare amerikansk medicin år af forskning-. Videre trak forsvarerne amerikanske «eksempler på malaria-forsøg med sorte amerikanske straffefanger» og andre forsøg med immigranter ud i søgene.

Derfor blev mediciner-sagen, som idéhistorikeren Peter Roosel viser i sin fremragende bog «Medicinsk etik», et almost opgør med lægevidenskabens brug af menneskeliv til forsøg.

Det blev fastslået, at læger stillet over for utiske fordringer har -en pligt til opror-, og at ingen nok så totalitær tvang kan retfærdiggøre knægtelse af patientens rettigheder.

Under dommen i 1948 formuleredes samtidig «Nürnberg-kodeks» ti bud. Det første ukrænkelige princip siger, at «forsøgspersonens frivillige samtykke er absolut nødvendig», og der gælder ingen undskyldning for at omgå det.

DENNE HISTORISKE lære blev groft tilsidesat i kældrene under Frederiksberg Hospital, da danske læger ifølge eget udsagn *ville se, hvad der skete* og derfor *ønd vilje*s undlod at orientere patienterne.

Lægerne i kældrene tiltie sig som videnskabelige pionerer, men de trog fejl og det kostede menneske-liv. Mydighederne ved det, men håber øjensynligt, at sagen kun glemmes af sig selv.

Det kan den her ikke.

Den LSD-afføre, som information bragte så mange gange og så viste optururksomhed på, er ikke kun en afdækning af et historisk overgreb med en fåtalig gruppe patienter. Den er lære et varsel om, hvordan samfundet og lægestanden forvalter sit ansvar, når der nye tuve en menneskelig pris på det videnskabeligt of viden i den fagtre nye verden.

Det ansvar kan ikke klares med en kollegial side-dommers trut i æreshornet.

Studenter mod Marcos

Studenter i Filippinernes hovedstad Manila danner kæde imod uroligheder under en demonstration imod landets præsident, Ferdinand Marcos. Studenterne ønsker flere penge til uddannelse og færre til landets militær. (Foto: UPI)

Guerillaer erobrer vandværk i El Salvador

SAN SALVADOR, 28. juni (AP) - Guerillaer har indtaget El Salvadors største hydroelektriske vandværk torsdag. Laget adskillige gjelder og trusse nu med at ødelægge selskabet, oplyser landets regering.

Guerillaerne har taget et stort antal regeringstropper og civile som gidsler efter angrebet på Cerron Grande-dæmningen, til sisimitiese oned for hovedstaden. En dring rapgeregendalde taldt i baghold, da de blev sendt til forståerkning af vandværket.

Oprørerne har over for radiostationer meddelt, at de vil ødelægge anlægget, hvis ikke regeringslæren indstiller forsøg på at tilbageerobre det.

Allerede i 1949 slår dannelsen af det israelske stat blev Yadin Israels andre generalstabschef og var i sine 50 år hans mest fremragende militærleder. Han forstærke sig i 1977 som politiker. Forud for valget dæt år grundlagde han partiet Den Demokratiske Bevægelse for Forandringer, som blev det tredjestærkeste grupper i parlamentet.

Yadin blev viceministerpræsident under Menachem Begin, men kom til at stå så meget i skyggen af den dominerende regeringschef, at han efterhånden fik valgets i 1981 trak sig ud af politisk liv. Han helligede sig i sinr senere år arkæologi og var en international anerkendt arkæolog.

Yigael Yadin død i Israel

TEL AVIV, 28. juni (DPA) Den israelske general og politiker Yigael Yadin døde torsdag af et hjertetilfælde, 67 år.

Jøderne kamp for al få deres egen stat affand i 1940erne Yadim uddannelse til arkæolog. I tresses slutede han sig til Haganah, der senere dannede grundlag for landets reguleire her.

Unge vælgere drejer til venstre

Mere myte end virkelighed, at unge vælgere skulle være specielt højredrejede

Den udbredte tale om højredrejning i befolkningen i almindelighed og blandt de unge-befolkningsgrupper i særdeleshed viser sig at være mere myte end virkelighed. En frisk analyse af til de konservative. KU har udsendt, tyder på, at blandt andre ungdommen om de unge vælgere » for at forekerere, Ingmar Glans og Jørger Goul Andersen.

Blandt de af de unge, som er kommet op i vælgerinteresse-røs i politik, er venstreflojsstillingen helt oppe på en part, mens de konservative kun får 19 pct. -under gennemsnittet for aldersgruppen. Fordelt på køn viser det sig, at kvinderne er langt mere markant end mænd mere stemmer på dt arbejderpartier.

Venstreflojen får samlet tilslutning fra en tredjedel af de unge vælgere. Alene SF får flere stemmer end de konservative og tvasten ligt at mange mod Socialdemokratiet.

«Disse tal demonstrerer entydigt løsne påstande om, at de unge vælgere skulle være på flugt fra venstreflojen over til blå de konservative. KU har opdaget i kampen om ungdommen omit kommer de unge vælgere hen til at forkerere, Ingmar Glans og Jørger Goul Andersen.

Klasseskel

Ser man på de traditionelle klasseskel, viser undersøgelsen for vælgervaren som helhed ikke blot en uventering man

en yderligere polarisering langs de traditionelle skillelinier.

Gunske viet får de konservative vi 10 pct. af arbejderstemmerne eller det samme som SF. Men den har de konservative start set støppet fra Fremskridtspartiet. Arbejderpartierne får i 1964 valget tilsammen 65 pct. af arbejderstemmerne, og dot er ventuvret det særlige med sammen valg fra 1977 og 1979.

Men hvor arbejderpartierne i 1977 og 1979 fik ca. 40 pct. af stemmerne fra Socialdemokratiet og havde mistet en del til venstrefløjen tilbageholdt deres parti på 64 pct. i dette har der i de senere år, mens borgelige partier to tredjedelene fem sammenlæggelsen af arbejderpartier.

Forskellen i partivalg mod arbejderne indere mod fort stemmes markant end for tredje års tidligere viste analyse af sognevalgene i de sidste 20 år, vi ser undersøgelsen par.

Lars Ingemar Glans og Jørgen Goul Andersen: gennemgang af undersøgelsen Side 4

Reagan mødt med kulde fra Sovjet

Alle præsidentens tilnærmelser afvises som valgfløs

MOSKVA, 28. juni (AP) De sovjetiske medier afvis torsdag, at den amerikanske præsident Ronald Reagan koncentrerer sig om «forbedrede» og «normalisering» af forholdet til Sovjet, idet han landet torsdag om ny dialog med Sovjetunionen, og De nyklager Washington for at «forsvurge eller føre se beret fra det sovjetiske initiativ, der rigter på at genetablere de sovjetiske amerikanske forhold og i rentkomnationen som helhed».

Det officielle nyhedsbureau TASS skriver, at Reagans tale nu bl.a. videreindhold og teknologisk nyforvikling dér stillen om

to supermagter er benægtet på at vinde stemmer ved at berolige amerikanerne og foregive, at der er sket en forbedring i dialogen mellem de to lande.

En kommentator end dot formelt balv-officielle Novosti-agentur, Alexander Mobrikin, skriver, at Reagan vil-cuanere på spørgsmål af andernagtshytstilling- og tignoner de sovjetiske nedrustningsforslag for at befrage sine konservative støtter. Efter Molydykins -afgivelse var præsidentens tale verden et «rødvenge eller bare en leret fra dde nedtrykke Sovjetaterne, for det sovjetiske amerikanske forhold og i rentkomnationen som helhed er og i vedrobrtbersmøblet hold og i rentkomnationen som helhed».

Det officielle nyhedsbureau TASS skriver, at Reagans tale mu bl.a. videreindhold og teknologisk nyforvikling dér stillen om meddeller, at Tornskovet krydsmissiler var blevet udstyret og amerikanske ubåde, ildendes at den angribes beslutninger om Reagans udtalelser ignoreret de sovjetiske nedrustningsforslag da at befange sine konservative støtter. Sovjetiske kommentatorer har iden senere tid hortil dt vivil tilere fra Reagan. Tatkabane tilbud. Iemmet i Dublin tidligere på måneden, om, at al-stil fra virkikakomtskaldsen av ut indbud sagde Kremlin tal-smand Leonid Zamjatin i nespotisk TV, at de sovjetisk-amerikanske forbindelser aldrig eller i 1963 har været dårligere-.

HUMMER-REKORD - Lene har de seneste dage oplevet rekordlandinger af hummer, men det har det blivet bl.a. fremmet forburgere i Frankrig og Spanien for de pladse af det (RB)

Kendt polsk marxist smidt ud af partiet

Adam Schaff ekskluderet efter pres fra Sovjet

WARSZAWA, 28. juni (AP) - Den marxistiske teoretiker Adam Schaff, som engang var en af Polens betydeligste hurre tælt Polens Fordispite for at have erklæret landet i antilagelsestilstand i december 1981, er blevet ekskluderet af det polske kommunistiparti, skriver partiets officielle dagblad torsdag.

Trybuna Ludu skriver, at den 71-årige professor og forfatter har givet sig skyldig i «gentaget alvorlig men» mod partiprincipperne » partie, og at dot er en kritisk reaktion imod fortjenesten af partilinien krav, at en polit lederne fortsat.

DENNE kommsen efter -at det sovjetiske månedsblad Vogrogi Filosofii (Filosofiske Spørgsmål) i maj forødteste Schaff for at fremme «fakte-tiple for det borgerlige og reformatiske ideologer sreselt, Hans forfatterskab er udkåst for angreb fra kommunistiske her for nansiser for.

Ventelandringer stiller sig fortdorst over for Schaffs fanklaning bedre idet i det mes tiske tilladrelt. Det n stand til at fortræ og for dese vivra dele ofentlig om udmeldelsessignen spate.

Schaffs nesteee bog -Hvis ringen fra Polens, er blevet af fortæller-jampi Vest (stelet. Her) argumenterer han for, at det polske kommu- nistparti mangler legitimitet, fordi sostelhonen er forkarste mit il Polen- med sovjetisk bøn han unsdd a oplyne tilstlae have. Mangelfuhle- hendstolle-moderne kommuns. Vore partiet fordi er, tydningse.

«Var partiet blevet oplyst, sille orskrong 70 procent af befolkningen have stemt dette regime» sagde Schaff et sted i sit interiv - og det amerikanske magasin.

Newsweek. Schaff har støtte kritiseret de vestlige socialdemokrat Josef Pińko omtaler uddeleget stavnet folkefra. Hans befattelsesbat et varen en forsetsverk omslut dlghedi-ahersta Stalin.

FINSK FORSVAR - Den finske regering godkendte torsdag, at der fin Sverige skal købes 150 luftvarnskanoner og et antal radaranlæg til forsvaret af den sørlige del af landet for i alt 285 millioner finmark. De finske Unto-Anttsia med aften om tilstandsrevisionen for de er af landets befolkning. Leverancer begynder i efter 1986 og vil have en være Veriheid den sister sig i sere al af varerne produceret i Finland. (RB)

tydning for [partiet] i partis - veistatsistiske ekspertense, som har er beplagtet i han nud hole -- nan havt og fortsanst i standens indledning- men den hviske herre i det polske kommunistparti har på det senere arbejdet-til en -eske eksklusion fordi de politiske opfatteles tidgese.

5.6. Serious reporting and discussion of domestic and foreign developments are found in *Information*. This issue features articles on occupational policy, medical experiments, and U.S.-Soviet relations. (Reprinted with permission)

The paper is not particularly attractive when compared to those papers that market their papers to a less literate and intellectual audience and rely upon style rather than substance to promote sales. *Information* has a daily circulation of about 35,000.

Jyllands-Posten. This originally regional newspaper has recently expanded from a paper intended primarily for distribution in Jutland into a publication distributed throughout Denmark. The paper has one of the country's most expansive business and economics sections and is noted for high quality coverage of Danish political issues and news (Fig. 5.7).

A highly attractive paper, *Jyllands-Posten* makes extensive use of charts and graphs, photographs, and graphic displays. The paper is politically independent but takes conservative stances on most issues.

Jyllands-Posten is published in one of the most modern publishing houses in the Nordic region and has a circulation of 110,000 daily and 230,000 on Sundays. The paper is usually 32–36 pages in length and expands to as many as 112 pages on Sunday.

Politiken. This liberal, independent paper is considered one of Denmark's and the world's most prestigious newspapers and carries a significant amount of national and international news. Its coverage of political issues and national occurrences rivals that of the best papers in any country.

Cleanly laid out in editions that average 40 pages, this paper provides significant commentary, debate, and discussion of social, cultural, and economic issues (Fig. 5.8). The paper takes a slightly more popular approach to news presentation than *Information*. Its main competitor is *Berlingske Tidende*.

Politiken is acquiring new presses that will permit four-color printing and production of up to 96 pages an issue. It has a weekday circulation of 140,000 and a Sunday circulation of 215,000.

Regional Newspapers

Aalborg Stiftstidende. The oldest existing paper in the provinces of Denmark, *Aalborg Stiftstidende* traces its history to 1767 when it was granted the royal charter to provide the news in Jutland. Today it has a

MORGENAVISEN
Jyllands-Posten

*** FREDAG 29. JUNI 1984 · UGE 26 · HVERDAGE KR. 4,00 · SØN- OG HELLIGDAGE KR. 5.00 · TLF. 06-14 66 77

ERHVERV & ØKONOMI

Kvalitetskontrol med pølser opgives måske

En ny, dansk lovgivning om kvalitetskontrol med pølser og andre charcuterivarer er i fare for at falde til jorden. Statens Levnedsmiddelinstitut har lavet et forslag til, hvordan en lov kan administreres, men oplægget har i følge underdirektør i Danske Slagterier, kemiingeniør Ole Jørgensen ikke store chancer for at blive godkendt, fordi kontrollen vil blive alt for bureaukratisk og dermed kostbar for forbrugerne og samfundet.

POLITIK   **SIDE 9**

Missil-sagen afgøres muligvis i Folketinget

Regeringen vil muligvis ignorere en opfordring fra et flertal i Folketingets forsvarsudvalg om at droppe missilretsagen og afvente en afgørelse i selve folketingssalen. Forsvarsminister Hans Engell og justitsminister Erik Ninn-Hansen er stærkt betænkelige ved at følge Socialdemokratiets, de radikales og SF's krav om, at sagen mod otte logkaptajn H. G. Olsen afgøres gennem politisk indgreben. Kaptajnen er ved byretten i København anklaget for pligtforsømmelse i forbindelse med missiluheldet fra fregatten Peder Skram.

Danskerne skyldte i 1983 skattevæsnet 5 mia. kr.

Danskernes ubetalte skat til skattevæsenet steg i 1983 med 214 millioner kroner i forhold til året før, så skatteværdens samlede gæld i 1983 var på fem milliarder kroner. En stigning på fem pct. Men i samme periode steg skatterne 18 pct., fremgår det af en beretning fra rigsrevisionen.

UDLAND   **SIDE 13**

291 syrere for seks israelere

For første gang i 10 år udvekslede arkefjenderne Israel og Syrien torsdag krigsfanger og omkomne. Det skete ved en libanesisk ceremoni, der blev ledet af Røde Kors i de israelsk besatte Golanhøjder. På tilfødet er det en israelsk kvinde der bliver befriet, er det israelsk korporal, der efter sin kedelige omfavner sin søn i Tel Aviv-lufthavnen. Tidligere på dagen havde Israel bombarderet, hvad det selv betegnede som terrorist-baser i det nordlige Libanon.

MIDTPUNKT   **SIDE 11**

Armenere bruger bomber for at blive hørt

En tyrkisk diplomat blev forleden dræbt i Wien af en libaneser. En armensk terrorgruppe har påtaget sig skylden for attentatet, ved at føre end 200 siden 1974. Armenske terrorstrategier bruger bomber, for at deres budskab om selvstændigt Armenien skal blive hørt, og som næsten fra dens verdens masakre for 60 år siden. Men kan få haver efter. Armgen kan være, at historieskrivning i vesten næsten udelukkende ser på armenerne med tyrkiske øjne. Det skriver cand. phil Gert Thomsen i Midtpunkt.

INDE I BLADET

Vejret	2	Midtpunkt	11
TV-anmeldelse	2	Læserbreve	11
Nyt om navne	6-7	Kunst og kultur	12
Politik	9	Udland	13
Ledere	10	Sport	14-15

De håber på godt vejr

Flere hundrede amatørskulptører skitter i spottekskekt forbrikke og mod akyerne i håbet om godt vejr. In. Anita Degn Niesen (billedet) fra Bushjerg. I den nærmeste fremtid skal de terdig vise resultatet af månedens slid og slørb på friluftsscenerne i i landskivs Bushjerg, Varde, Århus og Jels. Også i Roskilde er der trug for opholdsvejr. Her sætter rock-festivalen dem på ben i den kommende weekend. Læs herom i Det sker.

Modstand mod forsvars-forliget, men:

Regeringen er tvunget til at bøje sig

Af Carsten Juste

Det seneste udkast til et forsvarsforlig, som i går var lagt på forhandlingsbordet i Statsministeriet, er stadt på forbitret modstand i regeringspartierne. Regeringens forhandlere har bøjet sig så meget for Socialdemokratiets krav, at især CD er på nippet til at sige fra, erfarer Jyllands-Posten.

– Det urgente meg... Sådan betegner en af de borgerlige nøglepolitikere forligsudkastet, som ligger meget tæt på nullinstling ikke flere penge til forsvaret i de næste to år, bortset fra en begrænset pristalsregulering på 6 pct.

Det vil ifølge Jyllands-Postens kilder betyde, at forsvarsudgifterne udhules i forligsperioden, der skal vare indtil årsskiftet 1987/88.

Statsminister Poul Schlüter, finansminister Henning Christophersen og forsvarsminister Hans Engell forsøgte i går forgæves at overbevise Socialdemokratiets forhandlere med formanden Anker Jørgensen i spidsen om, at forsvaret skal have flere penge, og at den indtil nu tildige, gunstige pristalsregulering skal bevares.

Senere på dagen var repræsentanter for regeringspartierne til orientering hos forsvarsminister Hans Engell og forhandlingerne på nippet fortsætter samtrudig selv om forbitrelsen hos regeringspartierne er stor, synes regeringen imidlertid ikke et have andet valg end at acceptere den forsvarspolitiske afhængigheid af Socialdemokratiet og dermed det foreliggende forligsudkast, ser forlig kan offentliggøres. i dag

LÆS MERE SIDE 9

1100 til ung uge

Peder Pedersen fra Aabybro i Nordjylland er af de 1100 unge fra hele landet som i disse dage er i tagen i KFUM og K's landslejr. »Ung uge 1984« Brønning ved Esbjerg. Gymnastik, som Peder gang med, er sammen med seivforstar blandt mest populære tilbud, som lejren byder på.

Foto: Holger Bundgaard

LÆS SIDE

Præmie til Egon og »Bitten«

Egon Holm Andersen, Testrup ved Ålestrup (billedet), tager fra aartet til landbruget, da han holdt op som landmand for en halv snes år siden. I dag har han på et nødlagt husmandsbrug og har fjordhestene med hobby. At han er dygtig på det felt, anerkender Ungskuets dommere, da han i går fik æresspræmie for sin to-årige hoppe »Bitten«. Men Egon Holm Andersen har også mange års erfaring med fjordhestene, som han i sin tid brugte som arbejdsdyr på sit landbrug.

LÆS OM UNGSKUET I ERHVERV & ØKONOMI

Regeringen vil ofre millioner på kvægvirus

Regeringen vil opfylde landbrugets ønsker om at betale halvdelen af af de flere hundrede mio. kr., det vil koste at bekæmpe IBR/IPV-kvægvirus, som har angrebet mellem 80.000 og 100.000 danske malkekøer. Det gav landbrugsminister Niels Anker Kofoed tilsagn om ved Ungskuets officielle modtag i Herning i aftes.

– IBR/IPV skal udryddes så hurtigt som muligt, og regeringen er indstillet på at betale halvdelen af udgifterne, hvis landbruget vil betale den anden halvdel, sagde Niels Anker Kofoed.

Landbrugets organisationer har selv foreslået, at sygdommenes bekæmpelse betales efter denne formel.

– Om de samlede udgifter bliver på 200 mio. kr. eller 400 mio. kr., ved vi ikke endnu, sagde Kofoed.

Fagfolk skønner, at udgifterne kommer til at ligge på dette niveau. Men landbrugs-ministeren påpegede, at udgifterne lade være med at bekæmpe kvæggen, der angriber kaernen malkekøersorganerne, vil blive endnu større.

Bekæmpelsen, der vil komme strække sig over nogle år, går ud pełtheten at slagte de syge dyr, der er lekverg er fyldt på bayds med rasket.

Hvordan bekæmpelsen skal tilrettelægges er endnu ikke besluttet.

– Endnu mangler der veterinære tegtiser, før vi kan sige, hvordan en ekæmpes mest effektivt, sagde Anker Kofoed.

Han lagde dog vægt på, at beslutningen ikke kommer i gang i år, så fødslagtning sygdomsramte malkekøer kan få en fatale konsekvenser, vil blive endnu større. En dansk mælkeproduktion i skabsbert, der stutter med udgangen marts 1985.

LÆS ERHVERV & ØKONOMI

GRENZ-BASAR Toffer
syd for grense-overgangen
KRUSA-KOBBERMØLLE
Gyldig fra 25/6 til 5/7 1984

Billig BENZIN DM 1,29 pr. ltr = 4 kr. **4,77**

Fineste sherry, dry, medium, cream, 0,7 ltr	DM 3,90
Pinto Port Tawny portvin, 0,7 ltr	DM 6,95
Papillon, fransk rød og hviden, 0,7 ltr	DM 1,98
Pepsodent Mickelnkberg, 0,7 ltr	DM 2,50
Fineste Kabinetvine, alle sorter, 0,7 ltr	DM 2,68
Fineste kvalitetsvine, 0,7 ltr	DM 2,27
Læmaholdt, 0,7 ltr	DM 1,84
Fass-guldøl, 6 fl. incl. flasker	DM 4,95
Cola helse, 1 ltr	DM 0,59
Cola tonic, 1 ltr	DM 0,66
(Fortsæt lod for kursændringer)	

Fordel for Danmark med høj diskonto i udlandet

Mange danske virksomheder står stærkere i konkurrencen med udlandet, efter at Sveriges, Vesttyskland og øvrig i går forhøjede diskontorenten. Herhjemme sker der sandsynligvis ikke noget med Nationalbankens diskonto, som i øjeblikket ligger på syv pct.

Den primære naeves alle andre rentesatser, og en ændring i diskontoen mantes derfor af mange – lige fra den stærke virksomhed til den mindre virksomhed, og som føler sig kredt i kolli i butik.

Når virksomhederne i vore saholalde får en stærks trussomudgift, må de sandsynligvis sætte priserne op.

I Sverige har regeringen også opløkevet pristalsgæl, og fem det lateie til stigende priser, bliver ophøvelsen også til...

gavn for danske virksomheders geringsindgreb.

Den svenske forhøjer vil en anden lige forstrække at købe teks. en dansk frakke, hvis den er billigere end en tilsvarende svensk. Sverige er Danmark tredje-vigtigste eksportmarked, og alene i januar kvartal solgte vi varer for 4,3 mia. kr til svenskerne. Også på andre markeder end det svenske kan vi få fordel af den svenske kurs.

På det vesttyske eksportmarked opløver danske virksomheder også, at de er i skarp konkurrence med svenske virksomheder, og da de nu får et handicap i form af højere rente, står de danske eksportører også stærkere i Vesttyskland.

LÆS ERHVERV & ØKONOMI

jbs
BOXER-SHORTS

Den klassiske, lette underbuks eller shorts i let svensk-farvede Ensfarvede eller smalstribede.

ikke bare til mænd - men også til bare piger

5.7. This edition of *Jyllands-Posten* carries articles about policy flexibility in the prime minis[ter's] office, cattle virus, and the advantages of having funds in other nations. (Reprinted with permis[sion]

5.8. *Politiken* remains one of Denmark's most influential and serious dailies. This issue relates the attendance of 60,000 people at an outdoor concert, health concerns caused by the removal of cancer-causing construction materials, and a bank robbery by a 14-year-old youth. (Reprinted with permission)

MANDAG
2. juli 1984

Aarhuus Stiftstidende

Løssalgspris hverdage kr. 3.75 ● 191. årgang · Nr. 50445   Banntkegade 14, 8000 Århus C ● Tlf. (06) 12 40 00

AF i Århus reddet

Arbejdsministeren har trukket ekstra sparekrav af bordet

De godt 300 ansatte på arbejdsformidlingen i Århus Amt kan ånde lettet op. Regionschef Per Hansen meddeler i morgen på et møde med deres tillidsfolk, at fyringstruslerne er drevet over.

— Vi kan med meget stor sandsynlighed sige, at vi klarer neste år uden afskedigelser. Fem-seks mennesker er rejst i løbet af berkret, så selv om vi skal nedlægge enkelte stillinger, kommer det ikke til direkte fyringer, siger AF-chefen.

Også han ånder lettet op.
Dels har arbejdsminister Grethe Fenger Møller i fredags trukket sine » extraordinære sparekrav« på 45 mill. kr. på landsplan tilbage. De ville have kostet 90 stillinger i Århus Amt. Dels har Landsarbejdsnævnet godkjgert Arbejdsdirektoratets regnskrl, der betød, at Århus-området manglede henved 2.5 mill. kr. for at kunne dække det normerede antal stillinger.

lnger for 1985 og på 40.5 millioner kr. Desuden får amtet 700.000 kr. i form af en ekstrabevilling, fordi det er særligt belastet af stor ledighed.
Dermed godtgør de centrale myndigheder deres regnefejl med 2,5 mill. kr.

De redder alene omkring en halv snes stillinger, vurderer Per Hansen.

Land-

AF-chef Per Hansen oplyser, at rammebevillingen er på 40.5 millioner kr.

■ Læs iøvrigt side 14.

Kim Andersen må »nøjes« med at være på tredjepladsen:

Triumfen, der udeblev

Danskeren var uopmærksom et øjeblik, men avancerede efter flot kørsel

— Jeg var uopmærksom et øjeblik, og det kostede både triumf på etapen og den gule førertrøje, sagde en ærgerlig Kim Andersen (billedet til venstre), da han i går var sluttet som nummer to på anden etape af det professionelle cykelløb Tour de France. Jeg følte mig klart bedst i det fire mands udbrud, jeg selv havde etableret. Men kort før mål så jeg ikke franskmanden Marc Madiot satte fart på cyklen.

Kim Andersen havde med en førsteplads fået 30 sekunders tidsgodtgørelse med de 26, han fik for anderpladsen. Han er nu på en samlet tredjeplads i løbet, der har 170 ryttere til start. Danskeren er kun otte sekunder efter den førende hollænder, Jacques Hanegraff.

På Århus Cykelbane afvikledes i weekenden danske mesterskaber i både sprint og forfølgelsesløb. DL-rytterne indfriede deres forventninger — og hos de unge talenter gav der bevis for, at Århus Cykelbane har materialet til afløsning af den nuværende elite. Johnny Franck (billedet til højre) vandt sprint foran to klubkammerater — og en anden Århusianer, Klaus Lund fortjelsmeddelt.

■ Mere i sportens side 11, 12 og 13, hvor du også kan læse om TV-kampen i onsdag fra Wimbledon i eftermiddag.

(FOTO: Ib Hansen)

Thyrring sikker vinder

Thorkild Thyrring blev sikker vinder af genåbningsløbet på Ring Djursland i går i sport 2000-klassen. Han bevarede dermed føringen i kampen om Europamesterskabet. På intet tidspunkt var der fare om egentlig konkurrence om førstepladsen. Thyrring vandt foran Henry Vollenberg, Holland, og Erik Tinghøj, Danmark, der her får nogle dråber af sejrs-champagnen.

■ Læs mere om AMKA's succes på side 9.

(FOTO: Tom Andersen)

Dråberne blev dyre

Det koster en halv million kroner at fjerne mudderet efter Roskilde Festivalen

Det kan blive dyre regndråber, der faldt så tungt og heftigt over Roskilde Festivalen lørdag. Festivalens indtvlæ anstår, at det kan koste en halv million kroner at få fjernet det ankelhøje mudderærøte og nyt græs sået på den store dyrskueplads, hvor over 60.000 mennesker trods regn og kulde, mandefald blandt stjernenavnene og andre ubehageligheder oplevede en folkefest af format i weekenden.

Med cirka 55.000 betalende gæster — et par hundrede flere end i fjor — blev der tget sat publikumsrekord, og budgettet balancerede efter de første 40.000. Men regningen efter vejrgudernes casen kan gøre et alvorligt indhug i Roskilde Fondens overskud.

Efter fredagens episoder med bl. a. flaskekast mod scenen fortsatte lørdagen i mudderfest, og det gav, som festivalens indtvæ havde andre problemer at skils med. Efter afbudene fra The Smiths og The Band måtte også den er gelsøge sanger Paul Young melde fra i sidste øjeblik, så arrangørerne måtte lave en ny program i hele hovedmeuene.

■ Reportage fra den store rock-festival side 7.

Vand med nitrat kan vaskes rent

Ny metode udviklet i Århus

Forurenet drikkevand kan nu på det nærmeste vaskes rent igen. Billigt.
Medarbejdere ved Jydsk Teknologisk Institut i Århus har udviklet en ny metode til at fjerne de farlige gødningsstoffer nitrater. For antagelig en til to øre pr. kubikmeter kan nitraten dermed fjernes fra drikkevand, når gødning har gjort rent regnvand til sundhedsfarligt grundvand.

Metodens detaljer er foreløbig hemmelige. Teknikerne røber dog, at hvor tidligere kemile — dyre — metoder er fysiske, så er denne kemisk.

pp

■ Læs mere side 5.

Den nye metode til at rense drikkevandet er ikke dyr.

Flere forældre meldes

— Politianmeldelse skræmmer os ikke, siger far, der pillede lofter ned

Af Elisabeth Hansen

— Selvfølgelig melder vi forældrene til politiet, siger borgmester Thorkild Simonsen (S) om de forældre, der i weekenden tog sagen om de sundhedsfarlige karliflofter i egen hånd og pillede karlit ned i en børnehave og to vuggestuer i Århus Kommune.

Det kar ikke skræmt forældrene, at Århus Kom-

mune melder dem til politiet for hærværk og ulovlig indtrængen overisder til dem selv at passe hernne.

— Vi har sendt kommunen et brev om, hvorfor vi tog loftet ned i tolbørnerummet, siger formanden for forældrerådet i børnehaven Laurbærvænget 4, Trusbjørg Kurt Olsen. Vi har handlet i protest og nødværge. Mange børstitte er dybt bekymrede. På nogle børn kan det ses, så snart de har været i institutionen i et par timer.

Aktionen i Laurbærvænget blev besluttet for

tiden. På et møde torsdag gik det store flertal ind for at gøre noget selv. Forældrene har arrangeret pasning og laget et stort arbejde i det, for at aktionen ikke skal ramme børnene.

— Politianmeldelse skræmmer ikke?
— Nej, siger Kurt Olsen, for vi står solidarisk sammen.

■ Borgmester Thorkild Simonsen er utilfreds.
Læs side 3

Folkeværksted for de nye medier

Af Peter Poulsen

Århus bør have et offentligt støttet medieværksted.

Tiden er inde til at oprette et åbent hus, hvor folk kan komme ind fra gaden og prøve kræfter med de nye muligheder i vidal-medierne. Video-gruppen er i første omgang. To-vejs-video, computer-programmer og meget andet i næste.

Det forstag kommer fra den selvejende institution Århus Filmværksted.
Her arbejdes i dag med undervisning i og produktion af 8 og 16 mm. film. Det er et tilbud til alle om at udtrykke sig i levende billeder.

Samme mulighed bør oprettes for de nye medier, mener Århus Kommune og eller Amt bør starte bldt, men omgående.

med en investering på en halv million kr.

— To af forslagsstillerne, Steen Jørgensen og Jens Loftager:
— To-vejs satellitterte er da helt i orden. Det er jo nærmest et folkekrav at få mere fjernsyn. Men vi tror, at folk ret hurtigt vil finde ud af, at det stort set kun bliver gentagelser af Sport, shows og amerikanske film i større mængde.

Hvornår vil hurtigt spild for selv at komme til at bruge billed-medierne. Det skal der skabes en mulighed for i god tid, så de store muligheder i video-og computer-udviklingen ikke bliver hemholdt store, kommercielle interesser.

■ Læs side 8: Video for folket.

daily circulation of about 75,000 and a Sunday circulation of 105,000. It is recognized as one of the province's major news sources.

Aarhuus Stiftstidende. This is another paper granted an early charter that has survived to be an important conveyer of news and information (Fig. 5.9). It now has a daily circulation of approximately 70,000 and 90,000 on Sundays.

Frederiksborg Amts Avis. This paper published in Hillerød is the major regional paper for the outlying areas of Sjælland and publishes about 40,000 copies daily and 50,000 on Sundays. The paper is politically independent but tends to support liberal parties.

    Frederiksborg Amts Avis was started after the success of *Kolding Folkeblad* as the central paper for a group of local papers in Jutland.

Vestkysten. This 60,000 circulation paper published in Esbjerg in Jutland is an independent, liberal paper. A relatively young paper, it was started in 1917 and became one of the Liberal party's largest papers. The growth was accomplished, in part, because at its founding, smaller Liberal papers in the region were bought out and replaced by *Vestkysten*. It is no longer affiliated with the party.

CHAPTER SIX

Newspapers of Finland

National Newspapers

Helsingin Sanomat. The paper with the largest circulation in Finland, *Helsingin Sanomat* has a daily circulation of 450,000 and half a million on Sundays. As the country's most important paper, it carries a large amount of national, international, economic, and cultural news and political commentary.

The paper is usually published in two sections and consists of 32 pages. Unlike most major papers throughout the developed world, the first page of the paper is usually a full- or half pagc ad for a grocery or department store (Fig. 6.1). *Helsingin Sanomat* carries more advertising than any other paper in the country. Despite the high ad content, the paper provides serious information and commentary and is the newspaper of record for the nation. Although an independent paper, it tends to support Conservative policies on its editorial pages.

Hufvudstadsbladet. This attractive Finnish paper employs large photographs, modular layouts, and many graphic display devices to highlight its stories (Fig. 6.2). The paper carries a large amount of national and international news, cultural and political discussions, and other content of a serious nature.

A Swedish-language paper, *Hufvudstadsbladet* serves the needs of the minority Swedish-speaking population. Although an independent paper, it often supports the policies of the Swedish People's party. It has a daily circulation of about 65,000.

Ilta-Sanomat. The Finnish afternooon tabloid *Ilta-Sanomat* contains the requisite entertainment, personality content, and sensational news and photographs, but blends that material with hard national news and serious opinion (Fig. 6.3).

The paper, which usually consists of 40 pages, has a daily circula-

6.1. The use of ads on the front page is more common in Finland than elsewhere, even in the nation's most prestigious paper, *Helsingin Sanomat*. (Reprinted with permission)

HUFVUDSTADSBLADET

Vecka 29 Torsdagen den 19 juli 1984   Grundat 1864   001354-4-29   Nr 191   ★ 1 ★ Lösnr mk 4,00

Brittiska strejken

Färjtrafiken även drabbad

Hamnstrejken i Storbritannien drabbade på onsdagen även personbilar och semesterfirarna. Den vanligen livliga färjtrafiken mellan Dover och Calais på franska sidan om kanalen har inte fungerat på grund av blockader i de båda hamnarna.

Upprepade leverantörer blockerade infarten till hamnen i Dover med privatbilar i protest mot att strejken försvårar deras verksamhet. På den franska si-

dan i Calais förhindrade strandsatta engelska, franska och schweiziska långtradarbilsflottor den privata biltrafiken i hamnen. Strejken har avvärjt

försenat långtradarnas tidtabell. Senare på dagen sände de en tom man stark delegation till Dover för att förhandla om situationen.

Koivistos kritik aktuell

Processerna blir snabbare

Vårt långsamma rättegångssystem skall läggas om så att handläggningen av mål kan klaras av betydligt snabbare än för närvarande. Saken har emellertid kopplats till en planerad stor reform av underrättssystemet och konkreta förbättringar kan nås först om några år.

Per-Ole Träskman, professor i straff- och processrätt, efterlyser en övergång till ett system med så koncentrerad handläggning att våra underrätter i stället för det nuvarande systemet med prägeln av långa pauser mellan flera behandlingsomgångar.

Kanslichef Raimo Pekkanen vid justitieministeriet säger att

avräknas in att övergå till koncentrerad handläggning särskilt av civilrättsliga mål, men han väger inte lova särskilt snabba förändringar. Det handlar om mycket komplicerade frågor.

Båda instämmer i president Koivistos kritik av domstolsväsendets långsamhet.
● Se sida 6

Per-Ole Träskman

Dansgruppen Ngoma från Tanzania uppträder på den kanske bäst i nyhetsbevakade festivalen i Sommarfinland. Bara rundradion använder 50 km band på festivalen. Dessutom finns över hundra journalister från olika europeiska och utomeuropeiska länder närvarande under folkmusikveckan i Kaustby.

Kaustby

Pressens favorit- festival

□ Kaustby (Hbl – Stig Kankkonen) Frågan är om inte Kaustby är det mest "vakade" sommarevenemanget i Finland vad massmedia beträffar. Under festiveckan beräknas över hundra journalister från Finland, Norge, Sverige, Danmark England, Amerika, Tyskland och vem varifrån rapportera om händelserna.

□ Där tidningsredaktörerna skriver fotar kör Rundradion ut sin information både i ord och bild. Inte bara under festivalveckan utan längs med året. I k meter räknat bandar radion närmare km program under veckan! Till det ke mer ytterligare vad televisionen gör.

□ Sauli Koivukoski, som fungerat s presschef sedan den första festivalen 19 konstaterar att hela massmediaintresset festivalen mer eller mindre kom som chock det första året. Själv kallades Kauskoski 1968 att ta hand om massmedia presentanterna när han i logn och ro de i höbärgningsarbetet på "fädernins var Perho, några tiotal kilometer från Kausby.
● Se sida

En flyktig stund kan man beskåda passionsblommans prakt i Helsingfors vinterträdgård. Efter sex timmar har den blomnat färdigt.

Vinterträdgården

Blomster året om

De flesta luminiga grönområden i storstaden brukar kallas grönskande lungor eller oaser mitt i storstaden. En vinterträdgård är mera än en oas. Det är naturen inomhus. Oavsett om det är vinterns snöstorm eller sommarens hällregn eller solgass utanför så är trädgården avskild från yttervärlden.

Där kan du sitta i lugn och ro, lyssna på porlande springbrunnar och fågelkvitter och vandra om-

kring och studera både välkända och exotiska växter.
□ Stadens vinterträdgård är inte öppen enbart på vintern utan också sommartid kan du hitta ett och annat att beskåda. Bland annat passionsblomman visar under sommaren sina flyktiga blommor. Endast sex timmar är denna vackra blomma utslagen i vars delar folktron tolkat in Kristi lidande och död.
● Se sidan

Mondale väntar seger

SAN FRANCISCO (Hbl – Klas Bergman) Den 56-årige förre presidenten, norskättlingen från Minnesota, Walter Mondale, var sent på onsdagskvällen bli formellt nominerad till det demokra partiet s presidentkandidat.

För Mondale blir omröstningen kulmen på en lång och bitter och yrt enig jämn primärvalskampa j som trängde honom in i det sista att kämpa för sin slutliga seger.

Han i svånare och bittraste motel adaere, Gary Hart – senator från Colorado, höll strax före i omröstningen och omröstningen sitt tal till konventet, en mycket så vide uppgift efter de förregående dagarna då kampen en de frustrerades av News Yo s-guvernör Mario Cuomo och den svarte presidentkandida- ten Jesse Jackson.

Mondale nominerades formellt av Los Angeles svarte borgmästare Tom Bradley Hart j comineredes in senaten från Connecticut, Christopher Dodd, medan Jackson nominerades av Washingtons borgmästare Ma- rion Berry.

Mondales seger kunde ansedan under tisdagens omröstningar om partiprogrammet och de fem reservationer – fyra av Jackson och en av Hart – och där Mondales styrke vann övertygande segrar över hela linjen, även om en viss kompromissande skett.

Mondale mötte Hart halvvägs genom att acceptera uttrycks-reservationens formuleringar om USA bestäl visa lättahållsamhet i bruket av militärt väld utomlands.

Mondale gick också Jackson till mötes i frågan om diskriminering av minoritetterna mom arbetslivet. Men det skedde först sedan Jackson gått med på att stryka hänvisningarna till raskvoter i sin reservation.

Däremot fl Jacksons andra tre reservationer, och med övervägande stora siffror.

Hans reservation och hjuds s k första använd kärnvapen föll med i 1 405 mot 2 216. Hans en substantiella nedskär militärbudgeten föll skarpt siffror 1 127 mot 2 592. Mondales vinnare dag ytkar på rökningar nyligheterna men i långre takt in vad som nu ske Ronald Reagan.

Slutligen nisdades i förslag nor om avskaffa de s k primärna promär- dem, där val alter i fj gångar i tio vidmåter – denna röstförsortna blev i 1 2 500 eller av delsat s ett d natta delegaterna op och det karaktäris bättre mokret att slagmål natt al

Ont om hjortron

Jordgubbarna snart slut

Jordgubbarna är snart slut. Fyra femtedelar av frukten är sk dad i södra delarna av landet och tre fjärdedelar i Kuopiotak som är det huvudsakliga odlingsområdet.

Också tillbätor id mogna l hela landet. Hjortron finns det vidligt sra si på grund av jordgetroman. Vinbären se på conomarden var att förra...

med en nybad skörd. Men frosten har slot över livet.

Åkerväxterna ligger fortfarande en vecka före det mor mala i södra Finland, säger

borttavsternas t och på skolsåns vad...

Hiskonbäten boraknas den norrmalt så gillig i vålkrs...
● Se sidan

6.2. Stories about a strike closing British ports, Walter Mondale awaiting his presidential nor tion, and a local festival are featured on this front page of the Swedish-language Finnish p *Hufvudstadsbladet.* (Reprinted with permission)

Verilöyly hampurilais-ravintolassa

Raskaasti aseistautunut mies surmasi eilen San Ysidron kaupungissa, etelä-Kaliforniassa 20 ihmistä ja haavoitti 20 henkeä. Poliisin tarkka-ampujat surmasivat hampurilaisravintolaan linnoittautuneen ammuskelijan.
Sivu 12

Kurinpalautusta formuloissa:

Tyrrel ulos sarjasta Mansellille isot sakot

Kansainvälinen autourheiluliitto FISA kuritti kovalla kädellä formula-1:n rötöstelijöitä.

Tyrrel-talli suljettiin loppukauden MM-sarjasta ja kaikki sen saavuttamat pisteet mitätöitiin. Tyrrelin autojen alipainoisuutta oli peitetty lisäämällä jäähdytysvesisäiliöön lyijykuulia ennen punnitusta.

Keke Rosbergin Detroitissa kiroama Nigel Mansell sai roimat sakot vaarallisesta ajostaan. Lisäksi miestä uhkaa ajoluvan menetys jos tavat eivät parane.
Sivu 33

ILTA-SANOMAT

N:o 164 — 1984   TORSTAINA HEINÄKUUN 19. PNÄ 1984   ★★ 2,50 mk (sis.lvv)

IS-raportti

HULLUN KIRJOIHIN HELPPO JOUTUA

Joku on ehkä saanut väärän käsityksen jonkun puheista, aprikoi Matti Ruokola lääkintöhallituksen osuutta kohutussa Riitta Kauppisen tapauksessa.

Seinänaapuri päätti tehdä turkulaisesta Svante Jokelasta, 69, mielisairaan. Kun pitkällinen kiusanteko ei sekoittanut Jokelan päätä, oivalsi rauhanhäiritsijä kutsua ambulanssin ja poliisit viemään miestä pakkohoitoon. Terveyskeskuksen kesälääkäri vahvisti naapurin diagnoosin: "hullu on".

Niin alkoi terveen, mutta huonokuuloisen Jokelan kolmen vuorokauden pakkohoito Kupittaan mielisairaalassa.

Vaarallisia paljastuksia laukoneen pieksämäkeläislääkärin Riitta Kauppisen "hulluus" on puolestaan määritelty kestäväksi ainakin ensi syksyyn. Siihen saakka hän on hoitavien lääkäreiden mukaan työkyvytön.

Kauppisen tapaus hiertää kivenä lääkintöhallituksen kengässä, koska laitos oli mukana sopimassa pakkohoidosta. Pääjohtaja Matti Ruokola koettaa pehmentää:

— Joku on saattanut soittaa ja saada väärän käsityksen jonkun ylilääkärin sanoista.
Sivut 5 ja 6

Rattijuoppo diplomaatti törmäili Helsingissä
Sivu 5

Äiti pakeni — vauva jäi

Piiritys uuvutti haulikkomiehen

Haulikolla aseistautunut perheenisä linnoittautui kymmenkuisen vauvansa kanssa kotiinsa Valkeakoskella viime yönä.

Perheen äiti pääsi pakenemaan ammuskelevaa miestään ja poliisi ryhtyi piirittämään taloa.

Tilanne laukesi heti aamukuuden jälkeen haulikkomiehen nukahdettua.
Sivu 5

6.3. The threat of drunken diplomats in Helsinki and the humorous writings of a Finnish author are featured in this issue of *Ilta-Sanomat*. (Reprinted with permission)

tion of 120,000. It is independent of political parties but tends to support Conservative policies. About half of the circulation is in the Helsinki metropolitan area.

Ilta Lehti. Published by the same firm that publishes *Uusi Suomi,* a thoughtful regional paper in Helsinki, *Ilta Lehti* is the flashiest of the afternoon tabloids in Finland. A bright, bold paper, it contains large sports and entertainment sections and carries more national news and features than international stories (Fig. 6.4).

The paper is usually about 32 pages in length and a measure of its tabloid character is found in the entertainment section where the paper usually carries a photograph of a scantily clad woman. Such displays are rarely found in Nordic papers, especially in Finland where traditional values and conservative norms are prevalent.

Regional Newspapers

Aamulehti. Published in the industrial city of Tampere (Tammerfors), *Aamulehti* serves Finland's second largest city and the middle and upper central region of the nation. Usually about 32 pages in length, the paper is published in two sections that make much use of large photographs and four-color displays. Its daily circulation is approximately 135,000.

The paper emphasizes local news and has a large sports section, but does not neglect national and international news (Fig. 6.5). The layout is conservative, and printing is done with typestyles and layout that are not significantly influenced by the contemporary styles and layouts found on the European continent and in North America. The paper favors the National Coalition party on its editorial pages.

Etelä-Suomen Sanomat. A politically independent paper established in 1900, *Etelä-Suomen Sanomat* is published in Lahti in south central Finland. With a circulation of 60,000, this paper serves the predominantly agriculturally oriented readers of this area at the southern end of the lake country of Finland.

Kaleva. Published in Oulu, a town on the western coast of Finland near the Swedish border, *Kaleva* provides about 75,000 papers daily to

Tiistaina 24. pnä heinäkuuta 1984

ILTA LEHTI

UUDEN SUOMEN KOLMAS PAINOS

25130-4-30 N:o 196   Irtonumero 2,50 (sis. lvv.)

Huumeraportti jatkuu:
"KAI TÄHÄN KUOLEE"

Avioliitto laski osakkeita

SMP ANTAA KENKÄÄ URPOLLE

...iheuttaako rakkaus yli puoluerajojen Urpo Leppäsen poliittisen tuhon?

● Urpo Leppäsen kuherruskuukausi on nyt auttamatta loppu. Työvoimaministerin oma puolue SMP ei suostu enää lemmestä lurittamaan. Ensimmäinen käytännön toimi on Leppäsen pudottaminen puoluesihteerin paikalta. Samoin Leppäsen ministerinsalkku on vaaravyöhykkeessä.
● Osasyynä Urpo Leppäsen suosion katoamiseen pidetään tuoretta avioliittoa demarikansanedustaja Sinikka Hurskaisen kanssa.

Takasivu

Erkki Liikanen:
PAAVOLAN PALKALLA EI PITÄISI KADOTA
Sivu 5

ISSY — YÖN KUNINGATAR
Sivu 13

ISRAELIN KÄÄPIÖT VOITTIVAT
Sivu 3

Iltalehti mukana rajuilla jatkoilla
"URIAH HEEP JAKSAA JUHLIA"
Sivut 14—15

6.4. This issue of the Finnish tabloid *Ilta Lehti* features a story on labor minister Urpo Leppäsen and a popular club entertainer. (Reprinted with permission)

| Lauantai |

103. vsk. N:o 210 (32484)
Irtonumero 4,00 mk (als. hrv.)
Puh. 931-666 111

AAMULEHTI

PÄÄTOIMITTAJAT PERTTI PESONEN (vastaava), EERO SYVÄNEN

Lasten PUUVILLA-HOUSUT 26⁵
AHOLAI
LAUANTAI 4.

Lisää mitaleja luvassa

Kultaa — pronssia!

● Jouko Salomäki, 21, vyörytti Suomen ensimmäisen kultamitalin Los Angelesista.
● Ennen painijoita ehtivät mitallie kiinni ampujat — Rauno Biesin hermot kestivät uusinnan uusinnan olympiapistoolin pronssista.

● Narmon Jynyä edustava Salomäki paini 74-kilon sarjan loppuottelussa viisaasti ja pitti Rootsin Roger Tallrothin kurissa piinaavan jännittävillä loppusekunneilla.
● Rootsalaisen ohella Salomäki sai varoa tuomareita, jotka tarjosivat hänelle kolmatta varoitusta aivan ottelun loppuhetkillä.

Jouko Salomäen sinivalkoista riemua tyvältä sydämen pohjasta — nuori mies Narmosta on nyt olympiavoittaja.

● Salomäki ratkaisi olympiakullan loppuottelun kolmannen minuutin alussa, jolloin hän hankki puolilindenillä ja vyörytyksellä viisi pinettä. Tämella jakaista Tallroth kävi ankaristi päälle ja kavensi vähiin taistoon 4—5 -pisteisin.

● Vuosiien ehtyessä Salomäki turvasi ajatukseen ja takticksi Tallrothin vaarattomaksi tahallisilla allemenoilla.

● Summerin sudessa Salomäen 5—4 voiton sitetiksi nurmolainen heitti puolivoltin — yksi kaikkien aikojen tuntemattomista nuomialaisia olympiavoittajina tiolsi rellottomasti menestyksestään.

Sipilä tuskalla loppu-otteluun

● Joukon kunniaksi järjestetyisiä kahvitilaisuudessa ei kaikkua ahmittu — valaanpoitoisa sarvistelluin uusia kuhajuhlia Tapio Sipilän tahti kohti finaalia on ollut vaikuttava.

● Loppuuttelupaikan Ja väästään hopeamitalin 68-kilon sarjassa Sipilä varmisti mujtteessaa USA:n James Martinein pistein 5—2. Martinez ei luovuttanut finaalipaikkaa helpolla Muhokani voimanpeällle, vaan pakotti Sipilän jopa päätuomarin puhutteluun.

● Loppuottelussa Sipilä kohtasi Romanian Stefan Negrisan, jonka Sipilä voitti MM-kisoissa ja EM-painin pronssiottelussa.

● Myös Jarmo Övermarkilla oli pieni mahdollisuus jopa loppuotteluun, kun hän voitti Kreikan Dimitros Thanopoloksen uuvuttavan kamppailun jälkeen 6—1 pistein.

SIVUT 17—26

Niskavuori elää taas

● Hämeenkyrö ja Ylöjärvi ovat ollect viime päivinä tapahtumaympäristöinä Niskavuoren venhan emännän Lovilisan, hänen poikansa Aarnen, kylän opettajan Ilma Ahlgrenin ja nuiden Hella Wuolijoen henmien hahmojen elinympäristönä.

● 27 niskavuorettoman elokuvavuoden jälkeen saadaan heidän elämäänsä seurata valkokankaalla. 1980-luvun tekniikalla syntyy 1930-luvulla kituutettujen näytelmien uusi novitus, joka kunnioittaa Hella Wuolijoen teksti Suurelokuvan ohjaa Matti Kassila, ja sen ensi-ilta on 13 eri paikkakunnalla samanaikaisesti 21. joulukuuta.

SIVU 10

● Niskavuoren vanhan emännän, Levilisan, nimipäivän kunniaksi ovat Niskavuoren pihapiiriin löytäneet tiensä apteekkari (Esko Roine), opettaja (Saša Silvo) ja Aarne Niskavuori (Esko Salminen).

Eino Nieminen

Lentokonekaappauksesta selvityysneet suomalaiset Lars ja Mats Green illastivat Teheranissa Suomen suurlähettiläan Timo Jalkasen kanssa (vas.) Hilton hotellissa.

Kaapatut saivat lähteä Ranskaar

● Tiistaista asti jatkunut lentokonekaappausdraama laukesi lopullisesti perjantaina, kun ranskalaisen matkustajakoneen vapautetut matkustajat pääsivät poistumaan Teheranista Pariisiin. Orlyn lentokentällä vapautettuja vastassa oli mm. Ranskan pääministeri Laurent Fabius.

● Air France-yhtiön Teheranin lähettämä Boeing -727 -kone pääsi lähtemään Teheranista perjantaina iltapäivällä monien vörytysten jälkeen. Irakilaiset viranomaiset tutkivat mm. lähtijöiden matkatavarat kahteen kertaan ja selvittivät huolellisesti kaapatun koneen matkustajien kuuluneen pik-

● Kaikki panttivankeina olleet 55 matkustajaa ja viisi miehistön jäsentä olivat hyvässä kunnossa. Matkustajien joukossa on myös kaksi suomalaista.

● Ranskan lehdet syyttelivät perjantaina Irania kaappaukseen tukemisesta. Ranskan hallituksen edustaja

heltäkyti televisiohaastattelusa arvioituusta Iran osuutta koko mökkuuksen. Edustaja huomautti, kuitenkin, että ranskalaiset en saaneet osallistua panttivankien vapauttamisen hin, jotka käytyn Iraniin listuksen ja kaappareiden välillä.

Sivu 4 — poista

Tiedekunta ei synny hetkessä

● Tampereen yliopisten lääketieteellinen tiedekunta tai Suomen viidettä lääketieteellisestä tiedekunnasta muorin. Kahdessatoista vuodessa on kouluttelu puoli-ennatasa läkkirö ja tarkastetti 67 väitöskirjaa.

● Tiedekunta ei synny hetkessä. Kymmenen vuotta on minimiaika tietään (medliin kuomauksi, tutkijoiden kiinnittymiseksi, kansainvälisten kostakiien monneksi.

SIVU 6

Tomi Vuokolt

Sydän- ja verisonitaudit ovat tutkimaskohteina myös Tampereen yliopiston bioläketieteen laitoksessa, jossa tehdään perustutkimusta, pyritään selvittämään tautien syntymekanismia. Assistentti Matti Sala analysoi seerumin rasvahappokoostumien määrää kaasukromatografilla.

Maaherrapeli kuumenee

● Syksyllä vapautuvien kahden maaherranvakansin täyttö sujuu tuskin ilman puolueiden välisiä riitoja. Ennakkopuvailut Keski-Suomen ja Turun läänien uusien maaherrojen nimistä ovat lisääntynysä myös lehtien palstoilla.

● Keski-Suomen maaherran pekka vapautuu Kauko Sipposen (knsk) siirryessä EVA:n toimitusjohtajaki. Turun läänin Paavo Aitio (kd) puoleetaan jää eikkkeelle.

● Sosiaalidemokraatit pyrkivät todennäköisesti saamaan oman miehensä Tu-

run kuverniörivisi Keskutapuolue haluaa pitää koro Keski-Suomessa, multa huhuttu on myös Siidi n pe-heengehtajan Kalevi Kivistön nimttämieistä vaman kotiääänsä maa-berraksi.

SIVU 1

Hevoset vetivät Suomeen

● Hevosten hoito ja suomenkielen opiskelu ovat saaneet norjalaisen jääkärikapteeni Morten Frederikssonin Suomeen ja Ylöjärvelle. Mies opiskelee keski aikana Viitasaaren opistolla suomenkeelta. Sitä kun tarvitsee, jos mielii Pohjois-Norjassa kasvattaa hevosia.

● Ei siitä, että hevoset vain suomea tottelisivat, mutta kun Pohjois-Norjassa ei vihervissa juuri kasvateta on apua harrittava Suomen puolella. Eikä vähäinen syy kuu len opiskeluun on kylä Morten Fredrikssonin alun perin suomalaiset vaimo.

● Voimimaan tämänkokoiselle leelikuruelle osallistuu Fredriksonin lisäksi myös useeman muuta norjalasta Suomen ystävää. Kursi järjestetään opistolla Pohjola-Norden-yhdistyksen ja Työväen sivistysliiton tuella.

SIVU 14

OSA 1	
Kotimaa	4—5, 13—14
Pääkirjoitus	6
Mielipiteet	7
Tehtävät	8
Tänään	9
Kulttuuri	10—11
Talous	12—13
Ulkomaat	15—16

OSA 2	
Urheilu	17—26
Radio ja tv	29
Sarjakuvat	30

Morten Fredrikssonin parivuotias Petsamon Letukka ammentaa Toivos ravirataa tallilla. Isäntä itse käy hevostaan hoitamassa aamuin ja illoin.

Reino Branth

6.5. The top stories in this issue of *Aamulehti* herald the capture of gold and bronze medals in 1984 Olympics by Finns and the hijacking of an Air France jet. (Reprinted with permission)

the residents of this region. The paper is politically independent and faces local competition from smaller papers representing the People's Democratic party and the National Coalition party.

Keskisuomalainen. This 70,000-circulation newspaper in the city of Jyväskylä is associated with the Center party and serves the surrounding communities in the agricultural and lake country of central Finland. The paper averages about 24 pages an issue and is noted for its large photographs and attractive layout. It provides more international coverage than many regional papers, perhaps because of the importance of international issues and developments on agricultural exports.

Savon Sanomat. This important regional paper in Kuopio has a daily circulation of approximately 80,000. Usually 28 pages in length, the paper uses old styles of type typically found in regional papers in Finland, but mixes those typefaces with modern modular layouts and photographic displays.

Regional coverage is the most important feature of this paper and it provides a large amount of news about regional political issues, entertainment, sports, and educational activities (Fig. 6.6). The paper is affiliated with the Center party.

Turun Sanomat. This major regional daily is published in Turku (Åbo) on the southwest coast of Finland and carries a large amount of national and local information, but only a nominal amount of international news. The paper is independent of political parties.

Usually published in a 24-page edition, the paper employs modular layouts that often feature large photographs and four-color printing. It has a circulation of about 130,000 daily.

Like *Helsingin Sanomat,* half of the front page is often devoted to advertising and it is not unusual to find the entire front page taken up with advertising for department or grocery stores (Fig. 6.7).

Uusi Suomi. This tabloid-sized independent paper that serves the Helsinki region was established in 1847 and now has a daily circulation of about 85,000.

A serious newspaper, *Uusi Suomi* concentrates mainly on local and

SAVON SANOMAT

Perjantai 29. kesäkuuta 1984 ● Irtonumero 3,- ● 77. vuosikerta ★ 007260-4-26 ● N:o 174

Pieksämäellä ei ole epidemiaa

Rantasalmen kirkon urut
– yhdet Suomen parhaista

Päästöt torjuttava ennakolta
Ilman laadulle ohjearvot

Vaikka mutkia olikin matkassa...
Kolme lehteä syntyi uuden lehtikoneen tuotantoonajoyönä

Hinnat, verot ja maksut nousevat

6.6. Damage to one of the nation's finest church organs and a debate on educational policy are the main stories in this issue of the regional newspaper *Savon Sanomat*. (Reprinted with permission)

104

6.7. The effects of loss of part of the region's oat crop and the performances of an opera group are reported on this front page of *Turun Sanomat*. (Reprinted with permission)

008557-4-29 N:o 191 ●● Torstaina 19. pnä heinäkuuta 1984 Irtonumero 4,00 (sis. lvv

US tutki kannatuslukuvut - SDP menettänyt eniten

Vihreät vyöryvät etelän kaupunkeihin

● Vihreät suorastaan vyöryvät Helsingin ja muiden suurten kaupunkien valtuustoihin, ilmenee Taloustutkimus Oy:n Uudelle Suomelle tekemästä vaalipiirikohtaisesta mielipidetutkimuksesta.

● Pahimman tappion kärsisivät selvityksen mukaan sosialidemokraatit, joiden kannatus on jokseenkin tasaisesti laskenut Koivisto-kuumeen huippuajoista.

● SKDL:n tasainen alamäki jatkuu edelleen. Myös kokoomus ja keskustapuolue ovat maksaneet laskun vihreiden noususta.

● Helsingissä vihreät loikkaisivat lähes 13 prosentin kannatuksella kolmanneksi suurimmaksi valtuustoryhmäksi, jos maaliskesäkuussa havaittu mieliala on vallalla vielä vaaliuurnilla lokakuun puolivälissä. **Sivu 3**

Oikeusoppineet tukevat Koivistoa

● Oikeusoppineet tukevat presidentti Mauno Koiviston näkemystä siitä, että talousrikoksista syytettyjen oikeusturvassa on puutteita.

● Korkeimman oikeuden presidentti Curt Olsson myöntää, että juttujen käsittely voi venyä pitkäksi. Syytetyt joutuvat siksi odottamaan ratkaisua julkisessa puntarissa vuodesta toiseen.

● Asiantuntijoiden mukaan oikeudenkäynnit eivät Suomessa ole sen hitaampia kuin muuallakaan. Tosin vanhojen juttujen kaiveluvaa nähdään myös merkkejä tarkoitushakuisuudesta.

Sivu 6

Suomen korkotaso noussut
Sivu 19

Tuima taisto lintujärvellä
Sivu 18

Lakko sotkee turistimatkat
Sivu 8

Jackson luovutti taistelun

Rivit tiivistyivät Mondalen taakse

● Yhdysvaltain demokraattinen puolue valmistui yhdentynein rivein valitsemaan varhain torstaiaamuna Walter Mondalen presidenttiehdokkaakseen.

● Ensimmäisenä mustana vakavasti otettavan esivaalikampanjan käynyt Jesse Jackson johdatti demokraattien puoluekokouksessa San Franciscossa kannattajiansa Mondalen ehdokkuuden taakse.

● Pelko Jacksonin irrottautumisesta puolueesta väistyi, mutta hänen mustien kesskuudessa aikaansaamallaan innostuksella uskotaan olevan pysyviä jälkiä Yhdysvaltain politiikkaan.

Sivu 8

Viulunrakentajat kitkerinä verottajalle

Soitto raikaa sateessa

● Sade piiskaa Kaustisen kansanmusiikkijuhlia, mutta tunnelma on tuijissa lukemissa. Soitto raikaa litimärällä juhlakentällä, on tanssitupaa ja viulumarkkinoita.

● Pientä kitkeryyttä on vain viulunrakentajien puheessa. He eivät ole tyytyväisiä valtion verotukseen. Käsityöltä 1960-luvulla kokeilumielessä asetettu liikevaihtovero on yhä voimassa, ja se arsyttää viulunrakentajia.

Sivu 10

Tänä vuonna kaustisen erityisteemana on viulu.

Japanin-kaupan vaje kasvaa

● Suomen vientiponnistelut Japaninkaupassa ovat tuoneet alkuvuonna jopa huomattavia lisäyksiä kaupan volyymiin. Toisaalta Japani on edelleen kasvattanut kauppaansa Suomeen päin, joten kaupan alijäämäisyys vain kasvaa.

● Ulkomaankauppaministeri Jermu Laineetta keulakuvanaan käyttänyt vientikampanja Japaninmarkkinoille vuoden alussa ei ole riittänyt ennätysvajeisen kaupan kääntämiseksi Suomen kannalta suotuisemmaksi kursille.

Sivu 19

Walter Mondale on varmistanut itselleen demokraattien presidenttiehdokkuuden, mutta puoluekokouksen julkistaljoudessa riitti sitä mainosta myös pahimmalle kilpailijalle Gary Hartille, jonka vuoro voi tulla neljän vuoden kuluttua.

6.8. Improvement being made in southern Helsinki and a report on the Democratic Party Nationa Convention in the United States are featured in this issue of the city's tabloid *Uusi Suomi*. (Reprinte with permission)

regional issues and has one of the most complete and colorful weather sections in all the Nordic papers (Fig. 6.8). Although an independent paper, it usually supports conservative political viewpoints. *Uusi Suomi* usually consists of 32 pages and is a very attractive paper that features modular layouts and many four-color photographs and displays.

Vaasa. This paper, established in 1902 and a supporter of the National Coalition party, is published in Vaasa, a town located on the Gulf of Bothnia. As a major regional paper, *Vaasa* has a daily circulation of over 60,000 and serves much of the west central coast of Finland.

CHAPTER SEVEN

Newspapers of Iceland

National Newspapers

Althýdubladid. The organ of the Social Democratic party of Iceland, this paper sells about 3000 copies daily and provides news about party members, Icelandic politics, and foreign concerns (Fig. 7.1). This weekday morning newspaper had a circulation of 16,000 when it was a partner in the coalition government; the party believes circulation will rise again as political fortunes change.

In 1984 the paper changed to a half tabloid, 16-page format to conserve paper and reflect the scaled-down economy that forced a reduced circulation. For commercial income the managers of the *Althýdubladid* rely on legal notices and advertising income from businesses sympathetic to the party. The paper also produces an advertising supplement, which has a wide circulation and which helps to subsidize the paper itself. The paper is profitable again and recently managed to pay off a 10-million-kronur ($360,000) debt.

DV. This prominent paper resulted from the 1981 merger of *Dagbladid* and *Visir,* daily newspapers that each had previously attained circulations of about 20,000. *Dagbladid* began publishing in 1975 after staff members at *Visir* broke away from that supporter of the Conservative party to start an independent paper. Both papers were marginally profitable but unable to increase circulation and ad revenue. After resolving conflicts between staff members, the two papers were combined. *DV* now has a daily circulation of 35,000.

DV is the major competitor to Iceland's leading paper, *Morgunbladid,* and has a stronger circulation outside of Reykjavik than *Morgunbladid,* due in great part to its more extensive coverage of agricultural issues and other items of interest to rural readers (Fig. 7.2). *DV* is noted for its extensive classified advertising section and carries more classified ads than any other paper. Although physically the same

alþýðublaðið

Ályktun um landbúnaðarmál á atvinnumálaráðstefnu Alþýðuflokksins:

Fjárfestingamál í land- búnaði með ólíkindum

Á ráðstefnu Alþýðuflokksins um atvinnustefnu til aldamóta, sem haldin var að Illugastöðum í Fnjóskadal um síðustu helgi, var samþykkt ályktun um landbúnaðarmál, þar sem því er fagnað að vitræn umræða hafi hafist um landbúnaðarmál í landinu og að leysast sé um samkeppnishömlur á sviði kartöflu- og garðávaxta, þótt hægt miði. Í tvo áratugi hefur það verið baráttumál Alþýðuflokksins að litið verði á landbúnaðinn eins og aðra undirstöðuatvinnuvegi og athugað hvernig hægt sé að hagræða, lagfæra og spara í þeim atvinnuvegi. Þá segir í ályktun ráðstefnunnar:

„Útflutningsbætur og niðurgreiðslur eru þættir sem stuðla beinlinis að offramleiðslu í

landbúnaði. Sjálfstæðisflokkurinn og Framsóknarflokkurinn hafa byggt upp og staðið vörð um kerfi, sem virkar eins og vítahringur sóunarinnar. Í litilsigldri von um ódýrt atkvæðasnap slóst Alþýðubandalagið svo síðar í hóp sóunarflokkanna".

„Einkum og sér í lagi sú sóun á sviði milliliða sem á sér stað í landbúnaðarframleiðslunni á ekki hvað síst hlut í þeirri efnahagskreppu, sem íslendingar búa við í dag. Þegar launþegar verða að taka á sig 30% kjaraskerðingu, til að greiða niður verðbólguna, verður ekki lengur gengið fram hjá þeirri kröfu, að sóunarkerfi landbúnaðarins verði tekið til endurskoðunar. Sóunarflokkarnir eru farnir að

taka við sér, hægt og hikandi, og nú er dæminu stillt þannig upp, að þeim hafi allt í einu opinberast nýr sannleikur, og nú á helst allt að gerast í leiftursókn".

„Benda má á leiðir til úrbóta,

eins og eflingu nýrra búgreina, eflingu vísindalegra rannsókna til að stórbæta nýtingu í ullar- og skinnaiðnaði, betri og jafnari nýtingu sláturhúsa og síðast en ekki síst uppbyggingu lifefnaiðnaðar í sambandi við þau. Ljóst er að mikið og skipulegt átak verður að gera í þessum efnum og veita má því fjármagni, sem annars hefði farið í útflutningsbætur, til að standa straum af fjármögnun á nauðsynlegum framkvæmdum.

Alþýðuflokksmenn álita að mikilvægt sé að stuðla að skilningi og samvinnu dreifbýlis og þéttbýlis. Talsvert skilningsleysi hefur komið fram í ýmsum myndum, á högum og kjörum stétta. Þar verður að stuðla að friði.

Alþýðublaðið í breyttri mynd

Alþýðublaðið kemur nú út í nokkuð breyttu formi. Pappírsmagnið í því eykst ekki, en síðunum fjölgar. Handlagnir menn munu áfram geta komið blaðinu fyrir í eldspýtnastokk, en um jafnaðarstefnuna og áhrif hennar þurfa þeir stærri umbúðir.

Alþýðublaðið er og verður málgagn Alþýðuflokksins og jafnaðarstefnunnar, og mun aldrei reyna að dylja þann megintilgang með einhverjum huliðshjálmi. Það má líta á það, sem fréttablað um jafnaðarstefnuna. Blaðið vill fá að lifa og þróast á þeirri hugsjón, að svo megi bæta og breyta þjóðfélaginu að sem mestur jöfnuður og réttlæti geti ríkt. En til að svo megi verða hlýtur að verða að hvetja til meiri og öflugri pólitískar umræðu, þar sem hver og einn hefur tækifæri til að taka afstöðu til þeirra þjóðfélagsgerða, sem hann vill stuðla að.

Hingað og ekki lengra

Á aðalfundi Verkalýðsfélagsins Einingar sem haldinn var á Akureyri í síðustu viku var samþykkt ályktun um kjaramál, þar sem segir að nauðsynlegt sé að ríkisstjórn landsins sé gert það ljóst, að svo langt hefur nú verið gengið í því að skerða kjör launafólks í landinu, að nú er komið að alvarlegum hættumörkum.

„Verkalýðssamtökin hljóta að segja hingað og ekki lengra. Þessarri ríkisstjórn hefur verið sýnt fáheyrt umburðarlyndi að samtök launþega hafa látið sér lynda að gera kjarasamninga, sem aðeins bæta örlítið brot af því, sem aðgerðir stjórnvalda hafa skert kaupmáttinn. Ef ríkisstjórnin ekki skilur þetta og virðir með því að láta af kjaraskerðingarstefnu sinni, hlýtur óánægjan að magnast svo, að upp úr sýður með ófyrirsjáanlegum afleiðingum. Það hefur

vissulega tekist að hemja verðbólgudrauginn, og því fagna allir. Til þess færðu launþegar stórar fórnir, en það er ekki endalaust hægt að réttlæta nýjar og meiri kjaraskerðingar með því, að verið sé að lemja á draugnum. Nú er kominn tími til að menn sjái og finni, að fórnirnar hafi átt rétt á sér.

Reikningar ýmissa stórfyrirtækja í landinu, sem birtir hafa verið á síðustu mánuðum, sýna að í rekstri fyrirtækjanna hefur víða orðið góður bati. En hafa fórnirnar verið færðar til þess eins, að helstu stórfyrirtæki í landinu auki hagnað sinn, þá erum við ekki á réttri leið. Það verður einnig að koma til bati hjá litlu fyrirtækjunum, sem eru heimili launþega um allt land. Ef sífellt kreppir að þeim meðan aðrir græða, þá er stefnan ekki rétt.

7.1. *Althýdubladid*, the paper of the Social Democratic party, places great emphasis on social and economic news and commentary. This issue includes a discussion of the economic situation of households that raise sheep. (Reprinted with permission)

38.000 EINTÖK PRENTUÐ Í DAG.

RITSTJÓRN SÍMI 686811 • AUGLÝSINGAR OG AFGREIÐSLA SÍMI 27022

Frjálst, óháð dagblað

DAGBLAÐIÐ—VÍSIR   128. TBL. — 74. og 10. ÁRG. — ÞRIÐJUDAGUR 5. JÚNÍ 1984.

Austfirskir útvegsbændur stefna skipum sínum til lands:

VILJA HÆRRA FISKVERÐ OG SVO GENGISFELLINGU

— ef ég þekki þá rétt, segir forsætisráðherra

„Við vitum allir að útgerðin stendur illa og veldur þar mestu aflabrestur. En varðandi fyrirætlanir austfirsku útvegsmannanna um að sigla skipum sínum til lands síðar í þessum mánuði get ég ílíð sagt, til þess hef ég ekki kynnt mér málið nægilega vel. En ef að líkum lætur ganga óskir útvegsmannanna út á hærra fiskverð og svo gengisfellingu á eftir,

það er venjan," sagði Steingrímur Hermannsson í samtali við DV nú í morgun.

Ekki tókst að ná sambandi við Halldór Ásgrímsson sjávarútvegsráðherra en hann dvelur í Færeyjum þessa dagana.

„Málið er ósköp einfalt, þetta gengur ekki svona lengur. Það eiga

engin fyrirtæki peninga til að mæta sífelldu tapi," sagði Ólafur Gunnarsson, framkvæmdastjóri Síldarvinnslunnar á Neskaupstað, í morgun.

„Tapið á togaraútgerðinni var 21 prósent árið 1982 og 25 prósent í fyrra. Og það er fyrst og fremst vegna taps þessara tveggja ára sem vandinn er til kominn."

— En hverjar eru ykkar helstu kröfur? — Hvað viljið þið útgerðarmenn á Austfjörðum gera?

„Það er ýmislegt. Hækka endurkaupalánin, breyta vanskilaskuldum í 8 ára lán og að fiskverð sé ákveðið þannig að hvorki útgerð né vinnslan sé rekin með tapi."

— Áttu von á löngu stoppi?

„Ég vona að það verði ekkert

stopp. En miðað við undirtektirnar fram að þessu getur maður allt eins átt von á stoppi. Því miður, því að fólkið hér á Austfjörðum á þetta ekki skilið, allra síst.

Stjórnvöld verða að átta sig á að ef þau ætla að viðhalda byggð á landsbyggðinni, þá er ekki hægt að ganga á sjávarútveginn."

EIR/JGH

A gangi með orgel. Nei, þetta er ekki atriði úr kvikmynd heldur undirbúningur fyrir athöfn sem fram fór á Akureyri um helgina þegar tekin var fyrsta skóflustunga að nýrri kirkju þar. Sjá nánar frétt á bls. 2.

DV-mynd: JGH

Spánverjar vilja ólmir fá Íslendinga í æfingabúðir
— sjá íþróttir í opnu

Kvennagrátur er karlahlátur
— sjá Sviðsljósið á bls. 14

Úr á íbúðarverði
— sjá bls. 2

Starfsmenn stjórnmálaflokkanna segja álit sitt á skoðanakönnun DV
— sjá bls 4

Fyrsti Rollsinn kominn
— sjá bls. 2

Vírbinding líka fyrir tannlausa
— sjá bls. 5

Skemmdarvargar í Bláa lóninu
— sjá bls. 3

Þorvaldur í Síld og fiski fær viðurkenningu
— sjá bls. 4

Verkaður BÚR-karfi
— sjá Neytendur á bls. 8

7.2. A leading paper with extensive circulation outside of Reykjavik, *DV* places great emphasis on activities throughout the country. This issue reports on the changing fortunes of the fishing industry and a new organ for a church in Akureyri.

size as *Morgunbladid,* its layout and presentation is much more like that of tabloid papers.

DV supports the Conservative party and its chairman has been active in that party's politics for many years. The paper is published in the afternoon, Monday through Saturday.

Morgunbladid. This paper is Iceland's dominant newspaper with a daily circulation of 40,000. It enjoys the perquisites of additional advertising revenue that results from being the nation's premier paper. Begun in 1914, the paper has grown to an average of 48 pages an issue, with nearly half of its pages devoted to advertising.

Morgunbladid places the heaviest emphasis of Icelandic newspapers on foreign news, regularly devoting the full front page and as many as three other pages to news from abroad (Fig. 7.3). Much of its national news focuses on topics of interest in Reykjavik, where its circulation is concentrated. It is published Tuesday through Sunday.

Morgunbladid is an attractive paper, on par with the better looking papers of North America and Europe and is the only Icelandic paper profitable on the scale of the successful papers in Denmark and Great Britain. The paper is owned by members of the Conservative party and supports that party's viewpoints in its editorials.

NT (Nu Timmin). Like *DV, NT (Nu Timmin)* is both a new and an old Icelandic newspaper. It began in the spring of 1984, emerging from and replacing *Timmin,* which had been published by the Progressive party since 1916. The paper has a circulation' of about 18,000, and although now technically separate from the party, still supports its policies.

In an effort to increase circulation and advertising, the paper uses more color and graphic display techniques than *DV* or *Morgunbladid.* It offers less content than its two major competitors, however, running an average of only 28 pages each issue; about 20 percent of its content is advertising. This morning paper is published Monday through Saturday.

Despite the significant change in appearance when it replaced *Timmin, NT* has not managed to significantly increase its circulation or market position since that time (Fig. 7.4).

Morgunbladid

STOFNAÐ 1913

126. tbl. 71. árg.   ÞRIÐJUDAGUR 5. JÚNÍ 1984   Prentsmiðja Morgunblaðsins

Reagan býður grið en Rússar eru andsnúnir

<small>Dublin, 4. júní. AP.</small>

Ronald Reagan Bandaríkjaforseti kveðst reiðubúinn að semja við Sovétmenn um griðasáttmála fyrir Evrópu ef þeir fallist á tillögur ríkja Atlantshafsbandalagsins á Stokkhólmsráðstefnunni um að draga úr líkum á styrjöld. Sagðist Reagan í þessu sambandi reiðubúinn að stöðva uppsetningu nýrra meðaldrægra kjarnaflauga í Evrópu og jafnvel flytja burtu þær sem komið hefur verið fyrir.

Af hálfu sovézkra yfirvalda var tilboði Reagans hafnað og Chern-

enko, leiðtogi sovézka kommúnistaflokksins, sagði í ræðu að vonlaust væri að hefja að nýju samningaviðræður við Bandaríkjamenn um vígbúnaðartakmörkun meðan einsýnt væri að viðræður af því tagi myndu snúast um fjölgun kjarnavopna í Evrópu, eins og það var orðað.

Reagan sagði í ræðu í írska þinginu að Bandaríkjamenn vildu „meiri viðræður" við Kremlverja „til að koma í veg fyrir misskilning eða misskilning á ógnusvæðum eða hernaðarlega viðkvæmum svæðum". Tilboð Reagans þykir koma á óvart þar sem hugmynd Rússa um griðasáttmála fyrir Evrópu eru meðal tillagna á Stokkhólmsráðstefnunni.

Tillögur NATO-ríkja þar miða að því að minnka líkur á styrjöld í heiminum, m.a. með því að takmarka umfang heræfinga og skylda aðila til að láta vita um heræfingar fyrirfram, en tillaga Rússa gengur út á það eitt að gerður verði sáttmáli um að hervaldi ekki beitt í Evrópu.

Ræða Reagans í þinginu var hápunktur fjórða og síðasta dags Írlandsheimsóknar forsetans. Andstæðingar stefnu stjórnar Reagans í málefnum Mið-Ameríku og andstæðingar kjarnorkuvopna hafa annan heimsókninu til mótmælaaðgerða. Síðdegis hélt Reagan til London, en þar ræðir hann við Margaret Thatcher forsætisráðherra á morgun, þriðjudag.

Sjá nánar á bls. 21.

Fær Andrei Sakharov að fara úr landi?

<small>Moskva, 4. júní. AP.</small>

TASS-fréttastofan sagði í kvöld að Andrei Sakharov væri í fullenda tölu og að þeir sem héldu öðru fram væru að „grafa hans lífandi". Sagði TASS að Sakharov-hjónin væru við góða heilsu og hörð hungursverkfall.

Tatyana Yankelevich, stjúpdóttir Sakharovs, telur hugsanlegt að yfirvöld í Moskvu séu að leita leiðar til að leyfa Sakharov að fara til Vesturlanda án þess þó að gjata andlitinu, eins og hún orðaði það á blaðamannafundi í Stokkhólmi. Það þykir renna stoðum undir þær grunsemdir að tilkynnt var í Moskvu að Francois Mitterrand Frakklandsforseti kæmi þangað í opinbera heimsókn seinnihluta júnímánaðar.

Sú orðrómur hafði verið á kreiki í París að Mitterrand mundi fresta eða jafnvel hætta við Moskvuferð ef engar fregnir bærust um Sakharov og þó var hafi hann ætlað að þrýsta á Rússa að leyfa Sakharov-hjónum að fara úr landi til að leita sér lækninga.

Yankelevich ferðast nú um ríki Vestur-Evrópu og leitar eftir stuðningi yfirvalda til að komast að því hvað hent hefur Sakharov-hjónin. Kvað hún það hagsmuni Rússa að virsa frá á að stjúpfaðir sinn væri í tölu lifenda. Ef Rússar létu hann deyja í höndum sér væri Helsinki-sáttmálinn úr sögunni.

„Svo virðist sem yfirvöld séu ákveðin í að skýra í veg fyrir hvar foreldrar minir eru niðurkomnir eða heilsufari þeirra. Ég veit ekki hvort Sakharov er enn í Gorky, hvort hann er á sjúkr húsi og fæða nægð ofan í hann eða hvort hann er í lífs eða líðinn," sagði Yankelevich.

36 síkhar felldir í átökum í Amritsar

<small>Dehlí, 4. júní. AP.</small>

Í HLJÁTÍ og sex síkhar, sem höfðust við innan reggja Gullna hofsins í Amritsar, féllu í fimm klukkustunda bardaga við lögreglu og hermenn í dag, að sögn áreiðanlegra heimilda. Innanríkisráðuneytið staðfesti að til átakanna hafi komið.

Her- og lögreglumenn skipuðu

síkhum að yfirgefa hofið, en þeir svöruðu með byssukothríð, handsprengjum og hrökum, handsprengjum. Einn hermaður særðist alvarlega. Að sögn hafa hermenn ekki átt lagt til inngöngu í hofið, en verða að grípa til þess ef síkharnir gefast ekki upp. Sikharnir hafa hins vegar hótað blóðbaði ef hermennirnir gera áhlaup á hofið.

Einnig var skotið á hóp síkha, sem söfnuðust saman við annan helgistað og hugðust ganga til Gullna hofsins, og særðist fjöldi göngumanna. Og þrátt fyrir útgöngubann voru framin morð og rán í nótt og dag, sem standa í beinu sambandi við baráttu síkha fyrir trúfrelsi og sjálfsforræði. Sjö manns féllu í þremur skothar-

dögum í Amritsar á sunnudag í átökum síkha og hindúa.

Bannahur hefur verið fréttaflutningur frá Punjab-fylki og það var einangrað um helgina er stjórnarhermenn tóku sér stöðu við alla vegi og héldu undankomuleiðir. Ferðalog með járnbrautum og um þjóðvegi til og frá Punjab hafa jafnframt verið bönnuð. Stjórnarhernum var skipað til Punjab til að bæla niður uppreisn síkha, sem ábyrgð bera á láti 350 manna síðustu mánuði.

Gullna hofið er æðsti helgistaður síkha, en yfirvöld segja að íslamskir fleiri hundruð hryðjuverkamanna úr röðum sikha og vopnabúr.

Persaflóastríðið:

Alsírbúar reyna að miðla málum

<small>Alsír, Ankara, 4. júní. AP.</small>

FORSETI alsírska þingsins og sérlegur ráðherra forsetans fóru í dag til Teheran og Bagdad í umboði Chadli Bendjedid forseta til þess að reyna að miðla málum í Persaflóastríðinu. Var eigi skýrt frá ferð þeirra opinberlega vegna „viðkvæmni" aðila fyrir fregnum af formlegri milligöngu í deilunni.

Tyrkir íhuga að draga tyrkneskum skipum siglingar um Persaflóa í framhaldi af árás Írraka á olíuskipið Buyuk Hun suður af Kharg-eyju í gær. Í áhöfninni eru taldir af, en aðrir

komust í báta og var bjargað. Reiði ríkir meðal Tyrkja, sem halda því fram að Írökum hafi verið kunnugt um þjóðerni skipsins áður en þeir hófu flugskeytaárás.

Íranir halda því fram að það hafi verið Super Etendard-þotur búnar Exocet-flugskeytum, sem gert hafi árásina. Haffi verið skotið að skipinu úr mikilli fjarlægð í árásarferð til Kharg-eyju. Írakar sögðust hafa hæft tvö „stór" skotmörk í árásinni, en ekkert um minnst á eitt í fregnum frá Íran.

Indverskir hermenn standa vörð við Gullna hofið í Amritsar í Punjab, og kanna vígbúnað síkha í hofinu.

7.3. The dominant newspaper of Iceland, *Morgunbladid,* emphasizes foreign news. This front page includes stories on U.S.-U.S.S.R. relations, the condition of Andrei Sakharov, and an assault on a Sikh stronghold in India. (Reprinted with permission)

Þriðjudagur 5. júní 1984 – 135. tbl. 68. árg.

Vestfirðingur í samkeppni við vegagerðina:

Lagði einn 15-20 kílómetra akveg!

■ Þegar vegurinn kemur ekki til Lökinhamrabúa í Arnarfirði, leggja þeir hann bara sjálfir.

Það gerðist í síðustu viku, þegar Elís Kjaran stjóri frá Þingeyri lagði al-einn á nokkrum dögum 15-20 km vegarspotta frá Lökinhömrum inn að Stapadal í Arnarfirði, þaðan sem

fyrir var vegarslóði að Hrafnseyri og aðalþjóðveginum.

Nýi vegurinn styttir tölu-vert leið Lökinhamrabúa að þjóðveginum. Áður þurftu þeir að aka um Sval-vogu að Þingeyri til að kom-ast í þjóðbraut. Sá vegur var lagður af vegagerðinni 1974-75 og er hann lokaður

fyrir aðra en kunnuga, þar sem hann þykir með ein-dæmum hættulegur.

Elís lagði veginn að undirlagi íbúa Lökinhamra og hreppsnefndarinnar. Kostnaðurinn við fram-kvæmdirnar var 130 þúsund krónur. Hreppsnefndin lagði til 50 þúsund kr, og Sigríður Ragnarsdóttir á

Hrafnabjörgum 30 þúsund. Eftir standa 50 þúsund og ætlar ýtustjórinn að gefa vinnu sína.

Við vegagerðina þurfti Elís að fara um miklar skriður, en hann er þaul-vanur vegagerðarmaður og getur komið ýtu sinni hvar sem er. Heimamenn eru mjög hrifnir af framtakinu.

Eiga tækni-frjóvganir rétt á sér?

■ Á meðan læknavísind-in finna æ fleiri og flóknari leiðir til að hjálpa þeim sem ekki geta eignast börn með eðlilegum hætti hafa ýmsar spurningar komið upp um réttarfarslega stöðu barna sem verða til með aðstoð tækninnar og einnig um það hvort aðgerðir af þessu tagi eigi siðferðislegan rétt á sér.

Hér á landi hefur skipu-lagt tæknifrjóvgunarstarf verið stundað um tæplega fjögurra ára skeið. Í úttekt

í opnu NT í dag er fjallað um nokkur þeirra álita-mála sem komið hafa upp vegna tæknifrjóvgana hér á landi og erlendis.

NT-úttekt í opnunni

Eldur í tveimur strætis-vögnum!

– allt á huldu með orsök brunans

■ Um áttaleytið í gærkveldi kom upp eldur í tveimur strætis-vögnum við þvottastöð SVR. Upptök eldsins eru óþekkt en báðir bílarnir voru mjókomnir inn. Höfðu vagnstjórarnir yfir-gefið bílana fyrir utan, en fundu þá skömmu seinna logandi. Slökkvistarf gekk allgreiðlega, en alls notuðu slökkvimennirnir um 15 slökkvitæki, áður en slökkvihröð bar að. Nokkur slökkvitækjanna reyndust vera því sem næst tóm. Eldurinn logaði mest aftan til og undir vögnunum, og gæti verið að kviknað hafi í út frá kælinum í öðrum bílnum en síðan eldurinn breiðst út með olíu.

NT-mynd: Árni Bjarna.

Bláa lónið:

Óaldar-lýður herjar á baðhús exem-sjúklinga

– gífurleg skemmdarverk verið unnin

■ Gífurleg spjöll hafa verið unnin á baðhúsi psoriasis-sjúklinga við Bláa lónið í Svartsengi. Óboðnir gestir hafa heimsótt húsið að nýturlagi næst-um hverja einustu helgi um nokk-urra mánaða skeið og fengið útrás fyrir eyðileggingarfýsn auk þess að skilja eftir sig alls kyns óþrif, meðal annars manna-saur á miðju gólfi baðherbergis-ins. – Sjá nánar síðu þrjú.

Hreppsnefnd Eyjahrepps ekki sammála Thorssystkinum:

Samþykkir ekki að dótt-ir eiganda fái jörðina

– hafnar nýju byggingarbréfi og að jörðin verði rýmd

■ Hreppsnefnd Eyja-hrepps hafnaði á fundi sínum um helgina byggingarbréfi jarðarinnar Gerðubergs sem hljóðaði upp á að eigandinn Þórður Thors byggði hana dóttur sinni og tengdasyni í núverandi ábúandi Lárus Gestsson fari af henni. For-sendur hreppsnefndarinnar voru fyrst og fremst þær að Þórður hefði losnað aðra jörð í hreppnum, Akurholt úr

ábúð fyrir þessa sömu dóttur sína og þar hefðu þau hjónin nú þegar byrjað að koma sér fyrir. Þórður Thors sagðist í samtali við NT í gær álíta þessa ákvörðun sveitarfé-lagsins út í hött og að hann myndi eftir sem áður halda til streitu kröfu sinni á hend-ur Lárusi um að hann færi af jörðinni. Hann kvað hrepps-nefndina ekki hafa neinn um-

sagnarrétt um byggingarbréf þegar um svo nánin skyldleika eiganda og væntanlegs ábú-anda væri að ræða. Þó sagði Þórður að dóttir sín og tengdasonur færu að Gerðu-bergi þegar Lárus færi þaðan burt.

Svanur Guðmundsson oddviti Eyjahrepps kvaðst í samtali við NT þess fullviss að ákvörðun hreppsnefndar-

innar væri réttlætanleg og að henni yrði ekki hnekkt. „Ég vil bara bjóða þessu nýju sveitunga að Akurholti vel-komna og er þess fullviss að Eyhreppingar munu styðja við bakið á þeim til göngum á meðan þau eru að koma undir sig fótunum", sagði oddvitinn að lokum.

Sjá nánar í blaðinu á morgun.

Vestfirðir:

Verður sjómanna-verkfall í júlí?

■ Samninganefnd Alþýðu-sambands Vestfjarða hefur beint því til sjómannafélaganna á Vestfjörðum að þau afli sér verkfallsheimildar með það fyr-ir augum að verkfall geti hafist 1. júlí.

Samninganefndir Alþýðu-sambands Vestfjarða og Út-vegsmannafélags Vestfjarða komu saman til þess að revna að ná samningum á föstudaginn var og það tókst ekki. Í gær voru svo tilmælin um verkfallsheim-ild til þeirra félaga sem fara með sjómannasamninga, alls 10 félög, samþykkt.

Samningar hafa verið lausir frá því að login frægu um fryst-ingu kjarasamninga voru sett

---

7.4. The paper *NT* is struggling to gain a steady audience and features short articles on events that appeal to those who wish less serious news presentation. This issue reports on the progress of road work and a bus fire. (Reprinted with permission)

ÞJÓÐVILJINN

Listahátíðin á fullu. Umsagnir og frásagnir.

Bls. 6

5.

júní 1984
Þriðjudagur
125. tbl.
49. árgangur

Börnum misþyrmt á Íslandi!

500-4000 tilfelli árlega segja sérfróðir menn um þetta dulda ofbeldi

Við verðum mjög vör við ofbeldi gegn börnum, bæði andlegt og líkamlegt ofbeldi. Það er mjög erfitt að gera sér grein fyrir umfangi þessa en hugsanlega gætu hér verið um 500 - 4000 tilfelli á ári; kynferðislegt, andlegt, líkamlegt eða hrein vanhirða", sagði Aðalsteinn Sigfússon félagsfræðingur hjá Félagsmálastofnun Reykjavíkurborgar í samtali við Þjóðviljann.

Í gær héldu starfsmenn Félagsmálastofnunar ásamt starfsfólki á borgarstofnunum sem hafa með afskipti af börnum að gera ráðstefnu í Gerðubergi um barnamisþyrmingar.

Á ráðstefnunni fluttu erindi þau Pétur Lúðvíksson læknir á Barnaspítala Hringsins og Hulda Guðmundsdóttir yfirfélagsráðgjafi spítalans. Pétur vitnaði í erindi sínu til bandarískrar könnunar á ofbeldi gegn börnum en þar kemur m.a. fram að ofbeldið beinist einkum gegn börnum undir þriggja ára aldri og þá einkum gagnvart veikburða börnum eða þeim sem á einhvern hátt minna mega sín og ættu meður þar stærri hlut að máli en feður.

Séu skráð tilfelli í Bandaríkjunum hlutfallslega yfirfærð hingað væri hér um að ræða 52 slík tilfelli á ári.

Aðalsteinn Sigfússon benti hins vegar á að hér væri um mjög villandi tölu að ræða því skráningu væri mjög illa sinnt og menn álitu að umfangið hérlendis væri um 500 - 4000 tilfelli á hverju ári og þá væri átt við ofbeldi gagnvart börnum á einn eða annan máta.

„Þetta er falið vandamál, enginn vill láta vita af þessu. Við erum ekki í neinum vafa um að ein afleiðingin af þessu barnaofbeldi er það sem kallað er hegðunarvandamál unglinga. Orsakirnar oft á tíðum liggja í slæmri meðferð á þessum börnum í æsku".

Fók var mjög ánægt með þá umræðu sem fram fór um þessi mál á ráðstefnunni. Þetta er í fyrsta skipti sem allir þessir aðilar eru kallaðir saman og ekki vanþörf á að slíkt ætti sér stað. Það er mín von að þetta hafi aðeins verið byrjunin,

því hér vantar alveg samhæfðar reglur fyrir fólk til að starfa eftir sem þarf að taka á þessu vandamáli, sjá til að bætt verði úr skráningu og samstillingu og ekki síst farið að huga að fyrirbyggjandi aðgerðum", sagði Aðalsteinn Sigfússon.   –lg.

Þjóðviljinn í Oregon um helgina

Íþróttir á 8 síðum   bls. 9-16

Mikill baráttuhugur í kennurum:

Samningum verði sagt upp!

- *Vilja að BSRB boði til verkfalls 1. september*
- *Fjöldauppsagnir eru fyrirhugaðar*

Bláa lónið:
Brotist inni í baðhúsið

Bls. 24

Kennarar vilja að BSRB segi skilyrðislaust upp kjarasamningum sínum og boði til verkfalls hinn fyrsta september næstkomandi. Þetta kom fram í mjög harðorðri ályktun um kjaramál sem var samþykkt á fulltrúaþingi Kennarasambandsins nú um helgina. Jafnframt skoraði þingið á stjórn sambandsins að skipuleggja

fjöldauppsagnir kennara takist ekki að ná leiðréttingu á kjörum þeirra.

Formaður Kennarasambandsins, Valgeir Gestsson, sagði að „mjög greinileg samstaða ríkti á þinginu um uppsögn samninganna. Það er alveg ljóst að fólk er tilbúið í veruleg átök, og mun ekki veigra sér við verkföllum ef því er að skipta. Kennarar vilja standa að

sinni kjarabaráttu með öðrum félögum ef átök verða fyrsta september, bæði utan BSRB og innan. Og það er ljóst að menn eru tilbúnir í fjöldauppsagnir ef ekki fæst leiðrétting".

Í sama streng tóku aðrir þingfulltrúar sem rætt var við og mikils baráttuhugs virtist gæta meðal þeirra. Til dæmis sagði Hjálmfríður Sveinsdóttir úr Vestmannaeyjum að kennarar

væru mjög fúsir til aðgerða til að rétta stéttina við. „Menn eru hættir að tala um einn eða tvo launaflokka, þeir vilja almennilegar kjarabætur. Og ég sé fyrir langt verkfall ef lagt verður út í aðgerðir. Við eigum hreinlega ekki um annað að velja".

–Ös

Sjá bls. 3

7.5. The socialist paper *Thjódviljinn* offers strong sports and entertainment coverage, as well as coverage of important social issues.

Thjódviljinn. Published by the Socialist People's Union, this Icelandic paper was established in 1935 and has been more successful in recent years than *Althýdubladid.* A 24-page morning paper, *Thjódviljinn* has a circulation of about 10,000.

While an outlet for party opinion and news, the paper also serves as a guide to events in Iceland, provides a large amount of sports news, and carries information on the arts and cultural activities (Fig. 7.5). About 15 percent of the paper is devoted to advertising. The paper uses a clean modular layout that is heavily sectionalized. It generally does not cover foreign news unless it relates directly to Iceland or national political debates.

CHAPTER EIGHT

Newspapers of Norway

National Newspapers

Aftenposten. A serious paper, *Aftenposten* is Norway's most prestigious newspaper. It contains a higher percentage of hard national and international news and serious commentary than other papers. The paper usually includes many short articles in modular layouts and, although it sometimes uses color photographs, it tends to be "gray" because layouts feature long copy and small photographs (Fig. 8.1).

The paper is one of the few major newspapers in Scandinavia to publish both a morning and evening edition, although this is not an uncommon practice in Norway. The morning edition has a circulation of about 230,000 throughout the country and usually consists of 44 pages of copy, whereas the afternoon edition circulates mainly in Oslo, where the paper is published, and is usually 16 pages.

Aftenposten supports the Conservative party and is owned by the Schibsted Group, the only privately owned newspaper group in Norway.

Dagbladet. This Norwegian tabloid screams at passersby from the newsstands with colorful printing, large headlines, and heavy use of photographs. Usually about 40 pages in length, the paper provides readers with many national feature stories, little foreign news, and a slightly larger dose of national news.

Dagbladet features a large sports section and places significant emphasis on television and other entertainment information (Fig. 8.2). Despite its light news feast, the paper does offer political and cultural commentary in sufficient amounts to meet the minimum daily requirements of its readers. It has a daily circulation of 140,000.

VG (Verdens Gang). This competitor of *Dagbladet* is less frenzied in appearance and places more emphasis on national and international

I løssalg: Radio·TV-Magasinet

Aftenposten

Morgenutgave. Fredag 6. juli 1984. Nr. 304. 125. årg. Kr. 4,00. Flysendt/ekspress: Vest-Norge kr. 4,50. Nord-Norge kr. 5,00

LES

1. SEKSJON

Industri-
produksjonen
øker i Norge
Politikk, side 3

Helsedir. Mork
vil ha forbud
mot tatovering
Side 5

Liten fare for
blodkreft hos
elektrikere
Side 5

300 skip holdt
tilbake, sikker-
heten for dårlig
Side 5

80 millioner
betalt for
maleri
Utland, side 8

Nytt liv for
Pax forlag
Side 9

Moderate
indere trues
av landsmenn
Side 9

12 timers
politisk
Nordsjø-streik
Næringsliv, side 10

Begrenset
mengde av
olje-oppdrag
Næringsliv, side 11

ANNONSER
Kunngjøringer 12
Mistet · Funnet ... 12
Eiend.markedet ... 12
Næringsl.marked . 12
Båt · Bil · Fly 15
Dødsfall 19

2. SEKSJON

Norge møter
Mexico i
OL-fotball?
Sporten

Hjemmepraksis
ikke sidestilt
med skolegang
Siste side

Amnesty
forbereder
TV-innsamling
Siste side

ANNONSER
Reiseliv/et 25
Underv · Instr 26
Faglig assistanse . 27
Salg · Kjøp · Tjen. 27
Billing marked 28
Møter- og underh .. 27

Bensinboikott oppheves, krav om fast oljepris

● Bilorganisasjonene har trukket tilbake opp-
fordringen om å fylle bensin på NOROL-sta-
sjoner. Namsrettens kjennelse om at dette er
ulovlig blir respektert, men er anket.

● Prisen på norsk olje må bygge på samme
dollarkurs som i statsbudsjettet, kr. 7,30, mener bilorganisasjonene. Dette vil senke ben-
sinprisen med 20 øre literen.   Side 4

Gav alt for gullet

Dødssliten efter å ha tatt ut de siste kreftene mot slutten av løpet.
Men så ble det også gull til Øyvind
Lauritzen og hans tre lagkamera-
ter fra Lørenskog i en spennende
duell med Fana i sykkel-NM i lag-
tempo. Giåmdal tok bronsen.
(Foto: Dag Grundseth) Sporten

Livlig skattedebatt, men grunnlaget mangler -

Skattekommisjonens lekkasjer kommenteres fra
forskjellige hold: Kr.F. vil ha enighet om systemet,
men anser skattenivået som en adskilt sak. Høyre
ser et slikt skille som en svakhet. Sp. mener det er
et grunnlag å bygge videre på. Ap. sier det er et
godt debattgrunnlag. Aftenposten skriver på le-
derplass: Vent med vurderingen til utredningen
foreligger.   Side 2 (leder) og 20

Tusen dagers ledelse

Søndag er det 1 000 dager siden
Norge fikk en borgerlig regjering
ledet av statsminister Kåre Wil-
loch. Kamp mot arbeidsledighet
og statsfinansene, sikkerhets- og
utenrikspolitikk er hovedsaker
ved milepælen. Det satses på
fortsatt samarbeide.
Side 3

For mye privatliv i firma-regnskap

— Nye opprullinger av skatteunn-
dragelser vil komme, varsler skatte-
direktør Willy Ovesen. Svært mange
toppsjefer og firmaeiere har store
deler av sitt privatforbruk bokført i
firmaregnskapene, bemerker skat-
tedirektøren som nå har ihendeha-
verobligasjonene til observasjon.
Næringsliv, side 11

Hanoi anholder kritikere

Flere fremtredende opposisjonelle i
Vietnam er arrestert på ny etter å
ha tilbragt flere år i omskolerings-
leire. Blant de arresterte er tre kjen-
te forfattere. Pressen i landet har
hevdet at CIA har betalt vietname-
siske forfattere for å få dem til å un-
dergrave regimet. Myndighetene
har ifølge Amnesty International
ikke oppgitt noen grunn for arresta-
sjonene.   Side 8

Grethe-suksess

Brak-suksess, skriver vår anmel-
der om «The show must go home»
med Dizzie Tunes, Grethe Kausland og Benny Borg. Mye ros til
Grethe Kausland som «freser og
syder av talent». Yngvar Numme
(til venstre) og Tor-Erik Gun-
strøm (til høyre) spiller duo så det
svinger.   (Foto: Morten Uglum)
Side 9

Lokalt høytrykk

Revy i Vestfold betyr høysommer
og høytrykk, ikke minst på Hotell
Klubben i Tønsberg. Showet gikk
hjem for full musikk i nærvær av
hele Norges-eliten i show-bis, pre-
mièren er bransjens vennefest. De
gikk glipp av Dynastiet, men Grethe Kausland tok Alexis på kornet
(bildet).   Side 21

Klart for atomvåpen i DDR

Sovjetiske atomraketter som kan nå mål nord for
Trondheim, er under utplassering i DDR og Tsjek-
koslovakia. Raketten med betegnelsen SS-22, var
ikke tatt med i de avbrutte forhandlinger om mel-
lomdistanse atomvåpen i Genève. I Stockholm an-
viste Sovjet igår et forslag fra Sverige og Finland.
Det kunne fart til at konferansen om tillitskapen-
de tiltak ville gått inn i virkelige forhandlinger.
Konferansen tar nå pause.   Side 8

- Jeg tilbød Tiki!

Hvis Lars Monrad-Krohn i Kontiki
Data A/S har kjedeligheter efter
demnen i Oslo byrett, beklager jeg
dette, men han bare vær selv å
skylde på. Jeg foreslo at han kunne
bruke navnet på det polynesiske gu-
den Tiki og jeg var villig til å hjelpe
ham med å få kopiert gude-masken
til bruk som firmamerke, sier Thor
Heyerdahl til Aftenposten i telefon
fra sitt hjem i Italia. Men fabrika-
sjon under Kontiki-navnet gjorde jeg
det klart at jeg ikke ville godta.
Side 20

8.1. The completion of one thousand days in office by the prime minister and a protest over the price of gasoline are reported in this issue of *Aftenposten*. (Reprinted with permission)

STÅR PÅ

Dagbladet

Torsdag 5. juli 1984 • • • • Nr. 153 — 116. årgang. — Løssalg kr. 4,00

16 sider ekstra!

DYREST Forretningsbanken

BILLIGST Postsparebanken

BANKENES SKJULTE RENTER

Det er billigst å låne i Postsparebanken — dyrest i Forretningsbanken. Det er dramatiske rente-forskjeller mellom bankene. Like oppsiktvekkende er forskjellene mellom de renteopplysninger som de ulike bankene operer med i låne-kontrakten og det du faktisk må betale. Dette er konklusjonene i en undersøkelse av bankenes åpne og skjulte renter — som Dagbladet i dag presenterer.

Side 6 og 7

TV-DAGBLADET

■ ■ TV-Dagbladet står på også sommeren igjennom, med 16 sider hver torsdag. I dag med blant annet dette:

— over og ut!

■ Royalty-bølgen over oss: Alexis Ingalsad i den brennende hytta til Steven — slik tar NRK farvel med «Dynastiet».

Det nye TV-paret

■ Jon (Michelet) og Ellen Marit (Gaup Dunfjeld) blir sommerens TV-par.

Reagan-western

■ Gjer star til mandags-filmen Ronald Reagan i en western-film fra 1958.

Ingen tvil blant Dagbladets lesere: Ingrid Kristiansen var Månedens Navn i juni.

Det ble Ingrid

Midten

8.2. The interest rates of various banks and the TV listing for the week are heralded in this issue of *Dagbladet*, Norway's national tabloid. (Reprinted with permission)

news. It includes both serious and light news features, but like its counterpart places great emphasis on sports and entertainment reporting (Fig. 8.3). Its weekday circulation is 240,000, but its Saturday (weekend) edition has a circulation of 330,000.

VG makes little use of rules and boxed layout aids and has the appearance of being haphazardly put together. Its appearance is not greatly different from other Norwegian papers, however, because most Norwegian papers are not as cleanly designed as those found in Sweden and other nations.

VG is published in Oslo by the Schibsted Group, which publishes *Aftenposten*. Unlike *Aftenposten*, which supports the Conservative party, *VG* supports the Independent Liberals.

Arbeiderbladet. This 40-page tabloid is larger in physical size than *Dagbladet* or *VG* and employs the cleanest modular layout of Norwegian tabloids (Fig. 8.4). The paper carries a significant amount of national and Nordic news, but does not place much emphasis on news from other areas. It has a daily circulation of 52,000.

Arbeiderbladet contains a large sports section and provides a significant amount of commentary and opinion. The paper celebrated its 100th anniversary in 1984. The paper is owned by and is the official organ of the Labor party.

Regional Newspapers

Adresseavisen. This paper is published in Trondheim, a city on the central coast of the country. The paper serves the central and sparsely inhabited northern regions near and above the Arctic Circle.

Adresseavisen averages about 32 pages an issue and has a circulation of about 80,000. As a good regional paper, it places heavy emphasis on local and regional news and less emphasis on international issues, by which residents are less affected. The paper contains a reasonable amount of cultural and sports material and carries political commentary that is generally supportive of the views of the Conservative party.

Bergens Tidende. This major regional paper is published in Bergen and has a daily circulation of 95,000 on the western coast of the nation. It also publishes sections to editions especially suited for areas outside

8.3. A dispute between the ministers responsible for public health and social policies and the performance of two comedians grace the front page of *VG*. (Reprinted with permission)

8.4. Efforts of the wealthy to escape taxation are explored in the main article in this Labor party paper, *Arbeiderbladet*. (Reprinted with permission)

121

Bergens ⚓ Tidende

| 1. UTGAVE · Nr. 156 · 117. årgang | TIRSDAG 10. JULI 1984 | Nygårdsgt. 5-11, 5000 Ber |

Nordfjord:
Pent
Bergen:
Pent
Sunnhordland:
Pent
Siste side

1 NYHETER • LOKAL • SPORT

Ting-kvinner nyter ferien ____ side 5 /

Revansje for Bergens-syklist
side 13

ANNONSER
Møten:
underholdning .... side 6
Kunngjøringer .... side 9
Arbeidsmarkedet.... side 12

Sommerferdedelen

Bergens-gutter til «Drama» ____ side 15

Musiker i kamp med seg selv ____ side 27

ANNONSER
Forretn. - Kontor ... si
Service-kjøn-
næringsliv .... si
Reiseliv .... si
Kjøp-salg .... si
Bil-båt-maskiner... si
Eiendom-bolig....... si

Tips? Ring 𝔅𝔗 **(05) 32 76 40**

Løssalg: Bergen/Hordaland/Sogn og Fjordane .... kr. 4.0
Løssalg: Landet for øvrig .... kr. 5.0

Dyrere å eie hus i Bergen

Fra 1986 kan bergenserne vente en kraftig økning i eiendomsskatten. Taksten kan i mange tilfeller bli femdoblet. Kemneren er nå i ferd med å følge opp bystyrevedtaket fra tidligere i år, og 3—4 takstmenn er oppnevnt.

Med maksimal beskatning vil de nye takstene føre til en årlig økning i eiendomsskatten på 2800 kroner for en eiendom med nåværende takst på 100.000 kroner.

Dersom de nye takstene blir benyttet for beskatning av fordel ved å bo

i egen bolig, vil det dessuten skje en betydelig skjerpelse av inntektsskatten.

Eiendommene i gamle Bergen kommune har ikke vært taksert siden 1968. Etter kommunesammenslutningen i 1972 ble eiendommen i Fana, Laksevåg, Åsane og Arna også taksert. Takseringen startet i de mest tettbygde strøkene, og tett oppunder 100 prosent av eiendommene i Bergen er nå belagt med eiendomsskatt. Ettersom det har gått mange år mellom takseringen i de forskjellige by-

deler, er det oppstått store forskjeller i den reelle beskatningen.

Side 6

Fe de sekunder var den 38 fots store cabincruiseren fullstendi overtent.

Tiden knapp når båten brenner

Sekundene teller når det brenner i båten. Dette fikk eieren av den 36 fots båten som gikk opp i flammer i helgen, erfare til det fulle. Øyenvitner kan fortelle at etter et kraftig smell ble vrakbiter kastet opp i luften, og 30-fotern var overtent i løpet av et øyeblikk. Takket være tvittenårige Stig Helmers-Olsens raske reaksjon gikk det bra denne gangen.

I fjor ble 60 båter totalskadd av brann, og direktør Jan Erik Thoresen i Norsk Brannvern Forening oppfordrer båteierne til å gå nøye over motoren før de legger utpå.

Side 3

Stig Helmers-Olsen — lysraskt med redningsaksjon.

Rhodos-varme over Vestlandet

Foto: Oddleiv Apneseth

Foto: Jan T. Espedal

Nå konkurrerer Vestlandet med Rhodos og Spania i sommertemperaturer. I går ble det målt opp til 29 varmegrader i vest, og folk strømmet til badestrender, svaberg, parker og andre grøntanlegg for å slikke mest mulig sol. Også i dag

blir det varmt og nydelig vær på Vestlandet. Elisabeth, Trude og Elisa boltrer seg i en av fontenene i Nygårdsparken i sommervarmen i går ettermiddag.

Men det er ikke bare mennesker som svetter akkurat nå. Også en

stakkars Sanktbernhardshund (t.v.) synes det smaker med soft is. Han nøt isen under en et torg-besøk i går.

Side 9

Trygve J.-saken

«Frekt av Brann»

Trygve Johannessens overgang til Brann kan få etterspill. I Vidar raser man over Brann som har kapret seg kapteinen og toppscoreren til sin argeste opprykksrival ved halvspilt serie, uten en gang å ha henvendt seg til Stavanger-laget.

I et intervju i Stavanger Aftenblad i går truet Vidar formannen med å rapportere saken til Norges Fotballforbund.

Sporten, side 13

…med fløte

NORSKE MEIERIER

8.5. A boating accident and the warm weather in the western part of Norway are covered in storie on this front page of *Bergens Tidende*. (Reprinted with permission)

the city. Usually published in two sections, the paper does not place great emphasis on international news but concentrates on events within its coverage area, providing significant coverage of local and national events. This paper employs four-color photographs and clean modular layouts (Fig. 8.5).

Stavanger Aftenblad. This politically independent paper serves the city of Stavanger and the towns near the southwestern tip of Norway. Because of its regional importance, the paper covers news from throughout that region to a greater extent than other Norwegian papers; it is the primary source of foreign information for the area.

In recent years Stavanger has increased in national economic importance because it serves as the center for North Sea oil activities. As a result, the paper has increased its coverage of business and economic news, particularly that related to petroleum, to serve the increased needs for such information by the residents of Stavanger. It has a daily circulation of 60,000.

CHAPTER NINE

Newspapers of Sweden

National Newspapers

Aftonbladet. This brassy Swedish afternoon tabloid is associated with the Social Democratic party and traces its history to the liberal anti-monarchy movement of the 1800s. With a national circulation of about a third of a million copies daily, the paper is the largest voice for the party. As a tabloid, the paper concentrates less on international and economic information than the more serious papers, but it places significant emphasis on covering events inside Sweden and operates a dozen bureaus throughout the country for that purpose.

Content, which is usually displayed in modular layout with large accompanying photographs, emphasizes sports and entertainment, sensational news, and personalities (Fig. 9.1). It also contains a good dose of political news and commentary, which no Swedish paper is without, and it is noted for its feature stories. The paper is not as well organized as nor does it match the journalistic standards of the competing tabloid *Expressen.*

Expressen. The newspaper with the largest overall circulation in Sweden, *Expressen* is an afternoon tabloid published in conjunction with the morning paper *Dagens Nyheter.* A supporter of the Liberal party, the paper has a daily circulation of more than half a million copies and a Sunday circulation of two-thirds of a million copies.

Expressen operates 14 bureaus throughout the country and, like its competitor *Aftonbladet,* pays significant attention to less serious news than the morning papers. Television, cinema, music, and sports are widely covered, as are interesting occurrences that make good feature stories.

This afternoon publication has a popular format that appeals to readers who are less serious than those who read the morning papers; however, *Expressen* is noted for having the best journalistic standards of the afternoon papers and for maintaining consistent quality in writ-

GRUNDAD 1830 AV
LARS JOHAN HIERTA
TEL: 08/788 00 00

VARDAGAR 3:00
SÖNDAGAR 3:50

AFTONBLADET

XXX **FREDAG 15 JUNI VECKA 24, 1984** A160

3:35!
Här finns billigaste bensinen

Här är dagens billigaste bensin i Sverige. Det är ARA-Jets omskrivna mack i Täby

Foto: THOR LINDGREN

Yvonne, 21, vackrast i Sverige
UNG

Stor kalabalik utbryter idag på bensinmarknaden i Sverige. ARA-Jet har sänkt sitt literpris för sommaren med hela 49 öre på ett femtiotal platser i Syd- och Mellansverige. Aftonbladet har listan på den billigaste bensinen till midsommar.

De övriga bolagen tvingas, trots hårda protester mot ARA-Jet, att hänga med i svängarna på de orter där ARA-Jet finns.
– En ansvarslös dumping av priset, säger en arg OK-direktör till Aftonbladet.

SIDAN 6

Pengarna strömmar in till AIK:s kassör Jan Hallberg. Foto: LASSE HEDBERG

Klirr i kassan efter fotbollsfesten

Vilken fotbollsfest det var på Råsunda i går! Segerrusiga tågade AIK-fansen hem efter matchen och 1–0-segern över Hammarby. Men gladast

ändå var AIK-kassören Jan Hallberg. För i hans kassakista klirrade det efter derbyt.

MITTEN och SPORTEN

Det stora bråket (s) SIDAN 7

9.1. This recent edition of the Swedish tabloid *Aftonbladet* celebrates the falling prices of gasoline, the economic effects of a soccer festival, and the return of an international beauty contest winner to Sweden. (Reprinted with permission)

ing and presentation. It employs sectionalization to a greater extent than many Swedish papers and makes good use of graphic devices and stylish layout to highlight sections and stories (Fig. 9.2). Each issue is normally 44–48 pages in length.

Dagens Nyheter. As Sweden's largest morning paper, *Dagens Nyheter* circulates daily to more than a third of a million households throughout the nation and almost half a million on Sundays. The paper is politically independent but its political stance matches that of the centrist parties, as it has since its founding in 1864.

The paper places strong emphasis on political and local events in Stockholm and publishes more than a dozen suburban sections that localize news outside the city (Fig. 9.3). The paper also provides significant national and international coverage, although not to the extent of *Svenska Dagbladet.* A "fat" paper – 72 pages are not uncommon – *Dagens Nyheter* carries the largest amount of advertising of any of the national dailies.

Svenska Dagbladet. The most serious of the Swedish papers, *Svenska Dagbladet* concentrates on national and international news and economic and business information. Considered the most authoritative paper in the country, it is required reading for opinion leaders throughout the country and has a daily circulation of about 210,000.

Normally produced in two sections, the paper features a combination vertical and modular layout that is relatively easy to read, although its use of a large amount of boxed material and rules sometimes diminishes its normally attractive appearance (Fig. 9.4). The paper averages 48 pages, but is planning to purchase equipment that will permit it to double that size.

The paper is owned by a unique corporation formed by the largest companies in Sweden to underwrite losses the paper may sustain and to ensure its survival. In addition, it receives the largest amount of production subsidies available from the government.

Svenska Dagbladet takes a conservative political stance but clearly separates its opinion from reportage. Although independent of any party ties, observers in recent years have noted great similarities between editorial comments and policy decisions of the Moderate party.

EXPRESSEN

Sveriges största dagstidning — den har STING

Stockholm 08/738 30 00, Malmö 040/768 00,
Göteborg 031/80 19 10, Jönköping 036/11 85 70.

FREDAGEN DEN 15 JUNI

1984 nummer 160
från starten 13991

VARDAGAR 3:—
SÖNDAGAR 3:50

Expressen träffade LO-chefen i Schweiz

NY ATTACK MOT FELDT

Klyftan mellan LO-chefen Stig Malm och finansministern Kjell-Olof Feldt vidgas.

Expressen träffade Stig Malm i Genève i går. Då sa LO-chefen:

— Det känns som om några regeringsmedlemmar försöker forma om partiets politik. För dem är lösningen på alla problem större löneskillnader.

Kängan mot Kjell-Olof Feldt är klart markerad. Feldt har talat sig varm för vikten av att kunna hålla skillnad i löner.

□ MITTEN

Foto: GÖRAN ÅRNBÄCK

Derby-hjälten: Mitt härliga mål

■ ■ Vilken insats, Thomas!

AIKs målhjälte Thomas Andersson mådde utmärkt i morse när han studerade målbilderna från derbymatchen mot Hammarby.

— Det känns fantastiskt, summerar Thomas känslorna efter sin insats.

Exproffset köptes från Vasalund till AIK för att bli allsvensk skyttekung. Efter sex matcher utan en enda fullträff visade han i går vad han går för när han är som bäst.

SPORTEN OCH SIDAN 9

Foto: JAN DELDEN

□ LO-chefen Stig Malm går i Genève och ler åt Feldts uppmaning att Malm borde sköta sitt jobb i stället för att klandra finansministern.

Geting-guiden med stans alla nöjen

9.2. The afternoon tabloid *Expressen* was established after the Second World War by the morning paper *Dagens Nyheter*. This recent issue relates an attack on the policy statements of the minister of finance by the head of the chief labor organization in the nation. (Reprinted with permission)

9.3. A strike by ore workers and a major fire are covered on the front page of this issue of Da[gens] Nyheter. (Reprinted with permission)

SVENSKA DAGBLADET

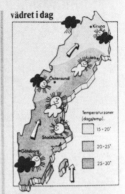

9.4. Unusually warm weather and a visit by the esoteric music group Urban Sax are covered on the front page of this edition of *Svenska Dagbladet*. (Reprinted with permission)

Regional Newspapers

Arbetet. This major Social Democratic paper, established in Malmö in 1887, has a circulation of more than 100,000 throughout southern Sweden and operates 16 bureaus mostly in the area it serves. It is the primary vehicle for party views in the south.

The paper is the primary source of national and international news for most of its readers and has maintained a relatively stable circulation in recent years despite competition by *Sydsvenska Dagbladet* and *Kvällsposten.*

Göteborgs-Posten. This major paper is published in Göteborg on Sweden's western coast and usually consists of 36 pages in two sections. The style of this paper is much more closely related to Danish and Norwegian counterparts than Swedish papers when it comes to layout and presentation; the first page usually includes some small advertisements (Fig. 9.5). Such advertisements usually are not found on the front pages of the better Swedish papers although they are common in the papers of Sweden's two neighbors to the west.

Göteborgs-Posten provides a significant amount of international and national news, as well as provincial and regional information in a modified modular layout, which tends to appear as many short news stories. Because of its size (about 285,000 circulation) and wide distribution in the western part of the country, it is the primary paper for many readers.

Sydsvenska Dagbladet. This provincial paper is published in Malmö and provides a blend of local, national, and international news; the local section is strong and there is also a significant amount of economic and business news. The paper normally employs a modular layout (Fig. 9.6). *Sydsvenska Dagbladet* has a daily circulation of about 115,000 and 150,000 on Sundays.

Although independent of political parties, the editorial stances clearly are similar to those of the bourgeois centrist parties.

Kvällsposten. This independent paper, which often supports Liberal party views, operates out of the southern city Malmö and has bureaus in nine cities. The circulation is about 110,000, which is competitive with *Sydsvenska Dagbladet* and *Arbetet* in the region that includes the cities of Malmö, Helsingborg, Trelleborg, Lund, and Kristianstad.

9.5. This issue of *Göteborgs-Posten* focuses readers' attention on the problems caused by beer consumption at soccer matches and the effects of exchange rates on the national economy. (Reprinted with permission)

Vädret: Askskurar
Dagens namn: Petrus
Soleu upp. 4.29, ned 21.52

SYDSVENSKA DAGBLADET
SNÄLLPOSTEN.

174   Lösnr Vardagar 3:—. Söndagar 3:25.   Tel 040-93 60 00 Tel-annonser 93 44 00 GRUNDAD 1848   Vecka 26.   Fredagen den 29 juni 1984

Prisstoppet bort
Räntan höjs

Ränteläget utomlands och den allt stridare strömmen av valuta ur landet, 4,4 miljarder kr sedan mitten av april, tvingade riksbanken att höja diskontot med en procentenhet och straffräntan med två procentenheter.

Höjningarna innebär en ordentlig åtstramning av kreditmarknaden. Det blir inte svårare att låna pengar, bara dyrare.

Regeringen slog till samtidigt och meddelade överraskande att man slopar prisstoppet från den 1 juli. Uppenbarligen är det Rosenbadsmötet med arbetsmarknadens parter som utlöst beslutet. Regeringen tror sig nu ha kontroll över både löner och inflation.

Slopandet av prisstoppet innebär också att den påbörjade taxströken upphör. Anledningen till den var att arbetsgivarna inte fick kompensera sig för lönehöjningen med höjda priser.

Sidorna 12—13

Dyrare att äta
Dyrare att bo

Höjningen av diskontot och slopandet av prisstoppet berör alla.

Villagarnas lån blir dyrare. Hyrorna stiger även om det tar en tid innan räntehöjningen slår igenom.

Matpriserna höjs. Detaljhandeln förvarnar om höjningar inom kort, livsmedel beräknas gå upp 1 proc.

Avbetalningsköp blir dyrare. Det slår mot bilhandeln som får avstanna att sälja.

Kontraderna för kreditkort går upp.

De stora väruarna blir bankspararna. Med av alla tjänar de som allemansuparar. 15,73 procents ränta. Skattefritt.

Samma näsa?
Videofilm hjälper polisen i jakten efter rånaren

Det här är en "hyst" bild ur videofilmen från den norska banken, som rikskriminalen visade för polisen och nämnderna. Rånaren, som polisen misstänker, är Alexander Matus, tar fram revolvern ur bältskran och rusar fram... till kassoriskan bakom disken

Jämför näsorna på de här båda männen. Den som sitter på den videofilmade bankrånaren i Norge är ganska lik Alexander Matus, storrånaren som rymde från Kumla där han avtjänade åtta års fängelse för åtta rån i Sydsverige...

Videofilmen som togs av den norska bankkameran stärker polisens misstankar mot samme rymmaren Matus, som tros vara inblandad i 3—4 bankrån i maj och juni.

Sydsvenskan var med när tre man från rikskriminalen visade polisen och nämndens i Alehult den unika videofilmen som togs i den norska banken i förra veckan.

I dag är det Malmöpolisens tur att titta på videofilmen.

Sidan 16

Sidan 2
Sidan 2

S lovar daghem åt alla

Efter 1990 ska alla barn som är över ett och ett halvt år få plats på daghem. Det lovar socialdemokraterna i sitt idé- och framtidsprogram som lades fram på torsdagen.

I programmet föreslår socialdemokraterna en utbyggnad av den kommunala barnomsorgen med tre till fyra miljarder kronor.

Vi har råd med ett fåtal reformer i framtiden och barnomsorgen är en av dessa, sade vice statsminister Ingvar Carlsson när han presenterade programmet.

Vi satsar på barnomsorgen lägger man stor vikt vid sysselsättningen och slår fast att svenska företag måste behålla sin konkurrenskraft gentemot utlandet för att full sysselsättning ska bli verklighet. En annan viktig förutsättning är att det svenska budgetunderskottet ska fortsätta att minska.

Sidan 2

M kräver 70 proc skattetak

Moderata samlingspartiet kräver ett marginalskattetak på 40 procent för normalinkomster och 70 procent för högre löner.

I det handlingsprogram för framtiden som presenterades på torsdagen föreslår moderaterna en rad skattesänkningar. Bland annat bör skattreskalan inflationsskyddas och på lång sikt vill moderaterna helt avskaffa statlig inkomstskatt för normalinkomsttagare.

När partiledaren Ulf Adelsohn presenterade handlingsprogrammet tog han tillfället i akt att angripa socialdemokraternas förslag om daghemsplats åt alla småbarn till 1990.

Det är en reform som skulle kosta 12 miljarder och den ger ingen valfrihet, sade han.

Valfrihet förutsätter att enskild barnomsorg ska finnas på samma villkor som den kommunala.

Sidan 2

Skandalscenen byggs om

För ett par veckor sedan invigdes nya scenen i Folkets park i Malmö. Redan nu står det klart att den måste byggas om.

När Herreys uppträdde i onsdags kväll var det många i publiken som inte såg någonting.

I mitten antogligen förhättra lutningen framför själva scenen, säger Bo Andersson, ordförande i Folkets parks styrelse. Det kan bli aktuellt att höja hela scenbyggnaden.

Sidan 17

Det fanns personer som klättrade upp i lyktstolpar och fick inte få se gamt av Herreys när de gästade Folkets park i veckan. Det var enda sättet att kunna se något

---

Hjärtläkaren avvisar kritiken

— Dödsbegreppet har ingenting med hjärttransplantation att göra. Här finns en behandlingsform för människor som annars är räddningslöst förlorade.

— Vissa uttalanden vittnar om okunnighet.

Det säger överläkare Göran Wilhaire-Olsson på Sahlgrenska sjukhuset i Göteborg och avvisar därmed den kritik som han och hans kolleger fått för sin insats med den första svenska hjärttransplantationen.

Han understryker att läkarna sett till patientens bästa.

Sidan 9

Tolv semesterveckor eller fem?

En lärare med lön från staten kan njuta av tio veckors semester varje år. Ett justitieråd får regeringsråd är 12. Längst ner på semesterskalan hamnar arbetare i olika yrkeskategorier. Än så länge har de fem veckors semester om året.

LO-tjänstemän, läkare och tandläkare får som regel ut tio veckors ledighet per år. Bankdirektörer och handelsresanden har rätt till sex och en halv. Kommunalt anställda som fyllt femtio får ta ut sju veckor och de spriker ut dem under året.

Skådespelare och musiker på Dramaten och Operan har tolv veckor.

Sidan 5

Längre semester LO-krav

Fyra dagars extra semester. Det kan bli resultatet av höstens avtalsförhandlingar på LO-området.

LO tar för första gången upp frågan om längre semester som ett huvudkrav efter att alla andra grupper har lyckats utvidga sin semester till mellan sex och tolv år.

— Om det inte går att förlänga semestern genom förhandlingar får man diskutera en översyn av lagstiftningen, säger Stig Malm.

1978 års semesterlag ger alla rätt till fem veckors semester, men i praktiken är det bara LO-medlemmarna som inte har lyck...

ta få ut några extra dagar i sina avtal. LO har i första hand koncentrerat sig på att höja semesterersättningen.

— Men betalning och ledighet är två skilda saker vill helt...

säger Lars Sundberg, jurist på LO.

Han får stöd av en färsk undersökning från Statistiska centralbyrån som visar att omkring en tredjedel svenskar inte har råd att åka någonstans på sin semester.

Av dessa är 635 000 LO-medlemmar

Sidan 12—13

31 proc lön lyft för Pal

Höjd månadslön och kronor kan statsminister Palme glädja sig åt. Hans månadslön höjdes från 21 000 och skall gälla retroaktivt från skiftet och börjar fr o m den 1 juli. Hela 1985 ut blir det nya höjningen på 22 000 kronor om året.

Wilander utslagen

Mats Wilander gjorde inget match i Wimbledon-dagen, men fick ändå komma i tredje omgångens ut. Australiern Pat Cash vann med 3—1 i set och det var längd i den första. Sundström är kvar, men nödrop.

7 dagar läggs ner

20 000 prenumeranter inne. Svenska Dagbladets tidning 7 dagar kommer att sitta nummer på fredag vecka. Tidningen har Svenska Dagbladet ut.

Castro släpper 26 fångar

Den amerikanske kandidaten Jesse Jackson lyckades övertala Fidel Castro att släppa 26 politiska fångar på Kuba.

Hysch hysch kring Roskilde

Roskildefestivalen är här inte valt att sitta villkor det bokat och det gäller både och både stjärnor allt dylika lösare.   Men Sydsvenskan dog presentera helt att granskat med tiden och sina lösare.

Victorias val avslöjas idag

Kronprinsessan Victorias kekjpis, talper "Chili", var samma dress ögfkndet var svenskan i går publicerade bilder av kungafamiljen på den. Vad heter resen, inte alla som mugde. Svaret det därtill, återfinns idag på sidan

OS-guld till Malmö

Malmö har redan klart en OS-guld. Det har skytten Åskult fixat sig. Han ska sin modligen Malmös ordls och denna olympiaveteran, en glänsande handikapp-OS i York.

Sparten

Kultur
Utrikes
Familj
Oss emellan
Ordet
Näringsliv 14-18

DEL 2
Malmö
Mellanskåne
Lund 14
Skåne 21
Sport
Sommarnöjen 23
Radio/TV

9.6. Discussion about the possibility of price freezes and the capture of a bank robber are fea on this front page of *Sydsvenska Dagbladet*. (Reprinted with permission)

Nerikes Allehanda. About halfway between the east and west coast of Sweden, in the heart of the agricultural and lake region, is the city of Örebro where *Nerikes Allehanda* is published. Like other provincial papers, this paper has a long history of concentrating on news directly affecting the residents of its region. With a circulation of 66,000 and more than a dozen bureaus in smaller cities, the paper continues to play an important role in meeting the informational needs of area residents. The paper supports the Liberal party.

Nya Wermlands-Tidningen. Published in Karlstad in the lake country of Sweden, this politically moderate paper has served the agrarian-oriented population of the region since 1836. It operates 17 bureaus, mostly in small towns in its market area, and is the primary newspaper for the region around Vänern, the largest lake in Sweden. *Nya Wermlands-Tidningen* has a daily circulation of about 75,000.

Östgöta Correspondenten. This provincial paper with a circulation of 66,000 is published in Linköping near the eastern coast of the country and serves the residents of the area with 12 bureaus scattered throughout the region. Associated with the Conservative party, *Östgöta Correspondenten* faces competition from several smaller papers in Linköping that represent the points of view of the Center and Liberal parties.

Västmanlands Lans Tidning. Published in Västerås, this paper with a circulation of 57,000 has served the region since 1831. Associated with the Liberal party, this paper serves the agricultural and lake region surrounding the city with nine bureaus in smaller towns for which it provides coverage.

NOTES

Chapter One

1. Ingvar Andersson and Jörgen Weibull, *Swedish History in Brief* (Stockholm, 1973), 10.
2. John C. Griffiths, *Modern Iceland* (New York, 1969), 20–24.
3. Ibid., 37–38; Knut Gjerset, *History of Iceland* (New York, 1925), 349; and Hjalmar Lindroth, *Iceland: A Land of Contrasts* (Princeton, N.J., 1937), 206.
4. Anthony Smith, *The Newspaper: An International History* (London, 1979), 26.
5. Andrew A. Stromberg, *A History of Sweden* (New York, 1931; 1969), 560.
6. Ibid., 25.
7. Edwin Emery, *The Press and America: An Interpretative History of the Mass Media,* 3d ed. (Englewood Cliffs, N.J., 1972), 2. See also Stig Hadenius and Lennart Weibull, *Massmedier* (Stockholm, 1978), 33.
8. Stromberg, *A History of Sweden,* 380–381.
9. Svend Thorsen, *Newspapers in Denmark* (Copenhagen, 1953), 7.
10. Annamari Mäkinen, How the Finnish Press Covers the World: A Content Analysis of the Foreign News in Keskisoumalainen (M.A. thesis, Univ. of Missouri School of Journalism, 1982), 33.
11. John C. Merrill, C. R. Bryan, and M. Alisky, *The Foreign Press: A Survey of the World's Journalism* (Baton Rouge, La., 1970), 82.
12. Thorsen, *Newspapers in Denmark,* 8.
13. B. J. Hovde, *The Scandinavian Countries, 1720–1865: The Rise of the Middle Class* (Boston, 1943), 1:130.
14. A. Y. Pers, *The Swedish Press* (Stockholm, 1963), 3.
15. Thorsen, *Newspapers in Denmark,* 8.
16. Mäkinen, How the Finnish Press, 34.
17. Sorren Bendrick and Paul Frisch, *Tidningen* (Stockholm, 1965), 45.
18. Svennik Høyer, "The Political Economy of the Norwegian Press," *Scandinavian Political Studies* 3(1968):86.
19. Gjerset, *History of Iceland,* 349.
20. Hovde, *Scandinavian Countries,* 1:210.
21. T. K. Derry, *A History of Scandinavia: Norway, Sweden, Denmark, Finland, and Iceland* (Minneapolis, 1979), 199.
22. S. T. Sheppard, "In Memoriam: William Moward Russell. The Genesis of

a Profession," *The United Service Magazine* (March 1907):570.

23. Halvdan Koht and Sigmund Skard, *The Voice of Norway* (New York, 1944), 67.
24. *Scandinavia Past and Present*, 3 vols. (Arnkrone, Denmark, 1959), 3:311.
25. Hovde, *Scandinavian Countries*, 2:541.
26. Thorsen, *Newspapers in Denmark*, 8.
27. Hovde, *Scandinavian Countries*, 2:541–42.
28. Stromberg, *History of Sweden*, 642.
29. Ibid., 643.
30. Hovde, *Scandinavian Countries*, 2:523.
31. Ibid., 557.
32. *Scandinavia Past and Present*, 3:311.
33. Høyer, "Political Economy," 86–88.
34. Thorsen, *Newspapers in Denmark*, 34.
35. Mäkinen, How the Finnish Press, 34–35.
36. Merrill et al., *Foreign Press: Survey*, 82.
37. Mäkinen, How the Finnish Press, 35.
38. Ibid.
39. Thorsen, *Newspapers in Denmark*, 9.
40. Ibid., 14.
41. Jóhannes Nordal and Vladimar Kristinsson, *Iceland 1966* (Reykjavik, 1967), 342.
42. Gjerset, *History of Iceland*, 399.
43. Jan-Otto Modig, "The Scandinavian News Agencies," *Gazette* 9(1963):143–44.
44. Ibid., 144–45.
45. *Scandinavia Past and Present*, 3:306.
46. Ibid.
47. Thorsen, *Newspapers in Denmark*, 20.
48. Ibid.
49. Karl Erik Gustafsson and Stig Hadenius, *Swedish Press Policy* (Stockholm, 1976), 32–33.
50. Mäkinen, How the Finnish Press, 35–36.
51. Ibid.
52. Merrill et al., *Foreign Press: Survey*, 82.
53. Smith, *The Newspaper: An International History*, 105.
54. John Logue and Gerd Callesen, *Social-Demokraten and Internationalism: The Copenhagen Social Democratic Newspaper's Coverage of International Labor Affairs, 1871–1958* (Göteborg, Sweden, 1979), 9.
55. Thorsen, *Newspapers in Denmark*, 19–20.
56. Merrill et al., *Foreign Press: Survey*, 77.
57. Thorsen, *Newspapers in Denmark*, 16–18.
58. Pentti Salmelin, "The Transition of the Finnish Workers' Papers to the Social Democratic Press," *Scandinavian Political Studies* 3(1968):73.
59. *Scandinavia Past and Present*, 3:306.
60. Thorsen, *Newspapers in Denmark*, 27.

61. *Scandinavia Past and Present,* 3:311.
62. Lindroth, *Iceland: A Land of Contrasts,* 206.
63. Griffiths, *Modern Iceland,* 195.
64. Salmelin, "Transition," 73, 74–75, 82.
65. Merrill et al., *Foreign Press: Survey,* 82.
66. Stig Hadenius, "Society and the Mass Media in Sweden," *Sweden Now* 29(April 1974):2.
67. Gustafsson and Hadenius, *Swedish Press Policy,* 33–34.
68. Thorsen, *Newspapers in Denmark,* 35.
69. Ibid., 29.
70. Salmelin, "Transition," 77.
71. Ibid., 80
72. Gustafsson and Hadenius, *Swedish Press Policy,* 35.
73. *Europa Year Book 1975,* (London, 1975), 1:631.
74. Stig Hadenius, Jan-Olof Sveveborg and Lennart Weibull, "The Social Democratic Press and Newspaper Policy in Sweden, 1899–1909," *Scandinavian Political Studies* 3(1968):52.
75. Lars Furhoff, "Some Reflections on Newspaper Concentration," *Scandinavian Economic History Review* 21(1973):16.
76. Hadenius, "Society," 2.
77. Pertti Hemánus, "Development Trends in the Scandinavian Press," *Gazette* 17(1971):1.
78. D. G. Kirby, *Finland in the Twentieth Century* (London, 1979), 86.
79. *Europa Year Book,* 1:599.
80. William L. Shirer, *The Challenge of Scandinavia: Norway, Sweden, Denmark, and Finland in Our Time* (Boston, 1955), 210.
81. Merrill et al., *Foreign Press: Survey,* 210. See also T. K. Derry, *A History of Norway, 1814–1972* (Oxford, 1973), 394.
82. John O. Thomas, *The Giant Killers: The Danish Resistance Movement, 1940–1945* (London, 1975), 81.
83. Thorsen, *Newspapers in Denmark,* 92–95.
84. Thomas, *Giant Killers,* 82.
85. Thorsen, *Newspapers in Denmark,* 90–91.
86. John Danstrup, *A History of Denmark,* 2d ed. (Copenhagen, 1949).
87. Richard Petrow, *The Bitter Years: The Invasion and Occupation of Denmark and Norway, April 1940–May 1945* (New York, 1974), 174–75.
88. Niels Thomsen, "The Danish Political Press," *Scandinavian Political Studies* 3(1968):147.
89. Yrjo Ahmavaara, Sirkka Minkkinen, Kaarle Nordenstreng, Max Rand, and Margaretha Starck, *Joukkotiedotus Yhteiskunnassa. Johdatus Joukkotiedotuskasvatukseen* (Helsinki, 1971), 91.
90. Mäkinen, How the Finnish Press, 37.
91. Frederick Fleisher, "The Swedish Press Subsidy Plan and the Collapse of the *Stockholms-Tidningen,*" *Gazette* 12(1966):179–86.
92. Hemánus, "Development Trends," 3–4.
93. Robert G. Picard, State Aid and the Press: A Case Study of Newspapers

in Two Swedish Cities, (M.A. thesis, California State Univ., Fullerton, 1979), 69–79.

94. Robert G. Picard, "State Press Aid During the Era of Economic Readjustment: A Case Study of Scandinavian Nations," *European Studies Journal* 3(1986):1–8.

Chapter Two

1. Harold D. Lasswell, "The Structure and Function of Communication in Society," in *The Process and Effects of Mass Communication*, rev. ed., ed. W. Scramm and D. F. Roberts (Urbana, Ill., 1971):98–99; C. Wright, *Mass Communication: A Sociological Perspective* (New York, 1959).
2. John C. Merrill, C. R. Bryan, and M. Alisky, *The Foreign Press: A Survey of the World's Journalism* (Baton Rouge, La., 1970), 114.
3. *Scandinavia Past and Present,* 3 vols. (Arnkrone, Denmark, 1959), 3:312.
4. David Jenkins, *Sweden and the Price of Progress* (New York, 1968), 262.
5. John L. Irwin, *The Finns and the Lapps* (New York, 1973), 159.
6. John C. Griffiths, *Modern Iceland* (New York, 1969), 168.
7. Björn Fjæstad and P. G. Homlöv, "Swedish Newsmen's Views on the Role of the Press," *Studier in Ekonomisk Psykologi* 87(1975):8.
8. Lars Furhoff, Lennart Jonsson, and Lennart Nilsson, *Communication Policies in Sweden* (Paris, 1974), 17.
9. Hans Dahl, "The Press, Most National of Media: A Report from Norway," in *Newspapers and Democracy,* ed. Anthony Smith (Cambridge, Mass., 1980), 96.
10. Svennik Høyer, Kjell Olav, Mathisen Helge Ostbye, and Anita Werner, *Maktutredningen: Rapporten om massmedier* (Oslo, 1982), NOU 1982:30.
11. Cited in mimeographed document, "The Press in Norway," Royal Norwegian Ministry of Foreign Affairs (Sept. 1983), 152:12–13.
12. J. B. Board, Jr., *The Government and Politics of Sweden* (Boston, 1970), 65.
13. Niels Thomsen, *Dagbladskonkurrencen, 1870–1970* (Copenhagen, 1972), English summary, 5.
14. Niels Thomsen, "The Danish Political Press," *Scandinavian Political Studies* 3(1968):160.
15. Jorgën Westerståhl and Carl-Gunnar Janson, "Politisk Press – Political Press," *Göteborgs Universitets Årsskrift* 64, no. 10(1958):98.
16. Annamari Mäkinen, How the Finnish Press Covers the World: A Content Analysis of the Foreign News in Keskisoumalainen (M.A. thesis, Univ. of Missouri, 1982), 43–44.
17. "World Press Freedom Review: Finland," *IPI Report* 31(December 1982):8.
18. Board, Jr., *Government and Politics,* 69.
19. Merrill et al., *Foreign Press: Survey* 75.
20. *Scandinavia Past and Present,* 3:312.

21. Svend Thorsen, *Newspapers in Denmark* (Copenhagen, 1953), 115.
22. UNESCO, *World Communications* (Paris, 1975), 375.
23. Bengt-Ove Birgersson, "Municipal Politics in the Swedish Press," *Scandinavian Political Studies* 3(1968):205.

Chapter Three

1. Carter R. Bryan, "Enlightenment of the People Without Hindrance: The Swedish Press Law of 1766," *Journalism Quarterly* 37(Summer 1960):431.
2. J. B. Board, Jr., *The Government and Politics of Sweden* (Boston, 1970), 36.
3. *Scandinavia Past and Present*, 3 vols. (Arnkrone, Denmark, 1959), 3:305.
4. *World Press Encyclopedia*, s. v. "Denmark," 1:291.
5. John C. Griffiths, *Modern Iceland* (New York, 1969), 195.
6. *World Press Encyclopedia*, s. v. "Norway," 2:703.
7. Raymond R. Nixon, "Freedom in the World's Press: A Fresh Reappraisal with Data," *Journalism Quarterly* 42(Winter 1965):3–14.
8. Ralph L. Lowenstein, Measuring World Press Freedom as a Political Indicator (Ph.D. diss., Univ. of Missouri, 1967).
9. Ibid., 48.
10. Lars Furhoff, Lennart Jönsson, and Lennart Nilsson, *Communication Policies in Sweden* (Paris, 1974).
11. Robert G. Picard, *The Press and the Decline of Democracy: The Democratic Socialist Response in Public Policy* (Westport, Conn., 1985), 97–130.
12. Ruth Link, "Open Government," *Sweden Now* 5(1977):42.
13. Lennart Groll, "Press Ombudsman: Mediator and Prosecutor," *IPI Report* (Oct. 1976):7.
14. Thorsten Cars, "How the Swedish Press Deals with Libel," *St. Louis Journalism Review* (January 1985):15.

Chapter Four

1. Jörgen Westerståhl and Carl-Gunnar Janson study, cited in R. F. Tomasson, *Sweden: Prototype of Modern Society* (New York, 1972), 211.
2. Olof Hultén, *Mass Media and State Support in Sweden* (Stockholm, 1979), 9.
3. Pertti Hemánus, "Development Trends in the Scandinavian Press," *Gazette* 17, 1(1971), 3.
4. Karl Erik Gustafsson and Stig Hadenius, *Swedish Press Policy* (Stockholm, 1976), 12.
5. Anthony Smith, "Subsidies and the Press in Europe," *Political and Economic Planning* 569(1977):2.

6. John Hohenberg, *Free Press/Free People* (New York, 1971), 409.

7. Lars Furhoff, "Some Reflections on Newspaper Concentration," *Scandinavian Economic History Review* 21(1973):9.

8. Karl Erik Gustafsson, "The Circulation Spiral and the Principle of Household Coverage," *Scandinavian Economic History Review* 26(1978): 1–2.

9. Ibid., 3.

10. Robert G. Picard, "Levels of State Intervention in the Western Press," *Mass Comm Review* 11(Winter/Spring 1984):27–35.

BIBLIOGRAPHY

Books

Ahmavarra, Yrjo, Surkka Minkkinen, Kaarle Nordenstreng, Max Rand, and Margaretha Starck. *Joukkoriedotus Yhteiskunnassa. Johdatus Joukkotiedotuskasvatukssen.* Helsinki: private publisher, 1971.

Anderson, Robert T. *Denmark: Success of a Developing Nation.* Cambridge, Mass.: Schenkman, 1975.

Andersson, Ingvar. *A History of Sweden.* New York: Praeger, 1968.

Andersson, Ingvar, and Jörgen Weibull. *Swedish History in Brief.* Stockholm: Swedish Institute, 1973.

Andrén, Nils. *Modern Swedish Government.* Stockholm: Almqvist and Wiksell, 1968.

Bendrick, Sorren, and Paul Frisch. *Tidningen.* Stockholm: Bonniers, 1965.

Board, J. B., Jr. *The Government and Politics of Sweden.* Boston: Houghton-Mifflin, 1970.

Butler, Ewan. *The Horizon Concise History of Scandinavia.* New York: American Heritage Publishing Co., 1973.

Christensen, Cai F., and Ulf Kjaer-Hansen. *Trends in Danish Advertising Expenditures 1958-78.* Copenhagen: Copenhagen School of Economics and Business Administration, 1981.

Dahl, Folke, ed. *The Birth of the European Press.* Stockholm: Royal Library, 1960.

Dahl, Hans. "The Press, Most National of Media." In *Newspapers and Democracy,* ed. Anthony Smith. Cambridge: MIT Press, 1980.

Danstrup, John. *A History of Denmark.* 2d ed. Copenhagen: Wivels Forlag, 1949.

Derry, T. K. *A Short History of Norway.* Westport, Conn.: Greenwood Press, 1968.

_____. *A History of Modern Norway, 1814-1972.* Oxford: Clarendon Press, 1973.

_____. *A History of Scandinavia: Norway, Sweden, Denmark, Finland, and Iceland.* Minneapolis: Univ. of Minnesota Press, 1979.

Emery, Edwin. *The Press and America: An Interpretative History of the Mass Media.* 3d. ed. Englewood Cliffs, N.J.: Prentice Hall, 1972.

Europa Year Book 1975. 2 vols. London: Europa Publications, 1975.

141

Fjæstad, Björn, and P. G. Holmlöv. *Dagspressen och Samhallët.* Stockholm: Norstedts Tryckeri, 1977.

Furhoff, Lars, and Hans Hederberg. *Dagspressen i Sverige.* 2d ed. Stockholm: Aldus/Bonniers, 1968.

Furhoff, Lars, Lennart Jonsson, and Lennart Nilsson. *Communication Policies in Sweden.* Paris: UNESCO Press, 1974.

Gjerset, Knut. *History of Iceland.* New York: Macmillan, 1925.

Griffiths, John C. *Modern Iceland.* New York: Praeger, 1969.

Gustafsson, Karl Erik, and Stig Hadenius. *Swedish Press Policy.* Stockholm: Swedish Institute, 1976.

Hadenius, Stig, and Lennart Weibull. *Massmedier.* Stockholm: Bonniers, 1978.

Hadenius, Stig, Jan-Olof Sveveborg, and Lennart Weibull. *Partipress: Socialdemokratisk och Presspolitik 1910-1920.* Halmstad, Sweden: Raben and Sjorgren, 1970.

Hohenberg, John. *Free Press/Free People.* New York: Columbia Univ. Press, 1971.

Hovde, B. J. *The Scandinavian Countries, 1720-1865: The Rise of the Middle Class.* 2 vols. Boston: Chapman and Grimes, 1943.

Hultén, Olof. *Mass Media and State Support in Sweden.* Stockholm: Swedish Institute, 1979.

Huntford, Roland. *The New Totalitarians.* New York: Stein and Day, 1972.

Irwin, John L. *The Finns and the Lapps.* New York: Praeger, 1973.

Jakobson, Max. *Finland Survived.* Helsinki: Otavia, 1984.

Jenkins, David. *Sweden and the Price of Progress.* New York: Coward-McCann, 1968.

Kihlberg, Leif. *I Annonsernas Spegel.* Stockholm: Bonniers, 1974.

Kirby, D. G. *Finland in the Twentieth Century.* London: Hurst, 1979.

Koblik, Steven, ed. *Sweden's Development from Poverty to Affluence, 1750-1970.* Minneapolis: Univ. of Minnesota Press, 1975.

Koht, Halvdan, and Sigmund Skard. *The Voice of Norway.* New York: Columbia Univ. Press, 1949.

Lasswell, Harold D. "The Structure and Function of Communication in Society." In *The Process and Effects of Mass Communication.* Rev. ed., ed. W. Scramm and D. F. Roberts. Urbana: Univ. of Illinois Press, 1971.

Lauwerys, Joseph A., ed. *Scandinavian Democracy.* Copenhagen: American-Scandinavian Foundation, 1958.

Lindroth, Hjalmar. *Iceland: A Land of Contrasts.* Princeton, N.J.: Princeton Univ. Press, 1937.

Logue, John, and Gerd Calleson. *Social-Demokraten and Internationalism: The Copenhagen Social Democratic Newspaper's Coverage of International Labor Affairs, 1871-1958.* Göteborg, Sweden: Univ. of Göteborg, 1979.

Merrill, John C. *A Handbook of the Foreign Press.* Baton Rouge: Louisiana State Univ. Press, 1959.

_____. *The Elite Press: Great Newspapers of the World.* New York: Pitman, 1968.

Merrill, John C., and Harold A. Fisher. *The World's Great Dailies: Profiles of 50 Newspapers.* New York: Hastings House, 1980.

Merrill, John C., Carter R. Bryan, and Marvin Alisky. *The Foreign Press.* Baton Rouge: Louisiana State Univ. Press, 1964.

_____. *The Foreign Press: A Survey of the World's Journalism.* Baton Rouge: Louisiana State Univ. Press, 1970.

Moberg, Vilhelm. *A History of the Swedish People: From Prehistory to the Renaissance.* New York: Pantheon, 1972.

Nordal, Jóhannes, and Vladimar Kristinsson. *Iceland 1966.* Reykjavik: Iceland Seolabanki Island, 1967.

Oakley, Stewart. *A Short History of Sweden.* New York: Praeger, 1966.

Olson, Kenneth E. *The History Makers: The Press of Europe from Its Beginning through 1965.* Baton Rouge: Louisiana State Univ. Press, 1966.

Pers, A. Y. *Newspapers in Sweden.* Stockholm: Swedish Institute, 1963.

Petrow, Richard. *The Bitter Years: The Invasion and Occupation of Denmark and Norway, April 1940–May 1945.* New York: Morrow, 1974.

Picard, Robert G. *The Press and the Decline of Democracy: The Democratic Socialist Response in Public Policy.* Westport, Conn.: Greenwood Press, 1985.

Präntare, Bo. *Presstöd och Presspolitik.* Stockholm: Pressbyrå Foretagen, 1978.

Scandinavia Past and Present. 3 vols. Arnkrone, Denmark: Edvard Henriksen, 1959.

Scobbie, Irene. *Sweden.* London: Benn, 1972.

Shirer, William L. *The Challenge of Scandinavia.* Boston: Little, Brown and Co., 1955.

Smith, Anthony. *The Newspaper: An International History.* London: Thames and Hudson, 1979.

Stromberg, Andrew A. *A History of Sweden.* New York: Macmillan, 1931; New York: Kraus Reprint Co., 1969.

Thomas, John O. *The Giant Killers: The Danish Resistance Movement, 1940–1945.* London: Joseph, 1975.

Thomsen, Niels. *Dagbladskonkurrencen 1870–1970.* Copenhagen: GEC Gads Forlag, 1972.

Thorsen, Svend. *Newspapers in Denmark.* Copenhagen: Det Danske Selskab, 1953.

Tomasson, Richard F. *Sweden: Prototype of Modern Society.* New York: Random House, 1970.

_____. *Iceland: The First New Society.* Minneapolis: Univ. of Minnesota Press, 1980.

Weibull, Lennart. *Tidningsläsning: Sverige.* Stockholm: Liberförlag, 1983.

World Press Encyclopedia. S.v. "Denmark," 1:291. New York: Facts on File, 1982.

_____. S.v. "Norway," 2:703. New York: Facts on File, 1982.

Wright, C. *Mass Communication: A Sociological Perspective.* New York: Random House, 1959.

Articles

"A Guide to Norwegian Mass Media Statistics." *Scandinavian Political Studies* 4(1969):204-23.

Andrén, Nils. "Sweden: State Support for Political Parties." *Scandinavian Political Studies* 3(1968):221-29.

Benson, Ivan. "Neutrality and Press Freedom in Sweden." *Journalism Quarterly* 17(March 1940):11-14.

Bermann, Tamar, and Bjorg Aase Sørensen. "Newspaper Environments: Journalists' Working Conditions in Norway." *NORDICOM Review* 1(1982):10-12.

Birgersson, Bengt-Ove. "Municipal Politics in the Swedish Press." *Scandinavian Political Studies* 3(1968):186-217.

Bryan, Carter R. "Enlightenment of the People without Hindrance: The Swedish Press Law of 1766." *Journalism Quarterly* 37(Summer 1960):431-34.

Cars, Thorsten. "How the Swedish Press Deals with Libel." *St. Louis Journalism Review* (January 1985):15.

_____. "The Structure of the Swedish Daily Press." *Swedish Journal of Economics* 77(1975):318-28.

Engwall, Lars. "Newspaper Concentration: A Case for Theories of Oligopoly." *Scandinavian Economic History Review* 29(Fall 1981):145 54.

Fields, Donald. "Finland: How Much Self-Censorship Remains?" *Index on Censorship* 2(1982):15-19.

Fjæstad, Björn, and P. G. Holmlöv. "Swedish Newsmen's Views on the Role of the Press." *Studier i Ekonomisk Psykologi* 87(1975):1-60.

Fleisher, Frederick. "The Swedish Press Subsidy Plan and the Collapse of the *Stockholms-Tidningen*." *Gazette* 12(1966).

"Freedom of the Press and Other Media in Sweden." *Fact Sheets on Sweden* (April 1976):1-2.

Freese, Jan. "The Swedish Data Act." *Current Sweden* 294(September 1982):2-9.

Furhoff, Lars. "Some Reflections on Newspaper Concentration." *Scandinavian Economic History Review* 21(1973):1-27.

Gothberg, John A. "Newspaper Subsidies in Sweden Pose No Dangers, Its Editors Feel." *Journalism Quarterly* 60(Winter 1983):629-34.

Groll, Lennart. "Press Ombudsman: Mediator and Prosecutor." *IPI Report* (October 1976):7.

_____. "Freedom and Self Discipline in the Swedish Press." *Current Sweden* 253(June 1980):2-7.

Gustafsson, Karl Erik. "The Circulation Spiral and the Principle of Household Coverage." *Scandinavian Economic History Review* 26(1978):1-14.

_____. "Mass Media Structure and Policy in the Early 1980s." *Current Sweden* 301(June 1983):1-10.

_____. "Press Subsidies in Sweden Today—Structure and Effects." *Current Sweden* 318(June 1984):1-8.

Hadenius, Stig. "Society and the Mass Media in Sweden." *Sweden Now* 29(April 1974):1-10.

_____. "Mass Media and the State." *Current Sweden* 133(October 1976):1-12.

_____. "Mass Media and the State in Sweden." *Gazette* 23(1977):105-15.

_____. "The Rise and Possible Fall of the Swedish Party Press." *Communication Research* 10(July 1983):287-331.

Hadenius, Stig, Jan-Olof Sveveborg, and Lennart Weibull. "The Social Democratic Press and Newspaper Policy in Sweden 1899-1909." *Scandinavian Political Studies* 3(1968):49-69.

Hemánus, Pertti. "Development Trends in the Scandinavian Press." *Gazette* 17(1971):1-15.

Hollstein, Milton. "Government and the Press: The Question of Subsidies." *Journal of Communication* 28(Autumn 1978):46-53.

Høyer, Svennik. "The Political Economy of the Norwegian Press." *Scandinavian Political Studies* 3(1968):85-143.

_____. "Recent Research on the Press in Norway." *Scandinavian Journal of History* 1(1982):15-30.

_____. "Power in Norwegian Society: The Report on Mass Media." *NORDICOM Review* 1(1983):1-3.

Hoyt, Stuart. "Survey of the Swedish Press Law which Faces Revisions." *Journalism Quarterly* 25(Autumn 1948):284-88.

Kristjánsson, Jónas. "Iceland's Press in Perspective." *IPI Report* (November 1981):10-11.

Lilius, Carl-Gustav. "Self-Censorship in Finland." *Index on Censorship* (Spring 1975):19-25.

Lindberg, Ulf. "A Study of Swedish Newspapers—From Initial Inventory to Corrective Measures." *NORDICOM Review* 1(1982):7-10.

Link, Ruth. "Open Government." *Sweden Now* 5(1977):42.

"Mass Media in Sweden." *Fact Sheets on Sweden* (September 1982):1-4.

Modig, Jan-Otto. "The Scandinavian News Agencies." *Gazette* 9(1963):143-48.

Nichols, John E. "Swedish Shield Law and Its Impact on Criminal Justice in Sweden." *Journalism Quarterly* 60(Summer 1983):253-61.

Nixon, Raymond R. "Freedom in the World's Press: A Fresh Reappraisal with Data." *Journalism Quarterly* 42(Winter 1965):3-14.

Nordenstreng, Kaarle. "American and Finnish Journalists Look at World Leaders." *Scandinavian Political Studies* 3(1968):107-85.

Nortamo, Simopekka. "The Finnish Press." *Look at Finland* 2(1984):6-10.

Olsson, Claes-Olof, and Lennart Weibull. "The Reporting of News in Scandinavian Countries." *Scandinavian Political Studies* 8(1973):141-67.

Pers, Anders. "The Swedish Daily Press Just Now." *Gazette* 9(1963):65-74.

Picard, Robert G. "A Change of Course for Swedish Subsidies." *IPI Report* 29(November 1980):12-13.

_____. "State Aid and Newspaper Marketing in Two Swedish Cities, 1965-1978." *Gazette* 28(1981):17-33.

_____. "Sweden Boosts Weeklies." *Grassroots Editor* 21(Spring 1981):12-13.

————. "Effekter av Presstod." *Meddelande* 100(February 1983):3–20.
————. "Levels of State Intervention in the Western Press." *Mass Comm Review* 11(Winter/Spring 1984):27–35.
————. "State Press Aid During the Era of Economic Readjustment: A Case Study of Scandinavian Nations." *European Studies Journal* 3(1986):1–8.
————. "Sweden Subsidizes Weeklies." *Grassroots Editor* 25(Winter 1984):5–15.
Pietilä, Antero. "Swedish Editors' Views on Government Support of the Press." *Journalism Quarterly* 48(Winter 1971):724–29.
Salmelin, Pentti. "The Transition of the Finnish Workers' Papers to the Social Democratic Press." *Scandinavian Political Studies* 3(1968):70–84.
Sheppard, S. T. "In Memoriam: William Moward Russell. The Genesis of a Profession." *The United Service Magazine* (March 1907):199.
Smith, Anthony. "Subsidies and the Press in Europe." *Political and Economic Planning* 569(1977):2.
Solokangas, Raimo, and Päiviö Tommila. "Press History Studies in Finland. Past and Present." *Scandinavian Journal of History* 1(1982):49–73.
Starck, Kenneth. "The Handling of Foreign News in Finland's Daily Newspapers." *Journalism Quarterly* 45(1968):516–21.
"Swedish Press and Other Media." *Fact Sheets on Sweden* (April 1981):1–4.
Teikarı, Erkki. "Mainly Political Changes in Finland's Daily Press." *Grassroots Editor* 12(July–August 1971):16–18.
Thomsen, Niels. "The Danish Political Press." *Scandinavian Political Studies* 3(1968):144–64.
Thorndahl, Bent. "No Winners in Denmark's Long Printing War." *IPI Report* (July 1981):7.
Thorsen, Stig. "The Flow of Foreign News into the Swedish Press." *Journalism Quarterly* 45(Autumn 1968):521–24.
Waldrop, Gayle. "The Daily Newspaper Press in Finland." *Journalism Quarterly* 44(Spring 1957):228–38.
Weibull, Lennart. "Newspaper Readership in Sweden." *Newspaper Research Journal* 4(Summer 1983):53–64.
Westerståhl, Jorgën and Carl-Gunnår Janson. "Politisk Press – Political Press." *Göteborgs Universitets Årsskrift* 64(1958):98.
Windahl, Swen, and Karl Erik Rosengren. "The Professionalization of Swedish Journalists." *Gazette* 22(1976):140–49.
"World Press Freedom Review: Finland." *IPI Report* 31(December 1982):8.

Brochures and Government Documents and Reports

Commission of the European Communities. "Evolution of Concentration and Competition in the Danish Newspaper and Magazine Sector." Evolution of Concentration and Competition Series, no. 10. Brussels, May 1978.
UNESCO. World Communications. Paris: UNESCO Press, 1975.

_____. "National Communication Policy Councils." Reports and Documents on Mass Communication, no. 83. Paris, 1979.

Denmark

Mediekommissionens. "Betænkning om de Trykte Mediers Økonomi og Beskæftigelse." Batænkning, nr. 972 Aarhuus: Aarhuus Stiftsbogtrykkerie, 1983.

Dansk Pressemuseum og Arkiv. Copenhagen: GEC Gads Forlag, 1962.

Finland

Facts about Finnish Newspapers. Helsinki: Finnish Newspaper Publishers Association, 1981.

Ministry of Foreign Affairs. "The Press in Finland." Finnish Features Series, Nov. 1981.

The Press in Finland. Helsinki: Finnish Newspaper Publishers Association, 1983.

Report of the Government Committee on Communication Policy. "Investigations and Recommendations Concerning the Press and News Agencies." Report no. 91, Pts. I and II (abridged), 1973. Helsinki: Government Printing Center, 1983.

Norway

Massemedier og Mediepolitik. NOU, 1983:3.

Norwegian Institute of Journalism. Fredrikstad: Institute of Journalism, n.d.

Rapporten om Massemedier. NOU, 1982:30. Oslo: Universitetsforlaget, 1982.

Royal Ministry of Foreign Affairs. "The Government and the Mass Media." DOC 042/79, Apr. 1979.

_____. "Newspapers in Norway." UDA 151/83 ENG, Aug.1983.

_____. "The Press in Norway." UDA 152/83 ENG, Sept. 1983.

Sweden

Budget Departmentet. Översyn av Presstödet 10,1978.

Finansdepartementet. Presstödet och Tidningskonkurrensen. SOU, 1974:102.

_____. Svensk Press: Pressens Funktioner i Samhället. SOU, 1975:8.

_____. Svensk Press: Statlig Press Politik. SOU, 1975:79.

_____. Svensk Press: Tidningar i Samverkan. SOU, 1975:11.

Justitiedepartementet. Dagstidningarnas Ekonomiska Villkor. SOU, 1965:22.

_____. Dagspressens Situation. SOU, 1968:48.

_____. Beskrivning och analys. SOU, 1972:7.

_____. Massmediegrundlag. SOU, 1975:49.

Presstödsnämnden. Dagspressrapport, 1977:1.

_____. Dagspressrapport, 1981:3.

_____. "Dagspressens ekonomi 1981." Dagspressrapport, 1982:1.
_____. "Dagspressens ekonomi 1982." Dagspressrapport, 1983:1.

Unpublished Materials

Braun, Lars. Press Subsidies in the Nordic Countries. A paper presented to the XIth Congress of the International Association for Mass Communication Research, Warsaw, Poland, 1978.

"Finnish Young People Read Newspapers and Weigh the Future." Finnish Newspaper Publishers Association, 1983. Mimeo.

Gustafsson, Karl Erik. "Press Research and Press Subsidies in Sweden." Dept. of Business Administration, Univ. of Göteborg, Sweden, 1979. Mimeo.

Hadenius, Stig. "Some Issues in Swedish Media Policy." Manuscr.

Liimatainen, Eila. "Finns Trust Their Newspapers More." Finnish Newspaper Publishers Association, 1983. Mimeo.

Loftin, Joseph E., Jr. The Origins and Development of the Swedish Newspapers Subsidies: An Interpretation. A paper presented to the Southwest Education Council for Journalism and Mass Communication, Las Cruces, N. Mex., Oct. 6–7, 1985.

Lowenstein, Ralph L. Measuring World Press Freedom as a Political Indicator. Ph. D. diss., Univ. of Missouri, 1967.

Mäkinen, Annamari. How the Finnish Press Covers the World: A Content Analysis of the Foreign News in Keskisoumalainen. M.A. thesis, Univ. of Missouri, 1982.

"98% of Finns Read Newspapers." Finnish Newspaper Publishers Association, 1983. Mimeo.

Nortamo, Simopekka. "Press Subsidies in Finland." Manuscr.

Picard, Robert G. State Aid and the Press: A Case Study of Newspapers in Two Swedish Cities." M.A. thesis, California State Univ., Fullerton, 1979.

_____. Government Subsidies and Press Freedom in Sweden. A paper presented to the Far West Regional Meeting of Women in Communication, Irvine, Calif., Mar. 14–16, 1980.

_____. Political Foundations of Swedish Newspaper History. A paper presented to the Association for Education in Journalism West Coast Historians Conference, San Francisco, Calif., Feb. 28–Mar. 1, 1981.

_____. Nordic Governments' Commitment to Press Aid During a Decade of Recession. A paper presented to the Nordic Conference for Mass Communication Research, Fugslø, Denmark, Aug. 18–21, 1985.

Pietilä, Antero. Government Subsidies and Press Freedom: The Case of Sweden. M.A. thesis, Southern Illinois Univ., 1969.

"Press Subsidy Granted by the Government in Finland." Finnish Newspaper Publishers Association, 1983. Mimeo.

"Professional Journalists' Training in Denmark." Danmarks Journalisthojskole. Mimeo.

Weibull, Lennart. Uses of the Party Press. A paper presented to the XIIth World Congress of the International Political Science Association, Rio de Janeiro, Brazil, Aug. 9–14, 1982.

INDEX

Numbers for pages with newspaper illustrations appear in boldface type.
Abbreviations: D = Denmark; F = Finland; I = Iceland; N = Norway; S = Sweden

Aalborg Stiftstidende (D), 6, 91
Aamulehti (F), 100, **102**
Aarhuus Stiftstidende (D), **94**, 95
Åbo. *See* Turku
Åbo Morgonblad (F), 6
Access to information. *See* Freedom of information
Accountability: legal, 51–55; self, 48–51
Adresseavisen (N), 119
Advertising, 56, 59–62, 70, 72. *See also* Cooperatives, advertising
Aftenposten (D), 13
Aftenposten (N), 116, **117**
Aftonbladet (S), 9, 12, 19, 22, 67, 74, 124, **125**
Aftontidningen (S), 22
Age of Freedom, 6, 43
Aktuelt (D), 12, **42**, 83, **84**
Åland Islands, xiv
Ålborg, 6
Alexander II, 12
Althing, xvii
Althýdubladid (I), 78, 108, **109**, 115
American Revolution, 7
Árason, Jón, 4
Arbeiderbladet (N), 68, 119, **121**
Arbejderbladet (F), 19
Arbetarpressens Forlagsaktiebolag, 18–19
Arbetet (S), 130
Århus, 13, 16
Århus Stiftstidende. See Aarhuus Stiftstidende
Arnarson, Ingólfur, 4
Association of Liberal Newspapers, 16

Belgium, 10
Berg, Chresten, 13
Bergen, 7, 119
Bergens Tidende (N), 119–120, **122**
Berling, E. H., 6
Berlingske Tidende (D), 6, 67, 83, **85**, 87
Bille, Carsteen Andersen, 10
Board of Denials and Corrections (D), 20, 49
Bording, Anders, 5
Børsen (D), 83, **86**
British Broadcasting Corporation, 21
B.T. (D), 35, **39**, 83, 87, **88**, 91
Business coverage. *See* Reporting, economic/business

Carlscrona, 7
Cars, Thorsen, 51
Catholic(s), 4, 5
Cavling, Henrik, 15–16
Censorship, 51, 52–54; Denmark, 6, 7, 10, 21–22, 44; Finland, 10, 15, 19–20, 44, 53–54; Iceland, 7, 44; Norway, 7, 9, 20–21, 44–45; Sweden, 7, 9, 20, 43
Christian VII, 6
Christiana, 14
Christian denominations, 8
Christianity, 3
Circulation, 56–59, 70, 72
Circulation spiral, 71–72
Cold-type production methods, 64, 65, 67
Comic strips, 41–42

Confederation of Trade Unions: Finland, 19; Sweden, 22
Cooperatives: advertising, 62; circulation, 58; production, 65, 66, 77
Copenhagen, 6, 12, 13, 16, 22, 32, 36, 59
Corantos, 4
Correspondents, 7, 40
Council for Mass Media, 49
Crime coverage, 38, 39

Dagbladet (D), 10, 12
Dagbladet (N), 14, 116, **118**
Dagbladid (I), 108
Dagens Nyheter (S), 12, 22, 66, 124, 126, **128**
Dagligt Allehanda (S), 7
Dagspressens Finansieringsinstitut, 23
Dalin, Olof von, 5
Danske Ugeskrift (D), 8
De Frie Danske (D), 21, 22
Demokraten (D), 13, 16
Den Danske Mercurius (D), 5
Denmark: cedes Norway to Sweden, 8–9; cedes parts of Scandinavian Peninsula, 7–8; German occupation in WWII, 20, 21–22; territorial disputes with Sweden, 3–4, 7–8
Den Svenska Argus (S), 5
Distribution. See Circulation
DV (I), 66, 108, **110**

Economic coverage. See Reporting, economic/business
Edhuskunda, xvii
Editorials, 37–38
Eidsvoll Assembly, 8
Ekstrabladet (D), 16, 22, 35, 83, 87, **89**
Enaeo, Olof Olfzson, 4
Erkko, Eero, 15
Esbjerg, 95
Essays, 27
Etelä-Suomen Sanomat (F), 100
Ett Tidninge Utgifne Af Ett Salskap i Åbo (F), 6
Expressen (S), 22, 66, 124, 126, **127**

Fædrelandet (D), 8, 10

Fair Practices Commission. See Pressens Opinionsnämnd
Faröe Islands, xiv
Ferslew, Christian, 13
Fich, Alfred, 11
Finland: anticommunist campaign, 19–20; ceded to Russia, 7; defeated by Soviet Union, 20; independence achieved, 18, 44; Swedish designs on, 3–4; tsarist control of, 10, 12, 15
Finnish Newspaper Publishers Association, 61
Finnish Union of Journalists, 62
Finno-Russian War, 19
Fixed responsibility, 10, 20, 51, 52
Folkebladet (N), 9
Folket i Bild/Kultur Front (S), 53
Folketing, xvii
Forsell, Carl Daniel, 9
Four-paper system, 16
Frederick III, 5
Frederick V, 6
Frederiksborg Amts Avis (D), 95
Freedom Council, Press Committee, 22
Freedom of information, 43–44, 46–47
Freedom of the press, xiii, 6, 43–47, 52–54; Denmark, 10, 44; Finland, 18, 33–34, 41, 44, 45; Iceland, 10, 44; Norway, 8, 44–45; Sweden, 6, 20, 43–44
Free Press, The, 16
French-language papers, 5
French Revolution, 7
Frit Danmark (D), 21, 22

German-language papers, 5
Germany, 5, 6, 8, 12, 20–23
Göteborg, 7, 9, 130
Göteborgs Handels-och Sjöfarts-Tidningen (S), 20
Göteborgs Handels-och Sjöfartstidningen (S), 74
Göteborgs-Posten (S), 130, **131**
Gotland, 4
Gotlands Tidning (S), 77
Great Britain, 8, 35, 87
Greenland, xiv
Groll, Lennart, 51
Gross National Product, xvi

Gustav III, 7
Gustav IV Adolf, 7
Gustavus Adolphus II, 4

Hanseatic League, 4
Helsingborg, 130
Helsingfors Dagblad (F), 12
Helsingfors Tidningar (F), 10
Helsingin Sanomat (F), 69, 96, **97**, 103
Helsinki, 10, 14, 20, 57, 100, 103
Hermes Gothicus (S), 4
Hierta, Lars John, 9
Hillerød, 95
Historical press developments: earliest
    printing, 4–7; growth of regional
    papers, 6–7
Holar, 4
Hørup, Viggo, 13
Hot type. *See* Production methods
Hufvudstadsbladet (F), 12, 96, **98**

Iceland: independence achieved, 44;
    settlement, 4
Ilkka (F), 17
Illegal Press Coordinating Committee,
    22
Illegal Press Joint Association
    Newsroom, 22
Ilta Lehti (F), 100, **101**
Ilta-Sanomat (F), 69, 96, **99**
Information (D), 67, 68, 87, **90**, 91
Information (news service) (D), 22
International news. *See* Reporting,
    foreign/international

Jeurling, Anders, 15
Jutland, 13, 91, 95
Jyllands-Posten (D), 91, **92**
Jyväskylä, 103

Kaleva (F), 100
Karl XIV Johan, 9
Karlstad, 133
Karlstadstidningen (D), 9
Kekkonen, Urho, 34
Keskisuomalainen (F), 103
Kjøbenhavnsposten (D), 8

Klausturposturinn (I), 7
København (D), 14
Københavnske Danske Post-Tidender
    (D), 6
Kolding, 13
Kolding Folkeblad (D), 13, 95
Kovisto, Mauno, 41
Kristianstad, 130
Kuopio, 103
Kvällsposten (S), 130

Labor issues, 14, 62–64
Lahti, 100
Land og Fog (D), 21
Lapps, 29
Lapua, 19
Libel, 54–55
Linköping, 133
Litzelius, Antti, 6
Loans to papers, government, 23, 73.
    See also State intervention
Lund, 7, 130
Lutheran(s), xvii

Malmö, 130
Matthiasson, John, 4
Monarchy(ies), xvii, 6; threatened by
    liberalism, 7–10
Morgenbladet (D), 12
Morgenbladet (N), 8, 9
Morgonblad (F), 10
Morgunbladid (I), 59, 66, 108, 111, **112**

Nationalism: cultural, 3, 11; Finland, 6,
    10, 11, 12, 15, 18; Norway, 9
National security, 51, 52–54
Nationaltidende (D), 13
Nazi(s), 20–23, 87
Nerkikes Allehanda (S), 133
News agencies, 11, 15, 17, 18
Newspaper mortality, xiv, 18-19, 23, 32,
    69–72
Newspapers: national, 36, 57, 58; pro-
    vincial/regional, 6–7, 36, 57, 58;
    shoppers, 60–62, 64; weekly, 23,
    36–37
Nordic nations, general description of,
    xiii, xvii, 3

Norrköping, 7
Norske Intelligenz-Seddeler (N), 7
Norsk Telegrambyrå, 11
North America, 4, 22
Norway: ceded to Sweden, 7–8, 9;
    Germany occupation in WWII,
    20–21
NT (Nu Timmin) (I), 111, **113**
Nya Wermlands-Tidningen (S), 133
Ny Tid (N), 53

Objectivity, 37–38
Odin, xiii
Ombudsman, xiv, 38, 48, 50–51
Ordinari Post Tijdender (S), 5
Örebro, 133
Organization for Economic Cooperation
    and Development (OECD), xvi
Oslo, 116, 119
Östgöta Correspondenten (S), 133
Oulu, 100
Ownership, 5, 56, 67–69

Päivälehti (F), 15
Palm, August, 13
Parliaments, xvii
Pay scales, 62–64
Pio, Louis, 12
Pjoöolfur (I), 10
Ploug, Carl, 8
Poland, 5
Political news. *See* Reporting, political
Political participation, xiii, 29–30, 32–
    34
Political parties, xvii; agrarian, 3; bour-
    geois, xvii, 13, 32; Center, 33, 74,
    75, 103; Communist, 9, 19–20;
    Conservative, 12, 32, 74, 83, 97,
    111, 116, 119; Farmers, 11, 17;
    Finnish, 12; Home Rule (I), 17;
    Hoyre (N), 12; Independence (I),
    17; Independent Liberals, 119;
    Labor, 14, 15–16, 119; Liberal, 11,
    12, 13, 14, 16, 32, 87, 124, 130,
    133; National Coalition, 100, 103;
    Populist, 24; Progressive, 111;
    Radical-Liberal, 16, 32; Social
    Democratic, 13, 14, 16, 17, 18, 23,
    32, 65, 74, 75, 78, 83, 108, 124,
    130; Socialist, xvii, 3, 12, 14, 19,
    24, 34, 115; Swedish, 12, 19, 96;
    Venstra, 12
Political party press, 8–9, 11–18, 29–35
Politiken (D), 13, 15, 16, 83, 87, 91, **93**
Popular press, 35, 36
Postal systems role, newspaper develop-
    ment, 5
Press councils, xiv, 17, 48–50
Pressens Opinionsnämnd, 17, 20, 48
Press freedom. *See* Freedom of the press
Prime minister(s), xvii
Printing and production issues, 63–67.
    See also Cooperatives, production
Printing press(es), 4, 7, 9, 13, 15, 22
Prior restraint. *See* Censorship
Privacy, xiv, 38
Production methods, 13, 63–67. *See
    also* Cooperatives, production
Protestant(s), 4

Quality press, 35
Quisling government, 21

Reader's Digest, 69
Religion, xvii, 3, 4–5
Reporting: crime, 38, 39; economic/
    business, 10, 11, 40; foreign/inter-
    national, 7, 9, 10, 38–41; political,
    5, 8, 33–34, 40–41
Responsible publisher. *See* Fixed respon-
    sibility
Reykjavik, 108, 111
Right-of-reply, xiv, 54, 55
Riksdag, xvii, 43, 48, 76, 77
Ritzau, Eric Nicolai, 11
Ritzaus Bureau, 11
Rode, Ove, 13
Roles of the press: cultural, 26, 27, 29;
    economic, 26, 29; educational, 26–
    27, 29; entertainment, 29; political,
    xiii, 26, 29, 30–35; social, xiii, 26–
    27
Runeberg, J. L., 10
Russia, 5, 7, 10, 14. *See also* Soviet
    Union
Russian Revolution, 18, 44

Sabmelas (F), 29
Safeguard Finland Association, 19
Saima (F), 10
Savon Sanomat (F), 103, **104**
Scandinavia, xiii, 4
Scandinavian Peninsula, xiv, 3
Sensationalism, 35, 38
Snellman, J. V., 10
Social-Demokraten (D), 12, 14, 16, 83, 85
Socialdemokraten (S), 13
Socialisten (D), 12
Social welfare policies, xvi–xvii
Society for the Beneficial Use of the Freedom of the Press, 8
Soelvold, Peder, 9
Sorting, xvii
Sources, protection of, 47
Soviet Union, 4, 19, 20, 41, 45, 53–54. *See also* Russia
Spectator, The, 5
State intervention, 72–79
Statsborgeren (N), 9
Stavanger, 123
Stavanger Aftenblad (N), 123
Stephensen, Magnús, 7
Stift papers, 6, 11
Stockholm, 9, 126
Stockholms-Tidningen (S), 15, 23, 74
Strangnas, 4
Subsidies, 23, 70–71, 73–79. *See also* State intervention
Suomen Julkisia Sanomia (F), 10
Suomenkieliset Tieto-Sanomat (F), 6
Suomen Sosialidemokraatti (F), 14
Suomen Tietotoimisto, Finska Notis-byrå, 15
Suometar (F), 10
Svenska Dagbladet (S), **28**, 67, 126, **129**
Svenska Telegrambyrå, 17
Sweden: cedes Finland to Russia, 7; control of Finland, 4–5, 5–6; territorial conflicts with Denmark, 3–4, 7–8, 9
Swedish Broadcasting Corporation, 46
Swedish Intelligencer (S), 7
Sydsvenska Dagbladet (S), 130, **132**

Tabloids, 22, 35, 57, 59
Tampere, 14, 100
Tatler, The, 5
Taxes and tax policies, 72–79
Television, 40, 57, 60–62
Thirty Years War, 4, 5
Thjódviljinn (I), **114**, 115
Thorlaksson, Gudbrandur, 4
Tidningarnas Telegrambyrå, 18, 46
Tiedonantaja (F), 20
Topelius, Z., 10
Trelleborg, 130
Trondheim, 119
Turku (Åbo), 6, 14, 103
Turun Sanomat (F), 103, **105**
Työkansan Sanomat (F), 20
Työmies (F), 13, 14, 16

Unions, 14, 62–64
Unitas, 19
United States, 15, 35, 51, 52, 53, 56
Uppsalla, 9
Uusi Suometar (F), 12
Uusi Suomi (F), **30**, 103, **106**

Vaasa, 17, 19–20, 107
Vaassa (F), 107
Valhalla (Valhöll), xiii
Västerås, 133
Västmanlands Lans Tidning (S), 133
Venstreblad papers, (D), 16
Verdens Gang (N), 14
Vestkysten (D), 95
VG (N), 116, 119, **120**
Vikings, 4
Visby, 4
Visir (I), 17, 108
Voltaire, François Marie Arouet de, 6

Wages, 14, 62–64
Westzynthius, Woldeman, 15
Wiinblad, Emil, 14
World War I, 17, 32, 35
World War II, xvii, 20–23, 40, 45, 71, 74